The Visual Theology
of the Huguenots

The Visual Theology of the Huguenots

Towards an Architectural Iconology of Early Modern French Protestantism, 1535 to 1623

Randal Carter Working

The Lutterworth Press

To my parents Kenneth and Marjorie,
and my brothers Russell, Jay, Jeffrey, and Thomas,
companions in life and ministry.

The Lutterworth Press
P.O. Box 60
Cambridge
CB1 2NT
United Kingdom

www.lutterworth.com
publishing@lutterworth.com

ISBN: 978 0 7188 9469 6

British Library Cataloguing in Publication Data
A record is available from the British Library

First published by The Lutterworth Press, 2017

Published by arrangement
with Pickwick Publications

Contents

CHAPTER 1

Introduction

La Parole de Dieu, dont nous puisons notre religion, nous com-
mande d'aimer ceux qui nous haïssent, et de croire que ceux qui
nous ont persécutés ont pensé, en ce faisant, faire service à Dieu.

The Word of God, from which we draw our religion, commands us
to love those who hate us, and to trust that those who persecute us
think, in doing so, they are serving God.
—Pierre du Moulin, *Bouclier de la Foi*

THERE IS GREAT INTEREST in visual culture within academia these days.
Nicholas Mirzoeff writes, "Visual culture is now an increasingly important
meeting place for critics, historians, and practitioners in all visual media
who are impatient with the tired nostrums of their 'home' discipline or
medium."[1] It is hoped that this work might not only be of interest to theologians and students of architecture and the built environment, but to historians and art historians interested in how to better access the past through
learning to see the way early modern citizens might have seen; and to understand how conceptions of space and religion manifested themselves in
buildings that still survive today. Although the Neoclassical style can now
be seen in Catholic churches, it was an innovation largely brought about by
Protestant architects. It is only in understanding the language and visual
quality of space that we can truly understand the resistance offered against
competing religious ideologies in their creation of the built environment.

1. Mirzoeff, *Visual Culture Reader*, 6.

CONFLICTING AESTHETICS

This work proposes that the Protestant architecture in francophone territories of the sixteenth and seventeenth centuries was laden with theological meaning. This will be explored by treating three contrasting examples: St. Pierre in Geneva, a Calvinist church taken over from Catholics, St. Gervais-St. Protais in Paris, a Catholic church finished by a Protestant architect, and finally a purpose-built Reformed church designed and built by that same architect. The time period will be approximately mid sixteenth-century Geneva, to be compared with the first two decades of the seventeenth century in France. The rationale for this period is that it encompasses the time of the first conscientious scrutiny of space fit for Protestant worship and the time of maturation of specifically Protestant church architecture. Together, the structures under consideration begin to suggest a Reformed approach to sacred architecture. Further, we will discern two distinct ways of seeing, one Catholic and one Protestant. Religious traditions incline to certain ways of perceiving what is good, true, and beautiful. This reality has much to do with architectural space, its style determined by how one sees reality. Finally, we will suggest that Protestant habits of design helped set the stage for the development of the Neoclassical style in France.

Yet even in the churches who found their identity in the exposition of Scripture, the habits of medieval Catholicism died hard. The 1659 *Registres du Conseil* of Geneva relate that concerned pastors and elders witnessed church members kneeling before a statue at the tomb of the Duke of Rohan in the Cathedral of St. Pierre, praying before the Huguenot leader's memorial.[2] The statues of Catholic saints had been excised and the Mass abolished for over a century, and yet old habits of devotion were not so easy to eradicate. Similar stories of the resiliency of "idolatry" emerge from continental and British settings alike. Especially in isolated country towns, "the results of the Reformed churches' endeavors to root out folk customs and magical practices, and to construct in their stead a new religious culture, were mixed, particularly when pastors and elders challenged popular traditions and time-honored social exchanges."[3] In the midst of monumental changes and reform, old customs sometimes still controlled popular practice.

Stories of enduring religious customs, as when women genuflected before a whitewashed church wall that covered a sacred image, illustrate

2. Guillot, "L'Église de St. Pierre," 84.
3. Mentzer, "Persistence of 'Superstition,'" 220–33.

the stubbornness of folk beliefs and the difficulty of reform, on one hand, and the lingering memory of sacred presence, on the other. Eliminating these practices and instilling new forms of piety was difficult work. These accounts also raise some interesting questions: do parishioners retain some dim recollection over generations of images that helped them cope with adversity or prepare for the experience of worship? Do they recall more explicitly what initially elicited their devotion? Is the act of praying to the image of a Huguenot hero meaningless, or worse? Do certain elements within a church building generate an impression of holiness? More broadly, what does Reformed worship space express, and how does it do it? How is space provided for worship intended to function, and how do cultural artifacts enhance it (or conversely, perhaps compromise its purity?) Or is Reformed architecture itself deficient in that it is incapable of meeting a need for sacred space in a horizontal community of peers, and in a vertical community through history? These are questions to which we will turn.

The medieval Catholic imagination, or manner of attributing meaning to what is seen, focused on images external to itself in which it found transcendence. However, the Protestant critique of this manner of seeing argued that the imagination focused on an image can only comprehend its interpretation of the image, whose reality takes form in the imagination. David Morgan, in *The Sacred Gaze: Religious Visual Culture in Theory and Practice* describes (sympathetically) how images work. He points out, "In every case, viewers experience an absorption in an image. They cultivate a variety of visual practices that engage them in this absorption . . . [this can be] contemplative, bringing the mind into deeper experience of itself . . . ."[4] But this was the very problem for Protestants. This work will argue that for them, this approach to the divine encompassed both the nothingness and the power of images, through which one perceived oneself and projected that image upon God. When faith orients itself toward objects, it is claimed, it becomes indistinguishable from one's idea of faith or from an experience of the religious imagination. The imagination that only contemplates itself reminds us of what Barth called "pre-judgment" toward Scripture, which he says "is not just a matter of our opinion . . . [Scripture is] not merely the probable echo of our own feeling and judgment, but objectively the witness of divine revelation and therefore the Word of God as the Word of our Lord and of the Lord of His Church."[5]

4. Morgan, *Sacred Gaze*, 2.
5. Barth, *Church Dogmatics*, I/2:147.

In these sentences, Barth reflects the Reformed fear of projecting human needs and presuppositions upon God, and states that authentic orientation toward God entails setting aside "our own feeling and judgment" to objectively receive revelation, that is, what God reveals about himself which is unknowable by human means without divine assistance.

For sixteenth-century Protestants, any religious fascination with an object as a manner of apprehending the divine is itself an idol—one thinks of Calvin's antipathy even for mental images—the object in this case fascinates because it reflects back an image of the self. Pursuing faith as an experience for its own sake could be seen as the cause of idolatry. In terms of visual/spiritual perception, the remedy to this dilemma is to learn to really see, to recognize the difference between one's experience of contemplation and the reality one seeks, in which one is seen and addressed by God.

The psychology of visual perception helps us understand why the issue of idolatry was of such elemental importance in the Protestant imagination. If God perceives the human person and speaks for himself, then an experience of worship that is valid refuses to put forth one's own image for God, which inevitably communicates a false god. For Calvinists, God cannot be portrayed in material form, a contradiction of Isa 40:18 ("With whom, then, will you compare God? To what image will you liken him?") The iconoclastic instinct, so fiercely and tenaciously held by early modern Reformed Christians, revealed a desire to remove any impediment to a vital relationship with God (see figure 1).

Figure 1: Protestant suspicion of images caused outbreaks of iconoclasm, though in many areas of Switzerland the dismantling of sacred art took place gradually, or in an ordered manner sanctioned by city authorities.

Iconoclasm suggests that its perpetrators did not consider images benign—or nothing at all—but rather found them to be powerful, magical, alluring, and negative. Further, David Morgan argues, following art historian David Freedberg, that no religion is truly "aniconic," explaining that iconoclasts "need the other to destroy in order to construct a new tradition in which to exist. And they often proceed by substituting one mode of imagery for another. Iconoclasm, in other words, is not a purging of images *tout à fait* but a strategy of replacement."[6] Protestantism would dismantle the medieval Catholic sacramental system, and would transfer religious affections to other objects, whether Protestant worship spaces, Protestant devotional works or martyrologies, or to a copy of the Bible. Regina Schwartz, in *Sacramental Poetics at the Dawn of Secularism: When God Left the World*, writes, "Instead of . . . God leaving the world without a trace, the very sacramental character of religion lent itself copiously to developing the so-called secular forms of culture and that these are often thinly disguised sacramental cultural expressions."[7]

Even if Protestants were not prone to imputing sacredness to objects or places of importance, they did come to see these as religiously significant or helpful to their collective memory. Gerrit Verhoeven explores the attitudes of Dutch Reformed travelers to both Catholic and Protestant sites of the Grand Tour in the seventeenth century in his article "Calvinist Pilgrimages and Popish Encounters: Religious Identity and Sacred Space on the Dutch Grand Tour (1598–1685.)"[8] "Geneva was bestowed with symbolic status," he writes, "as either starting point or terminus for the Calvinist Grand Tour."[9] Although motivations for undertaking such a journey included business, diplomatic missions, educational goals, and training in equestrian skills, many made a point of visiting places of importance in the Huguenot consciousness such as La Rochelle and Charenton. "Despite their dogmatic mistrust against the Catholic blueprint of sacred space, Calvinist burghers [in the Netherlands] soon established their own hallowed places,"[10] notably the burial place of Prince William of Orange. Reformed travelers to France frequently visited towns, monuments, and *lieux de memoire*. It would seem these sites held for them a kind of symbolism and sacrality.

6. Morgan, *Sacred Gaze,* 117.

7. Schwartz, *Sacramental Poetics,* 14.

8. Verhoeven, "Calvinist Pilgrimages," 615.

9. Ibid.

10. Ibid.

However, Protestants held that a true icon or representation of grace could not be a static symbol subjectively perceived, but rather was the obedience of the covenant community that is the church. In addition, the act of iconoclasm is many-layered, explained not only by theological polemics, but also by competing social narratives. To understand iconoclasm, one must grasp something of the power of symbol and why sixteenth-century Protestants repudiated the medieval Catholic understanding of it. Hans-Georg Gadamer helps us understand something of the way a symbolic works:

> A symbol not only points to something; it represents it by taking its place. But to take the place of something means to make something present that is not present. Thus in representing, the symbol takes the place of something: that is, it makes something immediately present. Only because it thus presents the presence of what it represents is the symbol itself treated with the reverence due to the symbolized.[11]

To approach Scripture in order to hear its objective claim on the reader is the foundation for understanding a Reformed manner of visual expression, particularly in the setting where the congregation gathered for worship. Reformed visual expression grew from a Reformed way of seeing. As it developed in specific contexts, the Huguenot style ranged from the classical fashion to a vernacular one, from basilica to barn, as appropriate for expressing a theology of the Word in a living community. This style expressed both simplicity and clarity, and in refusing to arrogate for itself any salvific power, ironically, it did communicate the biblical faith that alone had power to save.

MEANING OF SPACE

Catharine Randall has written a compelling and useful book called *Building Codes: The Aesthetics of Calvinism in Early Modern Europe*. She turns her attention to the Calvinist architects during the period following the wars of religion in France and into the time of the Edict of Nantes. These architects experienced in their work the tension of working for Catholic patrons. Responding to restrictions on their doctrinal expression, they contrived coded systems of iconology that subverted the Catholic religious and social

11. Gadamer, *Truth and Method*, 147.

systems. Randall asserts that the ornamental systems of their buildings would communicate on the surface, and on another level to scripturally-informed Calvinists. In this endeavor, they were influenced by the spatial elements of Calvin's *Institutes* and his understanding of the ideal ordering of a godly city, a response to the physical restrictions they experienced in France. However, her literary method perhaps limits the scope of her study by focusing too much on speculative aspects of French Renaissance architecture, which is after all a "concrete" art of brick, stone, and mortar. Care and restraint are needed in this project: it is not possible to trace hidden agendas in all elements of architecture. Calvinist architects practiced their craft in the face of ambiguity. This is not to dismiss the helpfulness of Randall's approach and insight into the character of sixteenth- and seventeenth-century design, and her work will be examined especially in chapters 4 and 6 in the discussion of Reformed perspectives on appropriate architectural design.

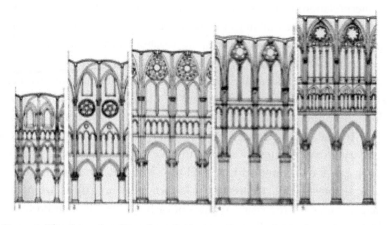

Figure 2: The above elevations show elements common to the Gothic style, including side aisles, clerestory windows, and pointed arches: 1. Laon; 2. Notre Dame, Paris; 3. Chartres; 4. Reims; 5. Amiens.

A more practical-theological approach helps grasp the meaning of Reformed sacred space, using an aesthetic analysis of built spaces in order to shed fresh light on the idea of sacred space in early modern Geneva and Paris (see figure 2). The approach will be to carefully examine three churches (or parts of those churches) that date back to the period, uncovering what can be learned through sacred spaces and architectural composition about Huguenot theology more broadly. Interpretation will take place by considering the visual rhetoric of buildings, which, it will be argued, architects built with such intent; further, this will shed light on the implications and theological priorities that can be understood through physical space, many of which are missed by modern observers. Andrew Spicer has written, "The limitation of such a broad approach [as nearly all previous studies] has been that these studies have not been able to examine closely the ways in which Reformed places of worship were influenced by local considerations and the status of the Reformed Church in a particular period."[12] There is much to be gained with a study that looks at specific contexts, engages in thick description, and seeks theological meaning through the aesthetics of material culture.

Several challenges arise in a study such as this. First, while one can contextualize the "visual theology" of the Swiss Reformed and the Huguenots, there lacks a settled discipline in which to locate this study. It is not a historical study per se, but rather a theological and aesthetic one, and thus a conceptual interpretation of architecture, albeit in a historical setting. The primary sources consist of the buildings themselves and what writings we can glean from the architects and their contemporaries about these constructions.

Second, a survey of secondary literature must draw from a larger concentric circle. Most secondary sources that relate to a study of Swiss and French Reformed architecture focus not on theology but on historical, sociological, or liturgical data. Others treat theological developments on the basis of textual evidence, not from architecture or other cultural artifacts. Secondary literature, therefore, tends to have a suggestive character, since our point of focus is not on historical texts and literary analysis, but on buildings, one of which, Charenton, is known today only by drawings. The principal source for the visual analysis of early modern French Protestant architecture is Catharine Randall, whose intriguing work on the subject has brought a more nuanced understanding of Reformed intentions in church building. Her work at times has a speculative quality. However, a theological interpretation of the built environment is by nature speculative, since architectural compositions are to be interpreted visually—conclusions cannot be definitive, but only tentative, and the intentions of those who designed or arranged worship space can usually only be suggestive.

Likewise, given the scarcity of research in this field, one must interpolate from general works, and locate the consideration of particular buildings within a brief survey of their local history, rather than embark on a

---

12. Spicer, *Calvinist Churches*, 3–4.

detailed examination of documents relating to other theological concerns. The most relevant textual evidence are the few writings of contemporary architects (there exist no known writings on the buildings in question by their respective architects), the commentary on two of these buildings by Randall, and a handful of other writers who give us some methodological tools in our search for meaning in buildings: Eric O. Jacobsen, Mark Torgerson, Robert Mugerauer, William Whyte, William Dyrness, and Jeremy Begbie. A survey of these writers will bring out the most relevant ideas in constructing our methodology of reading churches.

SOME FORMATIVE VOICES

In his book *The Space Between: a Christian Engagement with the Built Environment*, Jacobsen speaks of the importance of the space between buildings, the space for human interaction, and the space between Eden and the New Jerusalem where we are invited to live into the fullness of God's reign. The garden and the city are settings "where humanity is shown to be living in harmony with one another, with the rest of creation, and with God."[13] In the biblical accounts of creation and new creation, these settings are exemplified by shalom, a place of beauty and human flourishing. Something of the character of shalom can be experienced in current reality as it is marked by obedience to God's commands in the creation and cultural mandates. For this to be the case in human experience, attention must be paid to orientation. Jacobsen is referring principally to the organization or urban design of the city, but his insights apply to the architecture of specific buildings as well. He writes that orientation must be toward coordinates that reveal whether one is "properly directed toward shalom,"[14] and not merely toward geographic relationships or directional grids. What are these coordinates? They are gifts of the Creator: "embodied existence," "a place in which to thrive," "the gift of community," and "the gift of time." If these apply to the making and appreciating of urban space, then they would also seem relevant to the spatial relationships created within particular expressions of architecture and to the worship spaces we will examine in chapter 7. As embodied creatures, people need space for worship lest worship fall into Docetism—we need "a place in which to thrive." Further, the place of Christian worship, especially in its Protestant expressions, has tended to

13. Jacobsen, *Space Between*, 30.
14. Ibid., 31.

emphasize its common nature, or "the gift of community." Lastly, worship is an act that in its embodiment occurs within a span of time. These elements impinge on questions of architectural design.

Most relevant for the latter discussion is Jacobsen's chapter, "Loving Place," which we might paraphrase as "created space which is worthy of affection." Love is not only a characteristic of certain human relationships; it is also a possible response to places, and is "a key element to a city [or building] becoming great,"[15] and includes within it the factors of belonging and beauty. Belonging happens as strangers are brought into community—this can be enhanced by a physical structure—overcoming estrangement between God and people and between people themselves. Jacobsen's characteristics necessary for the "third place" can apply to churches as well as to neutral gathering places: "neutral ground" suggests a place where all are welcome; "the third place as leveler" insists that no one sharing in it has higher status than another; "conversation is the main activity" is analogous to the events of prayer and preaching that take place within; "accessibility and accommodation" remind us that one can expect to find community in this place; "the regulars" corresponds to members or congregants that gather for worship; "a low profile" parallels the Reformed value of avoiding ostentation—the church building should not point to its own grandeur, but to that of God; "the mood is playful" suggests that a sense of joy is key, and that no one using the space should "take themselves too seriously;" "a home away from home" parallels the comfort and support to be found in the community of faith gathered in a particular place. A building for the community provides for the experience of approach, for hospitality, and for enhancing relationships. All this applies to church structures.

But places worthy of our affection do more than encourage belonging. They also enhance the transcendent qualities of truth, goodness, and beauty. These characteristics, Jacobsen argues, go beyond personal taste; they are woven into the nature of reality. Beauty might be said to be foundational in that it attracts us and draws us to the excellence of the other qualities. As such it is an indispensible part of places that elicit our love. Drawing on Nicolas Wolterstorff, Jacobsen explains that art in the West is typically understood as something designed for contemplation, not for practical usage. The built environment, however, is an exception to this rule, for we understand architecture as belonging in the realm of art in spite of its usefulness. Another exception is liturgy and the arts conceived

15. Ibid., 240.

for the purpose of worship. Their aesthetic value is accepted even though their primary purpose is to enhance the context of worship.

Jacobsen then considers the basic aspects of a building which make it more or less aesthetically pleasing, aspects that go beyond questions of style. Drawing from Jonathan Hale, he lists "a few basic elements of beauty in buildings."[16] The first is the concept of "regulating lines," a "visual metric" of connections made in the composition of a building that enhance a sense of harmony. Applied to the relationships between buildings, the concept is equally important within a single structure, which, since created (usually) by a single designer, coheres more than within a collection of diverse structures.

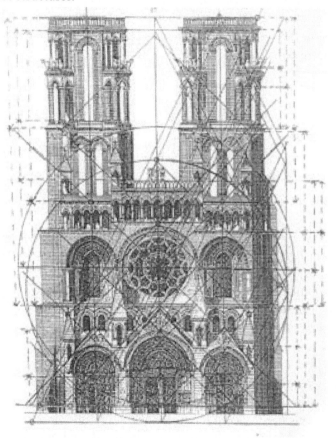

Figure 3: Regulating lines on the Laon Cathedral reveal the golden section.

16. Ibid., 264.

The second is the idea of the "golden section," or "proportion" (see figure 3). This is the ratio between the width and height of a rectangle which is intuitively pleasing to the eye. The ratio is 1 to 1.618, expressed also in the relationship between the numbers 3 and 5 (see figure 4). Pythagoras and Euclid considered its properties, as have many others, and the idea intrigued Renaissance thinkers as a pattern for satisfying proportions in art and architecture. De Brosse's façade of the St. Germain church in Paris seems to adhere to this proportionality. The golden section can be used in ways that "expand patterns in pleasing ways,"[17] including a perfect nautilus and five-pointed star. Jacobsen cites the example of the rose window on Chartres cathedral as an example of this proportion. "These patterns work, not for mystical reasons, but rather because these patterns correspond with the patterns that we perceive in nature and the patterns that are inherent in our own createdness."[18]

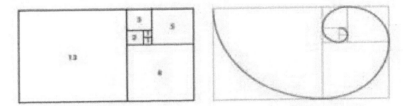

Figure 4: The Golden Proportion and the Fibonacci Series: 1, 1, 2, 3, 5, 8, 13.

Jacobsen concludes with some cautions about aesthetics, which he argues are *apropos* given the limitations inherent in human frailty and sin. First, concern for aesthetic quality can cover "more sinister motives." An example of this might be the urban design of Napoleon III and his engineer, Georges-Eugène Haussmann, whose designs imposed a unifying order to the city while eliminating narrow streets where insurrectionists' barricades could be easily erected.

Second, one needs to recognize the role of aesthetics even when not explicit within a system or a specific work. The example of Calvin's church in Switzerland and the churches of the later Puritans in America is highlighted. Many have insisted that these held no artistic values whatsoever, yet later scholarship has shown these were not devoid of aesthetic judgment. Instead, they display an aesthetic of sobriety, order, and simplicity.

17. Ibid., 265.
18. Ibid.

These qualities resonate in the design of many Calvinist churches, such as the New England meeting house.

Jacobsen concludes with the questions "How well does this environment point to and remind us of the Sabbath rest that is to come? How does this place measure up to the standard of shalom?" These are questions to be posed not only to the "space between buildings," but also to the buildings themselves.

Mark Torgerson contributes to the conversation on sacred space in his book *An Architecture of Immanence: Architecture for Worship and Ministry Today.* He lays the groundwork for understanding by discussing the divine attributes of transcendence and immanence, and the manner in which these are expressed in church design. Next, he considers the theological origins of an architecture of immanence, which he sees emerging from the ideas of Protestant liberal theology and its preference for God's presence among people rather than God's supernatural mediation in the earthly realm. Three movements—ecumenism, liturgical renewal, and modernism—converged to create the architectural emphasis on immanence that dominated church building in the twentieth century. The work of Frank Lloyd Wright, Walter Gropius, Ludwig Mies van der Rohe, and Le Corbusier formed the basic tenets of modernism in architecture, which were adopted almost universally for church building in the mid-century. This approach preferred attention to volume over mass, disdained what was perceived as thoughtless appropriation of historical styles, de-emphasized the distinction between clergy and laity, and stripped churches of ornamentation and explicit symbolism. Formally, the commitment to the language of modernism, especially as exemplified in the International Style, was seen in building features such as Spartan interiors, lack of exterior ornamentation, flat roofs, and extensive use of glass and other contemporary construction materials. The church was seen more as the house of God's people than the house of God, a notion seen in Reformed architecture from the Reformation of the sixteenth century and beyond, a subject to which we will return in chapter 2. In describing modern preferences, Torgerson cites Frédéric Debuyst, who claims "A church is not an architectural monument built to symbolize God's glory, but a 'Paschal meeting-room,' a functional space created for the celebrating of Christian assembly."[19] In this description, Debuyst echoes the sentiments of Calvin.

19. Debuyst, *Modern Architecture*, 30; quoted in Torgerson, *Architecture of Immanence*, 166.

Torgerson notes the tendency of some scholars to seek models for renewal in early church liturgies; this echoes the discoveries of sixteenth-century Protestant reformers that led to changes in order of worship and in church design. At the same time, these scholars took issue with the modern predilection for lack of symbolism and an ahistorical bias in church design. Many are now calling for a reemployment of the church's historical and symbolic vocabulary for church design. Memory must be considered in relation to sacred space, both in the sense of the continuity of the Christian tradition, and also in the sense of the usage over time of a particular worship space, which "is not always easily stripped of that experiential imprint [of religious and communal rites.]"[20] We will consider the role of memory in relation to conceptual space in chapter 3. Given Christianity's intrinsically historical nature, church design loses something in the radical break with the past favored by modernism. And given the ever present theological tension between God's immanence and transcendence, both attributes will find expressions in church building, notwithstanding periodic emphasis of one over the other. The Reformed tradition of architecture has tended to highlight God's immanence and the importance of the gathered community. In addition, churches throughout history have favored designs that accentuate the distinctive qualities of the church tradition, as did Protestants who wanted to differentiate themselves from Catholics. Torgerson provides a helpful analysis of modern and postmodern tendencies in church building, and aids understanding of the two poles of transcendence and immanence. However, his work does not construct a specific interpretive method for architecture.

Robert Mugerauer summarizes interpretive theory since the 1970s in his work, *Interpreting Environments: Tradition, Deconstruction, Hermeneutics.* Through the use of three case studies, he demonstrates the use of traditional, historical interpretation; of deconstruction; and of hermeneutics, all with the object of facilitating the use of deconstruction and hermeneutics for those working in environmental disciplines such as architecture, urban planning, and cultural geography. Mugerauer maintains that a shift took place since the 1970s as the work of Martin Heidegger, Hans-Georg Gadamer and others offered new ways of reading texts and discovering meaning. These approaches affected a variety of disciplines, including architecture and the visual arts. Mugerauer writes, "Only after the linguistically based disciplines had substantially shifted did architecture, urban

20. Torgerson, *Architecture of Immanence*, 204n57.

planning, environmental design, landscape studies, and cultural geography gradually begin to push beyond the dominant emphasis on language and textuality and pick up on the relatively obscure redefinitions of things, space, and the built environment contained in the new approaches."[21] The goal of these tools of cultural analysis is to "explicate space and built environments."[22] But for Mugerauer, given the proliferation of postmodern phenomenologies appearing in print, it is increasingly difficult to keep abreast of developments. The ever-expanding methodologies make for the "current, confusing situation."[23] In constructing a method of reading the meaning of buildings, it seems one can take the ground-breaking work of Heidegger, Gadamer, Michel Foucault, Jacques Derrida, or the writings Jean-François Lyotard, Jean Baudrillard, Gilles Deluze, Felix Guattari, Michel de Certeau, Luce Irigaray, Julia Kristeva, and others as a basis. Others like Jürgen Habermas and Alasdair MacIntyre would retain modern and classical traditions of interpretation. Still others, especially since the 1980s, have written specifically for architects, some using post-constructuralist interpretations of space. Again, Mugerauer summarizes the contemporary horizon,

> Even if the methodologies themselves are increasingly intelligible, however, it still is not clear how they apply to the built environment rather than to language, texts, and psychological-sociological practices . . . the available analysis of buildings and landscapes is fragmentary, scattered, and sometimes superficial or untrustworthy. All the activity has produced only a few sustained analyses that join theoretical mastery to professional familiarity with the built environment.[24]

Since hermeneutics (as does deconstruction) focuses on texts, seeing nearly everything as "language-signifier," the dynamics of the human environment are not normally treated. In response to the situation, Mugerauer focuses on hermeneutics. Through the course of human history "of explicit aesthetic and critical theory, the basic foundation remains the same: what we make has meaning because of its extrinsic relations." This statement synthesizes twenty-five centuries of aesthetic thinking, and is remarkably pertinent to this project. It is possible that Mugerauer himself, with his

21. Mugerauer, *Interpreting Environments*, xviii.

22. Ibid.

23. Ibid., xx.

24. Ibid.

focus on hermeneutics, overemphasizes the textuality of a building, which speaks a language that is less definitive and more suggestive than that of literary texts. We will argue that buildings, and in particular sacred space, hold meaning because of purpose and memory, of what has taken place within and around them. Said differently, they are meaningful because of their extrinsic relations.

William Whyte provides a clarifying perspective on architectural interpretation in his monograph, "How Do Buildings Mean? Some Issues of Interpretation in the History of Architecture."[25] He argues that architecture has and conveys meaning, and that it is widely understood to do so. Yet how the meaning is "inscribed" and communicated is unclear. He writes,

> For some writers, architecture—like all the arts—is an emanation of the Zeitgeist. For others, it should be understood as an expression of the underlying social order, or as an aspect of deep culture. Still others would interpret it as a self contained sign system, with its own grammar, syntax, and ways of meaning. What unites these authors, however, is the idea that architecture can be understood by analogy to language: either as a "code" capable of use to communicate the architect's 'intentions' to the users of their buildings," or more literally as an equivalent to spoken or written language in its own right.[26]

Following Mikhail Bakhtin, Whyte suggests buildings cannot simply be "read." Instead, they are understood, through the process of design, construction, and interpretation, through a process of "translation." Whyte makes three assumptions when considering a building. First, architecture is a human action, and as such, is a kind of text (as per Paul Ricoeur) capable of being understood. Second, architecture comprises many forms and genres, and as such is complex. It represents an intertwining of texts, and thus resists easy interpretation (perhaps as the ideas of regulating lines and the golden section, discussed by Jacobsen, tend toward.) Third, a structure evolves as conceived and executed by an architect, and again as interpreted by a user or viewer. Therefore, the evolution of a building is best understood as a series of transpositions, each with its own meaning. These transpositions together make up the character ("work") of architecture. "The historian's role . . . is to trace these transpositions, and in that way uncover

25. Whyte, "How Do Buildings Mean?," 153–77.
26. Ibid., 154.

the many meanings of architecture."[27] Finally, Whyte gives examples of changing understandings of buildings. Instead of attempting to determine which of these is correct, it is better to understand these various transpositions and contexts as together making up the sense of a building. Thus one can most accurately say that "architecture . . . does not convey meaning: it conveys meanings."[28] It is not "an artifact that can be simply described, but a multifaceted construct capable of multiple interpretations."[29] Whyte (and Mugerauer) does not discuss a spiritual dimension in the possible range of meanings, but his methodology makes it possible to be sensitive to the spiritual dimension inherent in a structure.

William Dyrness gathers together aesthetic approaches in "a kind of apologetic theology" in his book, *Poetic Theology: God and the Poetics of Everyday Life.* He contends that the habits of devotion, ritual, and community point to the essential nature of aesthetic experience, and help give expression to what is distinctively human.[30] He wants to restore the place of beauty to Christian life, insisting on its importance in shaping feelings and actions. Dyrness points out that aesthetic and symbolic practices are places that intersect with the presence of God in the world; insofar as they do so, they have a theological character. Yet he concedes that theology as normally engaged does not seem well suited to investigate the intersection between God and the forms of culture.[31] Although some theologians have raised questions of aesthetics and culture, theological approaches of the past few centuries have emphasized rationality to the neglect of the artistic, ritual, and image and their importance in religious life. Conversely, those who have investigated the importance of the "poetic" have largely employed philosophical or sociological methods that ignore the role of theology. These fail to come to terms with human desire and our ability to relate to God with our whole selves as embodied souls. Our relating to God takes place not only cognitively but also through imagination and the senses, and is rightly directed within the parameters of Scripture and of God's own Trinitarian relationship. This suggests that the will focused on God is animated by love, as argued by Augustine in his treatise on the Trinity. Dyrness writes,

27. Ibid., 155.
28. Ibid., 177.
29. Ibid.
30. Dyrness, *Poetic Theology*, 6.
31. Ibid.

The person, composed of memory, understanding, and will, becomes an image of the Trinitarian character of God. And Augustine believed that it is from this understanding of the person, grounded in God, that one moves to comprehend the world. This theologically-grounded self came to be fundamental for the humanists, and, later, for Calvin.[32]

In his investigation of historical approaches to aesthetics, Dyrness contrasts Roman Catholic and Protestant ways of understanding (seeing), the former tending toward forms in which God's work is embodied in the world, and the latter toward the human story as taken up in the narrative of the gospel and God's saving acts: "Here, then, are two quite different ways of understanding the possible role of aesthetics for human life. The one tradition stresses the splendor of *form* of the progressive revelation of the divine glory; the other stresses the *act*—one might say the drama—of a created order called to praise God."[33]

A distinctly Reformed spirituality relates especially to the drama of salvation. It is oriented toward text, and also to the auditory, and is historically suspicious of most images. But Dyrness provides an important corrective to the Word-centered tradition, arguing that God's glory can shine through beautiful objects produced by culture. Indeed, "The authority of Scripture must always take some historical shape to become visible," and in words quoted from Artur Grabowski, "Without the arts, the religion of the revealed Word will not have a representative in the world of phenomena."[34] Dyrness's argument is grounded in Scripture, which not only includes warnings against surrendering to "the lust of the eyes" but also descriptions of beauty in creation and in the divine character. In addition, he sees a connection between beauty and the pursuit of justice, which he explores in his chapter "Aesthetics and Social Transformation." A consequence of human sin, emphasized in the Reformed tradition, is that human culture expresses not only beauty and goodness, but also depravity. Therefore, cultural phenomena need to be evaluated critically in moral terms. How exactly this is done is an area that calls for more critical reflection, but this endeavor is essential in order to develop the "aesthetic criteria for the health of communities"[35] for which Dyrness rightly calls.

32. Ibid., 43.
33. Ibid., 291.
34. Ibid., 251.
35. Ibid., 268.

Jeremy Begbie proposes a theological aesthetic to bring theology to bear on the arts in his book *Voicing Creation's Praise: Towards a Theology of the Arts.* He explains two Protestant methodologies, those of Paul Tillich and of the nineteenth- and twentieth-century Dutch Neo-Calvinists before formulating his own aesthetic approach, concluding that "although Tillich and the Dutch Neo-Calvinists show a commendable concern to integrate theology and the philosophy of art, it is questionable whether they espouse a theology adequate to establish and sustain this integration."[36] Tillich explores the relation between religion and art, tying cultural artifacts to "ultimate concern," but for Begbie, he falls short in Christology and theory of symbol. Tillich "is prone to extreme generalizations and bizarre judgments," including his over-reliance on German Expressionism.[37] (67)

The Neo-Calvinists ground human creativity in common grace, seeing earthly beauty as reflective of God's beauty. Nonetheless, they overemphasize Law, downplay the relevance of Trinity and the Incarnation, and undervalue art that does not display outward beauty. Their claim that beauty is the "qualifying feature of art carries with it a number of drawbacks," including a movement toward Platonism. Drawing on the hermeneutics of Gadamer and Polanyi, Begbie argues that art concerns more than subjectivism, and defends its connection to knowledge and truth.[38] A concept of beauty should be embedded in creation and based on Christ's overcoming brokenness by entering into the world, shaped by the contours of the gospel. Begbie emphasizes art as metaphor and its irreducible quality; he points out, "Whatever meaning is disclosed in a piece of art is given in and with the work itself, not as an ingredient to be distilled out, but as a total impact which claims our attention and involvement."[39] This claim will be relevant to our study of particular works of architecture, which on account of their aesthetic, functional, communal, and historic contexts, cannot be divided into form on one hand and meaning on another.

In *Truth and Method*, Hans-Georg Gadamer provides a rationale for a hermeneutic of culture. He writes that *Bildung*, "culture," is the root word for "form" and "image." To make art is to formulate depictions of human experience. Since experience is a part of history and therefore changing, it is not immutably fixed, but rather has the quality of an event. Works of art,

---

36. Begbie, *Voicing Creation's Praise*, 167.

37. Ibid., 67.

38. Ibid., 199ff.

39. Ibid., 249.

then, are not experiences fashioned by genius, but "play" that transforms into structure. The creative event is not about the heroic individual making objects of veneration that exist in a timeless sphere, but is a participation in a game that "presents itself." In this process communication takes place, not simply as the passing of information, but as a subject matter making itself accessible.[40]

Hermeneutics, or the question of interpretation, "goes beyond the limits of the concept of method;"[41] it is not limited to science, but rather is a part of general human experience. Gadamer's claim that "the province of hermeneutics is universal and especially that language is the form in which understanding is achieved embraces 'pre-hermeneutic' consciousness."[42] Humility is called for in this endeavor, because in art truth is available that cannot be accessed through aesthetic philosophy or method alone.[43] All interpretation entails retelling. Gadamer holds that the human sciences "maintained a humanistic heritage that distinguishes them from all other kinds of modern research and brings them close to other, quite different, extrascientific experiences, especially those peculiar to art." While scientific method can still apply to the humanities ("the social world,") the objectives of knowledge are different than in science.[44] And understanding comes not simply through Kant's question, "What are the conditions of our knowledge?" but also through asking, "How is understanding possible?" Art–and in our investigation, architecture—seeks a different kind of truth than pure scientific method does, a subjective "being-in-motion . . . that constitutes its finitude and historicity."[45]

Gadamer argues that works of art "can assume certain real functions and resist others."[46] Two of its functions that pertain to the making of a place of worship are the space of memory and reverence. Thus particular works, including architecture, assume special significance as they point beyond themselves "to the whole of a context determined by them and for them. The greatest and most distinguished of these forms is architecture."[47]

40. Gadamer, *Truth and Method*, xii, xv.
41. Ibid., xx.
42. Ibid., xxxiv.
43. Ibid., xxii.
44. Ibid., xxvi.
45. Ibid., xxvii.
46. Ibid., 149.
47. Ibid.

A built structure "extends beyond itself in two ways," in its purpose and in "the place it is to take up in a total spatial context."[48] The duality between a building's purpose and its plasticity comprises its meaning, or "true increase of being." In this relationship a building can become a work of art. In these reflections Gadamer touches on two of the classic features of architecture, and offers a lens through which to view churches. (His discussion on decoration seems forced, suggesting that the term properly describes architecture's ability to embrace all "representational" forms of art.) He does helpfully remind us that part of the meaning of a museum, concert hall, or church originates from its context, or what Dyrness calls the "value-laden interaction between humans and their environment."[49] Gadamer concludes,

> Hence, given its comprehensiveness in relation to all the arts, architecture involves a twofold mediation. As the art which creates space, it both shapes it and leaves it free. It not only embraces all decorative shaping of space, including ornament, but is itself decorative in nature. The nature of decoration consists in performing that two-sided mediation: namely to draw the viewer's attention to itself, to satisfy his taste, and then to redirect it away from itself to the greater whole of the life context which it accompanies.[50]

Gadamer therefore expands Heidegger's hermeneutic circle, tying it to tradition in his "historical-hermeneutical activity."[51] (295) One's past, and the complex of expectations one brings to a work of art or a building influences the ways these texts, whether literary or visual, are perceived. Prejudgments are always present as we attempt to read culture and its artifacts. Rather than invalidating meaning, these enhance it and make it possible. These do not obviate the ability to arrive at truth; instead, as they are taken into account, they can lead to new understanding and new possibilities of meaning.

Lindsay Jones, in *The Hermeneutics of Sacred Architecture*, argues that the meanings of religious buildings are shaped by the rites and rituals that take place within them. Sacred architecture is perceived as an event within the community and for its later observers. A two-fold mechanism is at work in relation to architecture: first, allurement, and then transformation. Comparison across cultures is necessary to draw out meaning. Attentive

---

48. Ibid.
49. Dyrness, *Poetic Theology*, 82.
50. Gadamer, *Truth and Method*, 151.
51. Ibid., 295.

to the uniqueness of the larger culture around them, Jones draws on the hermeneutics of Gadamer, and allows for multiple possible interpretations in a "superabundance of meaning."[52] For him, sacred architecture demonstrates intentionality, revealing a designer's conceptions, and in turn shapes culture from its place in the cultural landscape. What takes place within a building continually adds to and changes its meaning. The limitations springing from the biblical prohibition against idolatry seem to make the interpretive task more difficult. An alternative reading could suggest, however, that this limitation channeled Protestant creativity in new ways. Jones repeatedly employs the phrase "religiously significant," but declines to define the term, and he leaves us on our own to develop characteristics common to all sacred architecture.

INTENTIONALITY IN ARCHITECTURAL EXPRESSION

Given the difficulty of reconstructing what the architects and designers of interior worship space were trying to express in Geneva and Paris, we will propose not conclusions, but hints as to their intentions. Theological reflection on these is scarce. There is necessarily a tentative, even a speculative character to the methodology used here. The substantial contribution being attempted in this work will be the result of comparing classically Catholic and classically Reformed space. The comparison suggests that the Reformed designers were drawn to Vitruvius and the classical vision as a part of a grand project of restoration and the idea of an ordered, rational world. Certainly other interpretations are possible—even that there is no theological meaning to their work. But this work will argue the contrary, based on both informed interpretation of the buildings themselves, and on inferences by other Reformed architects and designers. As a result, meanings of Protestant theology, ethos, and values will emerge that are inaccessible through verbal analysis alone.

The Reformed movement in France and Switzerland was motivated theologically, as well as by other concerns. The people that recovered the classical sources of architecture were Huguenots. Many of the members of the French Academy were Huguenots, as is demonstrated by Philip Benedict[53]. The examples of churches discussed in this study, while not definitive, suggest that Reformed architects and arrangers of space were in fact

52. Jones, *Hermeneutics of Sacred Architecture*, 21.
53. Benedict, "Calvinism as a Culture?" 34.

attempting to communicate theologically through their visual art. If they did not understand churches to be sacred space per se, insisting that all creation was filled with the presence of God and thereby sacred, they did see churches as special, set apart.

Thus the subject in question is the actual architectural monument. There are of course many others, but this study focuses on three. The most relevant texts are the architectural forms themselves, although their architects failed to comment specifically on them. The commentators on these buildings are nearly nonexistent. The one person that does write about them, Catharine Randall, is controversial. Thus we will take the approach of exploration, of looking for probabilities, and not settled conclusions. This is an area of investigation that will need the work of others, and this work can only begin that process.

There is a danger in assuming that Renaissance architecture was not built with conceptual, psychological, or pedagogical purposes in mind—that, unlike with the case of spoken or written rhetoric, buildings were somehow not meant to teach and persuade; or that Huguenots, in rejecting the Catholic religion, were only concerned with functionality and economy. Far from it, as this paper will argue—there was much thought and care in reflecting a new interpretation of God's Word through the space where its worshippers met. The human person is an embodied creature, and there is an inseparable link between architecture, beliefs, and the experience of worship. Therefore, the Swiss and French Reformed were concerned with creating representational sacred spaces. Their writings continually employ images of defense and of spiritual warfare, and they saw their worship spaces as emblematic of God's Word as a sure redoubt. We will examine the writings of Calvin and of French architects themselves, underscoring that the questions about sacred space are not anachronistic, but were at the heart of what early modern francophone reformers were trying to do.

How did French Protestants of the late sixteenth and early seventeenth centuries, a despised minority labeled by the Catholic majority as the "religion prétendue Réformée" (the "so-called Reformed religion") conceive of their faith? Specifically, how did they express their faith through the churches they occasionally adapted for their use or through the built structures in which they gathered for worship?

Part of the answer is that this persecuted marginal community sought meaning and attempted to evoke the classical past in the midst of religious and political tumult. French Calvinism in the seventeenth century helped transmit classical ideas. The architect Sebastiano Serlio, through his *Fourth Book,* spread the ideas of Roman architect Vitruvius. These were in turn diffused through Genevan and other printers and appropriated by Huguenot builders in France. Huguenots were able to see these ideas as consistent with their Calvinist faith, as classical forms appropriate for conveying notions of the nature of God and the character of the Christian community.

For sixteenth- and seventeenth-century Reformed Christians there was a link between architecture and worship. While Calvin proscribed images in worship space, his lacuna in specifications for worship space suggests that for him much of the arrangement of the setting for Reformed worship falls under the area of *adiaphora,* or indifferent things, allowing for various Reformed communities to arrive at their own conclusions about the meaning and utilization of space. An examination of some of the writings of Calvin, Serlio, Philibert de l'Orme, Jacques-Androuet du Cerceau, Jacques Perret, and Bernard Palissy will show this to be the case. In addition, as Randall C. Zachman argues in *Image and Word in the Theology of John Calvin,* the reformer was not opposed to all images per se, but only to humanly-crafted ones.[54] If Zachman is correct, then seeing as well as hearing was central in Calvin's theology. The manifestation of God is seen in the cosmos, in the Christian community, in pious individuals, in the sacraments, and in the ceremonies of Christian worship. It was Calvin's openness to God's self-revealing in creation and redemption which permitted the Calvinist architects to conceive of their own work both theologically and imagistically.

The study continues with an examination of the preference of Protestant architects, in particular Salomon de Brosse, for a more sober and rationalistic strain of Renaissance architecture, as opposed to post-Tridentine Catholic emotionalism and promotion of images for the instruction of the illiterate. Helping to lay the foundation for the Neoclassical style, Protestantism thus conveyed the ideas of Vitruvius to posterity in a minimalist interpretation.

Contemporary drawings of Brosse's "temple" in Charenton, as well as the St. Gervais church in Paris, compared with Protestant adaptation of St. Pierre in Geneva, provide insights into issues of an openly Huguenot designer in the employ of Catholic power during the period of the Edict of Nantes, which provided some toleration of the Protestant faith, within strict limitations. This project brings the prevailing conception of

54. Zachman, *Image and Word,* 19ff.

the origins of French classicism into question through positing of possible themes of investigation including alternative ways of remembering the past and signifying the present. At its core, Protestant architecture employed material mimesis to respond to a spiritual, social, and theological need to transform the stage for human experience. The Neoclassical style has its roots not only in antiquity, but in the architectural development of early modern Protestant architects.

The Catholicism of the late Middle Ages perceived nature as an unambiguous witness to the presence of God, with created things as clear markers of divine will and conduits for divine-human relations. There was spiritual energy throughout what seemed on the surface to be the realm of the profane. Medieval piety differentiated between the temporal and the eternal, between nature and grace, and yet, as Berndt Hamm has shown in *The Reformation of Faith*, the two polarities depended on and interpenetrated one another and holiness was imminent in material things, just as in the consecrated host of the Mass. The sacred intersected continually with the tangible and phenomenological, summarized in the sacramental view of Thomas Aquinas, who wrote that "Spiritual effects were fittingly given under the likeness of things [that are] visible."[55] While such a worldview emphasized a sacred/secular divide—some places are more touched by the divine than others—it also meant that anything might potentially serve as a connecting point to the spiritual realm. As Lee Palmer Wandel writes,

> [Catholic] Christianity . . . structured people's experience of space. Pilgrimage had carved a particular configuration of geography: shrines and paths to those places where Christians might touch relics of extraordinary holiness, might come closer to sanctity, where the likelihood of witnessing a miracle was greater.[56]

Just as pilgrimage was configured to the spatial and temporal rhythms of the human body and the time (and number of paces) required to move from one space to another, so the church buildings themselves were tied to the dimensions of the human body. Renaissance architects and engravers, including Da Vinci and Jean Martin, followed Vitruvius's description of a man with outstretched arms and legs whose body aligned to the geometry of a square and a circle. Images based on this dimension proved popular since it conformed to the Renaissance ideal of man (see figure 5), created in

55. Aquinas, *Contra Gentiles*, IV.61.2.
56. Wandel, *Voracious Idols*, 18.

the image of God, as the measure of all things. The "Vitruvian man" functioned, then, as a template for designs that were balanced and pleasing to the eye. In a similar vein, late medieval people saw the church edifice as an echo of the human body, with the altar as the head, and the entire consecrated structure as holy. This illustrates the division between sacred and secular, spiritual and physical, distinct and yet ambiguous in their relationship, one in which what was eternal depended in some way on what was temporal, corporeal, and passing away.

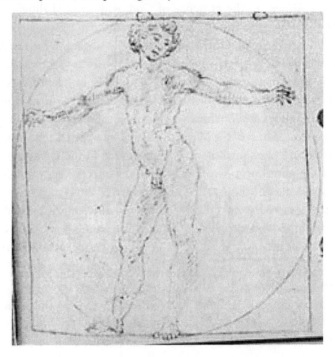

Figure 5: Giorgio Martini's "Vitruvian Man," demonstrating ideal human proportions.

For Protestants, in contrast, the stamp of the divine was found in the material world not in the union of materiality and metaphysics nor in their opposition, but in the presence of the Word of God, which provides the narrative of salvation and holds all things together in its creative power. A Word-oriented perception of the world is not forgetting of signs of the sacred in the world and thus losing an experience of the immediacy of God, nor what Max Weber called "the disenchantment of the world" in which the absolute transcendence of God and the isolation of the individual found few points of contact.[57] Weber's description of the rise of a Protestant worldview seems too facile. The created order echoes the will and active providence of God, and yet, a distinction remains between God and the creature, as the phrase *finitum non capax infinitum* ("the finite cannot contain the infinite") suggests. The incomprehensibility of God means that while certain mysteries will one day be revealed, humans cannot transcend their own finitude by touching holy relics or by occupying a holy place.

Because of this conceptual reorientation, Protestants sought to discard Catholic distortions and return to a more scriptural and Word-based way of communicating divine revelation. In architecture and the decorative arts, Protestants employed a mimetic tactic wherein visual space imitated and reproduced the words of revelation in order to represent the divine character. The real world was not so much a sacramental vehicle, as material to be recreated to recall or parallel salvific intervention in the world of human action and events. Space provided an auditorium for hearing of God's mighty acts in Scripture, and in more subtle ways visually represented that process. There was a dialectic between God and the world. The late medieval conception was to dramatize God's plan through the order of the world; but for Reformed believers oriented toward the text, tracing the divine in the material world was problematic, and needed to be seen through, as well as corrected by, the text. The relationship between metaphysics and the material was not transparent but rather suggestive. As Catharine Randall writes, "Divine light, when shone on earthly objects, will eradiate and shine through them. In and of themselves, however, they are opaque."[58] For this reason, in order to understand, one must delve beneath the surface of things to discern hidden meanings. This interest in occult and coded meanings was widespread in the sixteenth and seventeenth centuries, and informed the designing and execution of Protestant worship space, particularly when such spaces served a minority Reformed population within a larger, hostile Catholic culture, a theme Randall explores in *Building Codes*. The relative emptiness of Protestant worship space reflected the Reformed tendency toward iconoclasm, although, since it was filled with light, an analog for the Word, it was not entirely bereft of symbolism. By recasting the narrative of God's people, a pilgrim people in the world, Protestant architects used the materiality of the built space to *undermine* materiality, and to reconfigure the space that defined them.

57. Weber, *Essays in Sociology*, 290.
58. Randall, *Earthly Treasures*, 2.

Chapter 1, then, will consider the conflicting aesthetics and the meaning of space in the Reformed tradition. We will turn to some formative voices of secondary literature for help in evaluating buildings, and raise some questions about intentionality in architectural expression.

After establishing our methodology (chapter 2) and considering the context of medieval space against which Protestants were reacting (chapter 3), we look for evidence of a Reformed conception of space (chapter 4); then the theoretical background of Vitruvius and the sixteenth-century architectural treatise (chapter 5). Chapter 6 will trace the transmission of Vitruvian ideals through the work of Protestant architects. We will finally turn to three case studies to determine the nature of Reformed conceptions of sacred space (chapter 7).

PART ONE

PART ONE

CHAPTER 2

Iconology—Outline of a Working Methodology

ARCHITECTURE AS A VISUAL MEDIUM

Architecture as a visual medium envelops and influences emotional inter-action differently than do the other visual arts. That is because human actions include a spatial characteristic. In consequence, architecture has both a public and personal existentialist character. More than simply inviting the viewer into an imaginative scene, as in painting, or focusing on a particular object, as in sculpture, architecture envelops, creating literal environments and representational space, not simply representations of space. It includes nonrepresentational compositions but also, potentially, coded meanings of theological significance.

Therefore, in a study such as this we are compelled to use build-ings themselves as texts in order to assess their meaning. As J. H. Elliott argues in his book *History in the Making*, artifacts like the churches we examine played a cultural role of defining the faith of their communities.[1] Their architects' use of existing styles did not necessarily conflict with the new meanings intended by their designers, but expressed possibilities of expressing their ideas about a new creation, the right ordering of life, of rationality and the purposes of God. As we will argue, in utilizing these

1. Elliott, *History in the Making*.

styles, they edited the ideas of Vitruvius and helped recover a classical style and its visual language.

A methodology is needed to address the questions raised, a criteria to assess the meanings suggested by cultural artifacts in their own context, and in particular to ascertain what churches have meant for the communities who build them or appropriate and adapt them. Richard Kieckhefer provides a starting place for articulating a methodology that will approach the questions of interpreting liturgical space.[2] Using Kieckhefer as a point of departure, informed by insights from Jacobsen, Torgerson, Mugerauer, Whyte, and Dyrness, we will look at a sort of "architectural iconology" of French Protestantism, by which is meant an historical analysis and aesthetic investigation of architectural forms and images in their context. More specifically, this will help us to read French Protestant worship spaces, to determine what forms meant theologically to those that designed or used them.

WORD-ORIENTED AND FORM-ORIENTED CHURCH SPACE

All churches demonstrate characteristics that can be described as sacramental and evangelical. All Christian communities celebrate the sacraments, even if their major point of contact with the divine is in the hearing of the Word of God; all are evangelical in the sense of reading Scripture and recalling the gospel tradition, even if this is sublimated to the celebration of the Mass. However, churches tend to exhibit one of these factors as a "fundamental determinant of church design."[3] Some follow a long Eucharistic ecclesial and architectural tradition dating from the early period of Christian worship, seeing the approach to sacraments as this fundamental determinant of church design. Others follow the kerygmatic tradition that sprung up in the later Middle Ages and in the sixteenth-century Reformation, a tradition that understands the encounter with the Word of God to be the primary manner in which one accesses the holy. These influences can be seen to a greater or lesser degree in all churches, then, but one of these tendencies shapes the essential form.

Various contexts contribute to the experience of responding to a church, including cultural interaction, expectations, the ethos of its

2. Kieckhefer, *Theology in Stone.*

3. Krautheimer, *Early Christian*, 13.

community, and how it is being used liturgically.[4] One person, for example, might experience a liturgy as a meaningless show, and another not as a show but a sacred enactment. The meaning of architectural space is negotiated, then, between the intention of the architect and the experience of the building's users. Response to a church is learned and requires informed reflection, for "the meanings of a church are seldom obvious."[5]

Kieckhefer proposes four ways of looking at a church, undergirded by two foundational questions: How is it used? And, what sort of reaction is it meant to elicit? Both questions may be separated into two distinct refinements: when we ask how a church is used, we are enquiring first about the *overall configuration of space*: "how is it shaped, and how does its design relate to the flow, the dynamics of worship?" Another way of putting the question would be, Where is *"the central focus of attention,* if any . . . and how does it make clear what is most important in worship?"[6] The questions address the immediate impact and first impressions of walking into the church, of what the disparate elements communicate, and of the mood evoked. The center of attention communicates what is most important in the experience of worship, and pays attention to the "accumulation of impressions" that comes to the forefront through longer exposure. Marks of holiness, of the set apart nature of the worship space, lead to an intensification of experience and to deeper understanding.

To further elaborate Kieckhefer's methodology, he proposes four distinct questions to pose when looking at a church. They are:

1. *How is the space shaped, and how does its design relate to the flow of worship?*

2. *Where is the focus of attention?* (On the Lord's Table, an altar, or a pulpit? Is the focus on the worshiping community itself?)

3. *What is the aesthetic impact?* (Entering a church parallels our experience of coming into God's presence. A church's design—its aesthetic impact—reminds us of leaving behind the world for a time to enjoy community with God in prayer as well as with fellow believers.)

4. *What is its symbolic resonance?* (Does the church communicate rich associations that invite further exploration? Such connotations can take place both visually and verbally, but if little is communicated

4. Kieckhefer, *Theology in Stone*, 5–7.
5. Ibid., 9.
6. Ibid., 10.

that draws us into deeper meanings, then there is little to hold one's interest.)

Following Jacobsen, we might also ask of a church, Is it beautiful? Does it elicit our affection? How does the building provide for "the experience of approach, for hospitality, and for enhancing relationships?" As Lindsay Jones reminded us, buildings also have meaning because of how they are used as containers of religious activity. To grasp multiple meanings, we will look at transpositions between a building's designer, its users, and those who observe it. Dyrness's analysis of Protestant use of narrative applies as well.

First, however, a historical sketch of the development of the sacramental and the evangelical traditions will establish some context, and further define the two foundational orientations to church space that undergird discussion of churches. If Gadamer is correct that a structure's local history as an "event" and its social context help define meaning, then this survey is indispensible.

THE CLASSIC SACRAMENTAL TRADITION: ORIGINS OF SPATIAL ARRANGEMENTS IN CATHOLIC CHURCHES

The classic sacramental tradition emerged from the first decades of church building in the fourth century. Its most representative form is known as the basilican plan, a long hall-like structure with side aisles, completed by an apse form at the eastern end. The name basilica derives from the Greek *stoa*, a long covered walkway, and *basilea*, royal, a designation for a king's tribunal chamber in fifth-century BC Athens. In the second century BC, basilicas functioned as public halls for conducting business and deciding legal affairs.[7] Colonnaded aisles ran parallel along the sides, and a raised dais on the apse provided space for magistrates to sit. The central hall, being higher than the side aisles, permitted light to penetrate the building through clerestory windows. Christianity developed within the cultural framework of the Roman-Hellenistic world, and its organization as well as its architecture reflected this context (see figure 6). Familiarity with the historical development of the basilican form of church building, prevalent in the classic sacramental church, helps us understand the forms of medieval churches

7. Gietmann, "Basilica," line 3ff.

that sixteenth-century Protestants inherited in territories where the Reformation was adopted.

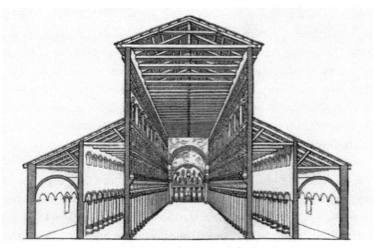

**Figure 6: A front section of old St. Peter's church in Rome
shows the Roman basilican form.**

Worship in the Late Roman Empire was a public obligation for its subjects, who were required to pray to the gods who assured the well-being of the state. In the private realm, citizens were free to worship or not without interference. As long as cults of personal salvation did not interfere with the cult of the emperor, explains Richard Krautheimer, no conflict need arise.[8] Indeed, in the first century of the development of Christianity, the faith grew with little notice. In officialdom or when under scrutiny, however, worship of the gods became a litmus test for loyalty to the emperor. As Krautheimer points out, "worship was a civic duty performed according to a state ritual."[9] Due to the work of St Paul, however, the Christian movement broke with Judaism, and could no longer be seen as simply an offshoot or as a heresy within its ranks.

Within the first century, Christianity spread to the Hellenized cities of Greece, Asia Minor, to towns and villages, and eventually to Rome. Organization of new congregations fell to lay administrators, overseers or bishops (*episkopoi*), and stewards or deacons (*diakonoi*), with preaching and guidance supplied by the itinerant disciples and by apostles and prophets.

8. Krautheimer, *Early Christian*, 23.
9. Ibid., 23.

By the mid to late second century, tasks included teaching and the leading of worship, works of charity, the teaching of catechumens, the care of cemeteries, the cure of souls, and the administration of property. Bishops and deacons, along with elders or presbyters (*presbuteroi*) formed a hierarchical class of clergy. Bishops eventually came to oversee the churches of each city, following the pattern of Bishop Dionysius in Rome (259–268). As Christians grew in power and influence, they came to be seen as challenges to state authority. Early persecutions had been local and sporadic, but after 250, Christian self-separation and refusal to participate in the cult of emperor worship caused ill feeling to issue in fierce persecution.[10] In the mid third century, authorities

in Alexandria, Carthage, and Rome confiscated property, executed church leaders, and prohibited Christians from meeting together. The church proved resilient, however, and Emperor Gallienus restored property, cemeteries, and the right to assemble. The larger churches owned property, either legally or overlooked by authorities. Smaller congregations continued to meet in homes, and large congregations would revert to this practice in times of persecution.

Built structures served spiritual needs as well as the exigencies of social welfare, for worship administration, and distribution of charity. Cemeteries allowed for memorials for the dead and particularly for the martyrs. The liturgy had been standardized by the early third century, and the common meal was no longer celebrated weekly, but on special occasions only, such as memorial banquets and meals for the poor.

A service consisted of two parts: the Mass of the Catechumens, for the catechumens as well as for regular believers, which consisted of prayers, Scripture, and sermon. The second part, the Mass of the Faithful, was for regular, confirmed members, and consisted of a procession for bringing offerings and contributions for the poor and for the maintenance of the church, and of the Eucharist.

The assembly hall had to be large enough to accommodate worshippers, and was divided into spaces for clergy and laity. The bishop's seat occupied a space on a raised platform to one end of the chamber, adjoined by chairs for the other assisting clergy. Men and women sat on opposite sides of the assembly. Furniture included chairs for the clergy, a table for communion, and a second table for the offerings. A confirmation room and a baptistery were also needed, according to the needs of the cult. Other

10. Ibid., 25.

requirements included rooms for clergy offices and quarters for clergy and their families; rooms for storing and distributing food and clothing for the poor; classrooms for the instruction of converts, and community gathering space. The scale and diversity of these usages determined that congregations needed more space than a private home could afford.

Krautheimer tells us such structures, occasionally purpose-built and often purchased and adapted, were dubbed *domus ecclesiae* or *oikos ecclesias*, or in Rome, a *titulus*.[11] Such houses that are known follow the general plan of local utilitarian domestic architecture of the third century. Christians shied away from religious forms of architecture such as temples and sanctuaries because of their association with pagan religious practices and Roman cultic customs. Christian meeting places were usually typical peristyle dwellings, following the manner of domestic middle class architecture, as was certainly the case at Dura-Europos in the eastern part of the Empire. This style comprised a courtyard faced on three sides by rooms, and by a columned portico on the fourth. In Rome, tenements seem to have been converted into Christian community houses in the third and fourth century to accommodate the needs of larger congregations.[12] Christians integrated classical forms into funerary architecture—mausolea, martyria, and banqueting halls—more readily than into worship spaces, since pagan funeral buildings did not carry the religious associations of public monumental buildings. Structures devoted to regular Christian worship and church administration resisted classical pagan architectural influences longer, preferring the purely utilitarian design of the *domus ecclesiae* into the late fourth century.

Gradually, however, churches began to emulate the more exalted architectural surroundings and ceremonial practices of a Roman magistrate. As Christianity gained official favor and eventually became the dominant religious power, the basilica was the principal form used for ecclesiastical building. From the time of Constantine, "Christian concepts [are] expressed in the language of the official architecture of Late Antiquity."[13]

Constantine's Edict of Milan in 313 insured official toleration for Christianity, and throughout his twenty-four year reign the church became increasingly enmeshed with the power of the state. The hierarchy of leadership that had developed in the years of peace for the church from 260 to 305

11. Ibid.

12. Ibid., 29.

13. Ibid., 37.

further solidified; the Mass was standardized across the Empire; and the bishops accustomed themselves to the privilege, rank, and insignia of high government officials.[14] In consequence, the church demanded an architecture commensurate with its social standing, and sanctuaries that stood on a par with the grandest of palaces and public buildings.[15] Sanctuaries contained "a lofty throne atop a dais, an audience chamber," and worship was accompanied by "the performance of acclamations upon entering the meeting room for services."

Today, variants of the basilican plan are seen in Catholic, Orthodox, Lutheran, Episcopalian, and other traditions. An extended nave contains seats for the congregants, and a chancel allows for the seating of clergy. Kieckhefer underscores that terminology and arrangements vary, but standard features include choir stalls and an altar, a symbolic place of sacrifice. This, in the classic sacramental church, is the point of focus. He writes,

> If a church of this type is based on a coherent aesthetic vision, it is usually one meant to evoke the immanence of God and the possibility among worshipers for transcendence of ordinary consciousness. Such churches often abound with symbolic forms and decorations, making them rich in symbolic resonance.[16]

That is, if the church was constructed with intentionality, the grandeur and immediacy of God will likely resonate in that space. Such spaces are usually replete with artistic pieces, but even without them, the structure itself communicates. It may be obvious that the scale of a classical sacramental church edifice communicates God's transcendence more than it does immanence due to the height and the expansiveness of Romanesque or Gothic styles. This dynamic is counterbalanced, however, with symbols and iconology, which convey a tangibility and imaginative locus for worshippers.

Even with the change in religious loyalty to Calvinist or Lutheran teachings, old perceptions of sacred space were not quickly or easily overcome. In addition, practical considerations insured that Protestants, where possible, appropriated classical sacramental churches, changing the utilization of space where that proved necessary for their purposes. Examples of this trend are numerous in the Rhineland-Palatinate, in Scotland, in the Netherlands, in the Alsace, in southwest France, and in the cities

14. Ibid., 39.
15. Ibid.
16. Ibid., 11.

of Protestant Switzerland such as Neuchâtel, Basel, Lausanne, Bern, and Geneva.

The basilican form, then, conveyed dignity, solidity, spaciousness, and grandeur, attributes suited to its original usage as a place of business or governance. As well, it was suited to express, in its adaptation for Christian worship, a theology of transcendence, power, and authority, as Krautheimer suggests. Churches were divided into spaces of increasing degrees of holiness, conjuring memories of the ancient Jewish temple in Jerusalem. The physical movement from the church yard, over the west porch and through the main doors, most often passing under carvings of Christ at the Last Judgment, would have relayed an impression of moving from the world into the heavenly realm. This form will be relevant to our later discussion of the Protestant adaptation of St. Pierre in Geneva, several centuries old by Calvin's time. Although in use as a Christian place of worship for over one thousand years, conceptualized through this long period as *domus dei,* perceptions of its nature would undergo a significant shift in the Reformation period, a return to the pre-Constantinian understanding of the church as *domus ecclesiae,* or *oikos ecclesias.*

THE CLASSIC EVANGELICAL TRADITION

The Protestant reformers of the sixteenth century rediscovered and returned to the ancient idea of a temple as the *domus ecclesiae* rather than as the *domus dei.* Harold Turner, who relies on his own observation of patterns in historic worship spaces, explains in *From Temple to Meeting House* that the reformers' new understanding of church space sprang from their changing view of the church itself and their recovery of the "primitive communal nature of worship."[17]

Kieckhefer describes the classic evangelical tradition as essentially an auditorium designed for the purpose of hearing the exposition of Scripture. All other visual elements are sublimated to this purpose, for as Calvin insisted, "Unless we listen attentively to [God], his majesty will not dwell among us."[18] Indeed, in this scheme in a place designated for Protestant worship there can be no place for symbols or images. In this space the pulpit, the focal point of the proclaimed Word, dominates the space. Rather

17. Turner, *From Temple*, 205.
18. Calvin, *Institutes*, 2.1.4.

than cruciform or rectilinear, the space is often broader, even square or octagonal. This enables all the individuals to clearly hear the preaching and be edified by it, even encouraging spontaneous interaction with the preacher. The building is stripped of ornaments, plain in style, most often lacking in chapels, images, frescoes, altars, and stained glass windows—all the elements charged with theological meaning in the classic sacramental church. Kieckhefer reminds us that the style would be appropriated by nineteenth-century urban revival preachers, following the pattern of exposition of Scripture and call to faith above all else, and once again by twentieth-century evangelicals "with the latest technology at their command."[19]

Figure 7: "Purging the Temple" (upper portion), receiving the Scripture (lower left) and the typical features of Protestant worship, with the two biblical sacraments and the congregation gathered around a pulpit to hear the preaching. (From *Foxe's Book of Martyrs*, 1563 edition.)

19. Krautheimer, *Early Christian*, 11–12.

DEVELOPMENTS IN THE CLASSIC EVANGELICAL
TRADITION

The classic evangelical tradition in church design developed in response to needs of new Protestant worshiping communities. For Luther, churches' physical significance paled in comparison with the believing community itself, and churches were not consecrated as holy spaces but approached from a perspective of practical concern. In purpose-built Protestant worship spaces, there was no altar and the Lord's Table became predominant. Turner points out that the first Lutheran architectural treatise appeared only in 1649 at the end of the Thirty Years War in response to the need for guidance in matters of design. The city architect of Ulm, Joseph Furttenbach, penned *Kirchenbau* as a guide to construction of sanctuaries in rural territories devastated by war. "He recommended plain domestic rectangular buildings, with pulpit, table and font together where all could see and hear."[20]

This arrangement was a shared characteristic with Reformed spaces, although in contrast with Huguenot churches, the exterior as well as interior space in Furttenbach's church designs was adorned with crosses, and in contrast with Reformed churches in general, his church designs included ornate altars. Along with Jacques Perret, he was one of two architects of the period writing about the arrangement of Protestant churches per se; it was not until the eighteenth century that a theoretician of Protestant temples properly speaking would appear with Leonhard Christoph Sturm, "a Lutheran converted to Calvinism and author of works on architecture and theology."[21]

There was much deliberation over the nature of the church, whose distinguishing characteristics Calvin held to be "the Word of God purely preached and heard, and the sacraments administered according to Christ's institution."[22] One implication of this conviction was that appropriate worship space included a visible and centralized pulpit for proclamation, a baptismal font visible to the congregation, and a Lord's Table accessible for the Eucharistic meal. Calvin recognized that buildings themselves are neutral: even pagan temples can serve as spaces where God encounters his people.[23]

---

20. Turner, *Theories of Culture*, 206.

21. Germann, "Les Temples Protestants," 346.

22. Calvin, *Institutes*, 4.1.9

23. Turner, *Theories of Culture*, 207. Turner cites Calvin's reflections on the nature of

In his sovereign freedom, God deigns to meet his people in the place where they gather; Julie Canlis, in her work *Calvin's Ladder*, reminds us that "Calvin will emphasize time and again that we are to be drawn up to God rather than dragging him down to us—whether it be in the Lord's Supper, idolatry, or carnal ways of conceiving of God. . . . 'For our affections must ascend to heaven, or otherwise we would not be at all united to Jesus Christ.'"[24]

Nonetheless, it is possible to construe some preferences of Calvin, which accentuate the Protestant predilection for simplicity, practicality, and accessibility. Church space is consecrated by the Word and yet is not sacred more than any other place; it can be put either to godly, edifying use, or used to erect idols in the minds of believers. He writes, "As God in his Word enjoins common prayer, so public temples are the places destined for the performance of them."[25] Calvin recognizes the practical need for gathering space dedicated to prayer, arguing for the gathered worshiping community and against what he sees as the inadequacy of merely individualistic devotion. His language speaks of the church's public prayers, but seems at times to refer as much to the worship space itself. God invites the prayers of the faithful, and therefore buildings set aside for those prayers, which are contrasted with the Christian's private "chamber," have their necessary place. In the prayers (and the buildings themselves?) "there [should] be no ostentation, or catching at human applause." Calvin betrays some

---

the pagan temples. To quote the pertinent section from Calvin, "All the temples which the Gentiles built to God with a different intention were a mere profanation of his worship, —a profanation into which the Jews also fell, though not with equal grossness. With this Stephen upbraids [Israel] in the words of Isaiah when he says, 'Howbeit the Most High dwelleth not in temples made with hands; as saith the Prophet, Heaven is my throne,' . . . For God only consecrates temples to their legitimate use by his word. And when we rashly attempt anything without his order, immediately setting out from a bad principle, we introduce adventitious fictions, by which evil is propagated without measure. [Yet] it was inconsiderate in Xerxes when . . . he burnt or pulled down all the temples of Greece, because he thought it absurd that God, to whom all things ought to be free and open, should be enclosed by walls and roofs, as if it were not in the power of God in a manner to descend to us [emphasis added], that he may be near to us, and yet neither change his place nor affect us by earthly means, but rather, by a kind of vehicle, raise us aloft to his own heavenly glory, which, with its immensity, fills all things, and in height is above the heavens." (*Institutes*, 4.1.5)

Here Calvin lifts up the principle that space is only sanctified by God's Word—an implicit denial of the validity of Catholic space, since in Calvin's view the Romanists did not handle Scripture properly—yet he leaves open the possibility that any space can in theory be so consecrated as to be fit for worship.

24. Canlis, *Calvin's Ladder*, 119.

25. Calvin, *Institutes*, 3.20.30.

ambivalence at this point: he consistently emphasized human participation in Christ, but is nearly mute on the effectiveness of the material sphere for such a connection. He only tentatively ruminates on the relationship of the Holy Spirit to the created order, contributing to "a historical reticence toward the arts and images."[26] Calvin's reluctance here seems to be in part a reaction to the ostentatious display of medieval imagery. He does confer a certain dignity on the actual place of common worship when he says, "lest the public prayers of the Church should be held in contempt, the Lord anciently bestowed upon them the most honorable appellation, especially when he called the temple the "house of prayer." Calvin continues,

> If this is the legitimate use of churches (and it certainly is), we must, on the other hand, beware . . . of imagining that churches are the proper dwellings of God, where he is more ready to listen to us, or of attaching to them some kind of secret sanctity, which makes prayer there more holy. For seeing we are the true temples of God, we must pray in ourselves if we would invoke God in his holy temple. Let us leave such gross ideas . . . knowing that we have a command *without distinction of place,* [emphasis added] "in spirit and in truth."[27]

The former temple of Israel was indeed consecrated by prayer and sacrifice, but above all it prefigured God's dwelling within the people of God, the true church. The Old Testament prophets insisted that God could not be contained in a temple made of human hands. Turner rightly observes that the temples or churches possess only a kind of derived or secondary sanctity that depended entirely on the kind of worship offered there (see figure 7). God has honored humanity by making people (i.e., the Christian community) to be his literal temple, his sanctuaries, and we should not debase the dignity of our calling by venerating walls and ceilings. However, Calvin left room for churches to work out an appropriate physical setting for worship. Andrew Spicer explains,

> Although the Reformed attitudes towards places of worship and their appearance were largely shaped by the theology and writings of Jean Calvin and the second generation of Reformers—ideas which were enshrined in the Second Helvetic Confession—there

---

26. Canlis, *Calvin's Ladder,* 244.

27. Ibid.

was no architectural model or blueprint of an ideal Reformed temple. Such matters were regarded as *adiaphora* by the Reformers.[28]

Calvin's reflections thus provide a theological foundation for Reformed approaches to church architecture, not as specific designs but as biblical guidance on appropriate attitudes, particularly toward the church buildings that Reformed Christians inherited. The majesty and glory of God were best perceived not through decorative adornments, but rather were heard in the Word of God read and expounded upon. The lack of specific and extensive architectural and design directives may not be so much a lacuna in Reformed ecclesiology as an expression of the freedom to develop forms appropriate to the settings of various diverse communities. Calvin is more concerned with what takes place within a church than with its specific shape.

The first spaces designed expressly for Reformed worship appeared in Huguenot strongholds of France, and later in Holland, Scotland, the Palatinate, Transylvania, and eventually in the plain meeting houses of colonial New England. These spaces were created for dignity rather than magnificence, with symbolic reticence and focus on the preacher. In the course of time and with the rise of the modern liturgical movement in the twentieth century, buildings displaying the characteristics of the classic evangelical model borrowed stylistic elements from the classic sacramental tradition as well, though reinterpreting these elements for their own purposes.

In the era of Renaissance architectural treatises, we find little explicit conceptual basis for Protestant space, in spite of the fact that many architects in sixteenth- and seventeenth-century France were themselves Protestants or at least crypto-Calvinists. Turner writes that "there were no major [written] treatments of the church building, and nothing at all comparable to the great treatises that provided a theory for the Catholic symbolism of the Renaissance churches."[29] This is doubtless attributable to the conflictual religious context in which they labored, where architects in the employ of Catholic royal power would naturally attempt to avoid costly ideological debate. In the context of Protestant territories, it seems that builders' attention centered on practical concerns. "Reformation activity was focused more on the development of liturgies, and explicit statements

---

28. Spicer, *Calvinist Churches*, 2.
29. Turner, *Theories of Culture*, 206.

about the buildings tend to be rather incidental or limited to their internal arrangements."[30]

Reformed Christians saw themselves, rather than an architectural edifice, as the church of God built from "living stones" on the foundation of Christ. The primary consideration in most built spaces was functional rather than aesthetic. Specific modifications in the practice of Protestant churches included a diminishing of the distinction between clergy and the laity, the reception of communion in both kinds, the reunification of preaching and sacrament, the extinguishing of the cult of the saints, and a new distaste for luxury and ostentation. These changes necessitated a rethinking of the space of worship, resulting in bringing the pulpit into new prominence, eliminating the high altar, restoring the table as a locus for communion, doing away with divisions of interior space, and generally cultivating space that reflected the people themselves as the temple of God. The priority was making possible a gathering of the people in physical proximity to hear the gospel proclaimed and to join in common prayer rather than establishing, as in Catholic churches, a physical separation that echoed spiritual progression from the entryway to the pulpit and beyond it to the altar.

OTHER CONTRIBUTORS TO THE CLASSIC EVANGELICAL TRADITION

Zwingli must be noted as well for his contribution to Reformed habits in use of worship space. His is a voice for simplicity and what may be termed visual concentration in the locus of common worship. One of the dramatic acts of the Reformation would be when he prepared communion in Grossmünster at Zurich in the Reformed manner on Maundy Thursday in April 1525. Having removed the church altar, he served at an ordinary domestic table, dressed in secular garb, facing the congregation rather than with back turned and facing the altar as per custom of the Catholic Mass. Instead of costly accoutrements, simple wooden cup and plates were used. Rather than the consecrated host, ordinary bread was used. In so doing, powerful new visual symbols were implemented, ones insisting that a life of holiness was not reserved for the cloister, but penetrating secular and family life in the place where one fed physically and spiritually.

30. Ibid.

Martin Bucer in Strasbourg is another voice in formulating a Reformed sense of space fit for worship. His conclusions are consistent with Calvin's theological approach to worship, yet he provides a few more specifics, and he embarks on a program to rearrange interior space to better facilitate intelligible worship. Reflecting on his approach, Turner writes:

> After recognizing the need for churches, which was not true of all sections of the Reformation, [Bucer] declared "that the choir should be so distantly separated from the rest the temple, and the service (which pertains to the whole people and the clergy) be set forth in it alone, is anti-Christian." This arrangement suggests that the ministers are "nearer to God than lay people," and also "confirms the pernicious superstition by which reading . . . the Scripture and prayers without intelligence and without understanding of faith is thought worship pleasing to God." For these reasons, and from a misapprehension as to the frequency of round churches in antiquity, Bucer favored a building of this shape as the ideal form.[31]

Bucer explicitly directed, then, that the worship space must be in proximity to the choir, enhancing the connection between the clergy and the laity. That he would give this rule is evidence that the reformer understands the power of visual elements to symbolize and instruct—in this case, that worship is for the whole people of God; that all have equal status in worship; and that fitting worship entails understanding. Few others were as clear on the matter as Bucer was, but other Protestant communities practiced a similar manner of translating theological convictions into the arrangement of worship space.

Margarite de Navarre, who was attracted to the teachings of Luther and sympathetic to reform, is another illustrative voice in forming a view of Reformed worship space. In her creative piece *Heptameron* she reflected on what she considered appropriate design and appointment of spaces for worship:

> Truly, I have often wondered . . . how [Catholics] think to make their peace with God by means of things, means of things which he himself reprobated when he was on earth, such as great buildings, gildings, painting, and decorations, But if they rightly understood what God has said, that the only offering he requires of us is a humble and contrite heart, and another text in which St. Paul says that we are the temple of God in which he desires to dwell,

31. Ibid., 208.

they would have taken pains to adorn their consciences while they were alive, and not have waited for the time when a man can no longer do either good or ill.[32]

Margarite is expressing, in the artistic form of a novella, her convictions on what pleases God in the sanctuary. This is, no less, a form in which she frequently reflects on the meaning of material objects and works of art, as Catharine Randall has shown.[33] The place of worship is to be marked by simplicity, as the appropriate focus in preparing for worship is repentance and return to God in humble faith, a beauty not "from outward adornment, such as braided hair and the wearing of gold jewelry and fine clothes."

Heinrich Bullinger, too, in a section of the *Second Helvetic Confession* titled "Decent Meeting Places," includes instructions for the arrangement of worship space:

> Moreover, the places where the faithful meet are to be decent, and in all respects fit for God's Church. Therefore, spacious buildings or temples are to be chosen, but they are to be purged of everything that is not fitting for a church. And everything is to be arranged for decorum, necessity, and godly decency, lest anything be lacking that is required for worship and the necessary works of the church.[34]

Bullinger insists that places of worship which honor God are to be modest, governed by the principle of humility. There is to be a sense of fittingness in houses of worship. Beauty in such places will be seen in sensitive arrangement; aesthetic concern is appropriate, suggested by his terms "fair," and "comeliness," but these terms are held in balance by the words "necessity," "seemliness," "decency," and what is needful for the rites and orders that comprise the liturgy of the church. There is here a dynamic in which the faith of the church, not external elements like architecture, is the essential component of the community ordered by the Word of God; nonetheless Bullinger suggests a kind of set-apart quality of the buildings themselves that were dedicated to worship. Built structures are to enable and enhance the worship offered within them, and yet it is appropriate to conduct oneself with reverence, a kind of anticipation that God will be

---

32. Marguerite, *L'Heptameron*, 313.

33. Randall, *Earthly Treasures*.

34. Bullinger, *Second Helvetic Confession*, XXII.4.

pleased to meet his people gathered for worship in this place in a way distinct from other places.

> And as we believe that God does not dwell in temples made with hands, so we know that on account of God's Word and sacred use places dedicated to God and his worship are not profane but holy; and that those that are present in them are to conduct themselves reverently and modestly, seeing that they are in a sacred place, in the presence of God and his holy angels.[35]

Here, Bullinger goes so far as to suggest that the places used for worship are made sacred by the activities that take place within them. He shared the sentiments of nearly all reformers, that the places where God's people meet were not intrinsically holy by any magic they possessed, however, these were places to be treated with due reverence. Their special function demanded a fittingness or appropriateness of response, a humility that recognized the nature of the true ornaments of the church. Whether on the continent, in Scotland or elsewhere, all Reformed parties were attempting to return to an ancient Christian understanding of the church building as the *domus ecclesiae*. So the place itself is not holy, until inhabited by God's holy people, sanctified by prayer and by God's Word, among whom he dwells. In "The True Ornamentation of Sanctuaries," Bullinger continues, seemingly blurring the line between human and architectural ornamentation:

> Therefore, all luxurious attire, all pride, and everything unbecoming to Christian humility, discipline, and modesty, are to be banished from the sanctuaries and places of prayer of Christians. For the true ornamentation of churches does not consist in ivory, gold, and precious stones, but in the frugality, piety, and virtues of those who are in the Church. Let all things be done decently and in order in the Church, and finally, let all things be done for edification.[36]

Externals, such as apparel, reflected internal reality, and therefore the putting aside of pride and the adopting of "humility, discipline, and modesty" were to be reflected in simplicity of manner, just as in sobriety of decoration in the meeting place itself. Simplicity of design reflects godliness just as does appropriate clothing or virtuous comportment. Michel de Montaigne, a Catholic whose mother was a Protestant and who was sympathetic to the

35. Ibid., XXII.5
36. Ibid., XXII.6

cause of reform, reflected on pretentiousness of manner and the obsession to impress among the nobility and aspiring nobility. This pretentiousness made everyone look ambitious and foolish. Clothing might ostentatiously show "superficial errors," but was also enough "to inform us that the whole fabric is crazy and tottering."[37] Just as the recognized importance of laying aside excess in clothing highlighted the value of unadorned simplicity, so the simplicity of design reflects godliness and deference.

Théodore de Bèze, the successor pastor/reformer in Geneva following Calvin's death in 1564, is another voice in our brief survey of influences in shaping a Reformed practical theology of worship space. Using the language of the church as the "house of God," he employs a series of "opposites" to illustrate the quality of ordinary/extraordinary in the church. In his *Sermons on the Song of Songs* he refers to the "extraordinary vocations" as the "architects" of the church, and the "ordinary vocations" as the "custodians." The function of the architects was to build the church on the foundation of Christ as mediated by the apostolic witness, and the function of the latter to maintain what was given for the ages. In the case of corruption in the church, the custodians' function became to restore the church to the purity of the apostolic foundation. In using "architect," "building," and "foundation" metaphorically, perhaps De Bèze suggests that the real built space of the church is not for the purpose of grandeur or innovation, but for clarity and fidelity to the biblical faith.

PROTESTANT CHURCH BUILDING IN FRANCE AND THE CLASSIC EVANGELICAL TRADITION

The churches of France drew from these multiple influences. Principally, they drew from the theological inspiration of Calvin and of Martin Bucer. Calvin's influence was profound, as seen in his work behind the Gallican Confession of 1559, in his sending de Bèze to represent the Reformed party at the Colloquy of Poissy, and in his commissioning scores of Geneva-trained missionary pastors to serve in France.

Nevertheless, the traditions and discipline of the French Reformed churches drew from wider sources than Strasbourg and Geneva. Glenn Sunshine underscores the influence of the Pays de Vaud through the work of Pierre Viret on the system of the *classe* of the French polity.[38] In addition,

37. Montaigne, "Of Sumptuary Laws," 65.
38. Sunshine, *Reforming French Protestantism*, 4, 41.

the French church may have drawn on the organization of the diaconate from the Catholic Church, though perhaps by way of Strasbourg or Zurich. Most importantly, perhaps, the Huguenots made a number of structural innovations in response to their particular contexts. The French developed a presbyterial or synodical representational government to deal with matters of discipline and doctrine. In the Swiss cantons of Bern and Zurich Reformed theologians envisioned a system where church and state cooperated for the management of the church, in which the state insured outward conformity in behavior and the church established theological and organizational norms. There the system of called synods envisioned by Calvin devolved into a structure led by a single pastor or church rather than a full representational organization. In France, however, where the government never considered the Reformed Church as anything but seditious, a threat to the state to be eliminated, such a symbiotic relationship between church and state was impossible.

The implications for the built space of churches in France were diverse. Reacting against practices that smacked of popery, the congregations tended to extreme simplicity. In places where Protestant congregations were forced to meet in secret, the faithful gathered in homes or even in barns, usually outside the major cities. When Protestants were free to build temples, they demonstrated a preference for large basilican (longitudinal) or centralized forms such as the octagon or circle, providing maximum sight lines for all worshipers.[39] As the drawings or engravings of Huguenot churches in Charenton, Lyons, La Rochelle, Rouen, Dieppe, and Chermont reveal, Reformed Christians in many cases eschewed crosses on (and in) their buildings. In the cases where Catholic churches could be requisitioned and adapted for Protestant usage, such as in Languedoc, the church of St. Fiary at Agen, and St. Étienne de Capduel at Nîmes, chapels and niches would be "cleansed" of images, pulpits moved to more central positions, Lord's tables repositioned or introduced into the worship space. Kieckhefer describes the essential options when adapting a Catholic worship space:

> The early Reformers adapted existing churches more often than they built new ones, and their greatest ingenuity was often devoted to the reconception of medieval longitudinal space. They often set pulpits midway down one side of the nave, turning long spaces into wide ones. In a church with a distinct chancel, three main possibilities presented themselves. First, the nave could serve as

---

39. Guicharnaud, "Introduction," 136.

the main worship space, and the chancel could be reserved for other occasions (for smaller services such as weddings). Second, the first part of the service (the liturgy of the Word) could be held in the nave, after which the entire congregation could be invited into the chancel for the remainder (the Eucharist), with the altar placed either "altar-wise" against the east wall or "table-wise" down the center of the chancel. Third, the chancel could become the space in which privileged individuals or families sat while the service was held in the nave. Along with any of these uses, the chancel could serve also as a space for burials.[40]

It seems there were variations on adaptations for Protestant worship. Some would gather toward the choir, others in the nave but turned toward the short side. At times there would be movement during the service as when the lay worshipers gathered on the chancel to receive the Lord's Supper.

The meanings conveyed by a seventeenth-century Protestant building differed from earlier churches in part because of the distinctively Word-centered worship which takes place within it. This is not because the form of the building is itself indifferent, but because the meaning of other forms is always amplified and explicated by the spoken Word. In a service stripped of extraneous elements and lifting up the gospel, aspects of Roman Catholic heritage are excised. When Reformed churches do borrow from the classic sacramental churches, they reinterpret these features. Classical liturgical churches, on the other hand, tend to serve a multiplicity of purposes, with varying aspects based on different principles. Speaking a language that much contemporary culture no longer understands, they can be more difficult to interpret. Either tradition can be coherent, and enhance the functioning that takes place within. Both the adaptations of the classical liturgical church-building and the innovations of the classical evangelical church-building expressed in their own manner a sense of sacrality. For Krautheimer, this is achieved not so much by separation from the profane, but rather in a church's "symbolic associations," or connections to profound human narratives.[41]

Theological meanings arise, then, from the intersection of design with actual uses of buildings, in particular with liturgical usage. In addition, buildings' inhabitants adapted them in light of physical deterioration, changing uses, evolving surroundings, and the vagaries of fashion, and

40. Kieckhefer, *Theology in Stone*, 46.
41. Krautheimer, *Early Christian*, 18.

especially in response to their quest for renewal and reformation. In this sense, buildings are perpetually metamorphic, "growing" in a kind of evolutionary fashion, artifacts whose use adapts to changing needs over time.

In summary, the classic evangelical tradition sees the church building as a frame for worship, not one that is holy in and of itself, but as a space which enables and enhances an encounter with God through the hearing of his Word in the gathered community. In France and Switzerland as elsewhere, decorative elements in such a scheme tended to be few; visual components intended for didactic purpose were missing; everything contributed to the experience of approaching, hearing, reflecting upon, and responding to the words of the Bible. In time, decorative elements such as tombs, tablets of the Ten Commandments, or coats of arms of civic leaders were introduced (which also made their way into the classic sacramental churches adapted for Protestant worship), and later expressions of the evangelical tradition would reflect some stylistic elements of the other basic church types. For the Protestant reformers of the sixteenth and seventeenth centuries, design preferences reflected a return to the pure and unadulterated worship of the early church. The context for these developments in both architectural theory and design was the early modern climate of reflection and discovery that drew on the theories of an ancient architect and engineer. First, however, we present a case study of a Catholic conception of space to make clearer what the sixteenth-century Protestants were reacting against.

CHAPTER 3

A Catholic Conception of Space
The Visual World of the Middle Ages

A CATHOLIC WAY OF SEEING

Since architectural meaning derives in part from the context of its various users, it is necessary to consider Catholic understandings of space in contrast to that of Protestants. Catholic conception of space came about organically through a uniquely Catholic manner of seeing and understanding reality. The medieval mind sought transcendence through liminal space and by means of holy objects, material artifacts saturated with power and meaning. Churches teemed with symbolic forms, lending semiological resonance. These visual artifacts gave order to the cosmos, relating everything to the Catholic world view and to the power of the divine. This spatial understanding engaged viewers and encouraged them to find holy things to be means of grace.[1] Matthew Milner, considering the role of visual perception on the English Reformation, argues that fifteenth-century religious experience had followed the medieval Catholic habit of seeing. He writes,

> Any mediating speculation, sight of the image of pity, the Crucifixion and the Passion, let alone the image of a saint or the experience of liturgy, especially the mass . . . offered "vivid verisimilitude[s]"

1. For a study on the role of sensation in the changes in religious culture of the sixteenth century, see de Boer and Göttler, *Religion and the Senses.*

through which deeply felt piety caused the percipient to be pulled into the depiction in a kind of "personal relationship" or "confrontation" [as Robert W. Scribner argues in *Popular Piety and Modes of Visual Perception in Late-Medieval and Reformation Germany*, 456] . . . late medieval piety [was] not simply a "way of seeing" "the symbolical character of the world" . . . but an unfolding . . . of religious sensing as an aesthetic immersion in the sacred, replete with visual mediation.[2]

Milner's description applies not only to England at this point, but to the general Catholic habit of perceiving reality and the way it is intersected by the divine.

From here we turn to investigate a medieval Catholic way of understanding sacred space, setting a point of comparison for the new Reformation program. This is important in order to see what the reformers were reacting against and what they achieved. Fourteenth-century Florence serves as an example of the spatial results of the Catholic manner of perception, especially in its ecclesiastical and civic design.[3] This provides a means of exploring the intersection between the physical space of a Renaissance city and the "mapping out" of conceptual/ spiritual space. It also demonstrates a theological reading of space through its schemes of damnation and salvation. Florence has been chosen because the city was particularly representative of a Catholic way of seeing. Furthermore, it exerted a strong cultural influence beyond the Italian territories as the Renaissance expanded into France and beyond. Protestant attitudes towards Catholic monuments were mixed, given the fascination of early modernists in general with classical influences from Italy. A rejection of Catholic ideas did not mean there was no admiration or interest in Italy, as Gerrit Verhoeven has shown.[4] Calvinist travelers to Italy express ambivalence built on a sense of wonder and curiosity, if also criticism and a sense of superiority, Verhoeven suggests.

As was seen in the classic sacramental tradition of church design, ecclesiastical building most often followed two general patterns, the rectangular or basilican plan, such as in the Florence Cathedral of Santa Maria del Fiore, and the octagonal plan, as in its baptistery. Most common was the former, featuring either a single or double aisle without a gallery, in which

2. Milner, *Senses and the English Reformation*.

3. See Rubin, *Images and Identity*.

4. Verhoeven, "Calvinist Pilgrimages."

at one end was an apse, an often semi-circular projection from the main hall. Separated by an arch over the altar, this allowed space for the clergy to sit, with cantors to each side and the faithful seated in the main chamber. The New Testament Revelation of John echoes the essential features of the arrangement. *The New Catholic Encyclopedia* describes the conceptual space of John's vision,

> In the midst, we see the throne, whereon there sits One enthroned, of whom the Christian bishop is the representative; and with Him are four and twenty presbyters, who are "priests" (*hiereis*), ranged in a semicircle (*kyklothen*), twelve on either hand (Apoc., iv, 2, 4). Within the space bounded by these seats is a pavement of glass "like to crystal" (possibly of mosaic), and in the centre the altar (Apoc., iv, 6; vi, 9; viii, 3; ix, 13; xvi, 7). On the hither side of this are the one hundred and forty-four thousand "signed" or "sealed," who "sing a new canticle," and who incidentally bear witness to the very early origin of the *schola cantorum*, at least in some rudimentary form (Apoc. vii 4, xiv, 1–3).[5]

The citation is interesting for its description of an imaginary, visional space that possibly both reflected and shaped the built space of the worshiping community. In a similar vein, the Prophet Ezekiel's vision is structured in spatial terms, and he goes to great lengths to describe the dimensions of the temple courts and precincts, along with its internal layout. The liturgy of the church responded to these visions, focusing on the altar, which was often surmounted by canopy veils or in proximity to a chancel screen, or, in the Eastern Church, by the iconostasis.

The design of the medieval church served as a container for the holy, a meeting place with God. Although its multiplicity of meanings—spiritual, social, legal, and economic—cannot be fully encompassed in a single function, its primary purpose was to serve as liminal space, opening up the numinous more intensively than elsewhere. Florentines went to churches and other holy places in the expectation of meeting the divine.

PROCESSIONS AND RELICS IN THE MEDIEVAL CITY

Social and religious values were not simply shaped by space. In a reciprocal relationship, they acted *upon* space to claim it. Human movement, and indeed the human body, is necessary to worship, giving it embodiment and

5. Lucas, "Ecclesiastical Architecture," paragraph 6.

therefore reality. The church blessed the corporeal, and churches were often built on the burial sites of saints. In turn, processions delineated the city and gave it meaning, turning it into sanctified space.

Relics conveyed spiritual power and protection, and city leaders actively promoted them to the populace. In addition, they conveyed legitimacy on political claims against a city's rivals, as well as potentially increased the number of pilgrims coming to a city, which added to the coffers as well as to the spiritual stature of the city. Following major feasts of the festal year, processions took place in defined areas, gathering outside city gates, and making their way past ring walls, over bridges, through piazzas to terminate in churches. These orchestrated movements formed a sacred imagination of built space that reinforced Catholic identity and reminded citizens of their place in the cosmos. These liturgical actions helped re-imagine the space of the city as sacred space and a part of the saving narrative of faith, encompassed by the physical movement of the processional through the city's built environment.

Relics, processions, and public ceremonies channeled popular devotional feeling and afforded important means of religious expression in the late Middle Ages.[6] They helped give meaning to church and urban space alike, defining it in the minds of worshipers. Understanding of these visual and kinesthetic arts in the service of worship helps to understand what Reformed Christians would later react against as well as reconstitute for their own purposes.

THE CATHOLIC USE OF SYMBOLS

The use of symbols is the art of endowing things or actions with an inner meaning for expressive purposes; for Catholics, using symbols expresses their sacramental view of reality as upheld by God. Karsten Harries, in her work *The Ethical Function of Architecture*, helps us discern how this takes place when she writes,

> Both symbol and representation stand for or signify something else. Both may thus be considered signs, but a representation must in some way resemble what it represents; a symbol may but need not resemble what it symbolizes (i.e., some symbols are representations).[7]

6. For a picture of the relationship of Florence to its patron saint, see Cornelison, "Art Imitates Architecture."

7. Harries, *Ethical Function*, 98.

It can be said that symbolic objects and actions have always facilitated apprehension of the divine, and have therefore always been central to worship. The Genesis creation account relates that God created humans in his own image, a kind of symbol of God's reign and stewardship over creation. Other examples from the Old Testament include circumcision, the burning bush, Aaron's budding staff, the Tabernacle and its furniture, including its spatial configuration, Solomon's temple, and the prophets' visual metaphors such as Jeremiah's pot and loincloth. The New Testament records other instances of symbolic acts and objects, including ritual washing, Jesus' use of mud to heal the blind, the laying on of hands, the wind, fire, and dove that embodied the presence of the Holy Spirit, and the bread and cup of the Lord's Supper. Insofar as the worship of Israel and the church expressed itself through tangible means, all the sacrificial rites and sacred actions pointed through the material beyond itself to God. Each of these examples serves to arouse an emotive and cognitive response and to amplify the meaning of a spiritual reality. The cross, the central symbol of the Christian faith, clearly pointed to Christ's sacrifice for the redemption of the world. If the cross was not used as a literal symbol in the New Testament era, its meaning as an event was clearly definitive even before it was depicted visually: the Apostle Paul writes, "For I resolved to know nothing while I was with you except Jesus Christ and him crucified" (1 Cor 2:2). The post-apostolic period saw the usage of numerous symbols and images, many of which were drawn from the Old Testament, such as Christ the Good Shepherd, loaves and fish, the palm of victory, the Lamb of God, the ship, the heavenly city, the lamp to represent Christ the light of the world, the *chi rho* as the first two letters in Greek for "Christ," and anointing with oil.

The medieval church developed a rich lexicon of symbols, from the liturgical vestments to the layout of the church itself, echoing the geometry of the Latin cross. Symbols embellished church architecture as a way of augmenting the divine office. Churches and cathedrals, given the focus of the Mass on the divine mystery, expressed in stone, wood, and glass a sense of awe and transcendence. The space was oriented toward the East, perhaps echoing the depiction of Christ as the Sun of Justice. Figures around the western porch frequently portrayed the Last Judgment, drawing worshipers to contemplate the transitory nature of mortal life, and reassuring of the sovereign reign of God. Numbers recalled significant numbers of Scripture, such as the Trinity, the four Gospels, the five books of the Law, the seven sacraments, the eight Beatitudes (and also the eighth day of creation, or the era of grace), the Ten Commandments, and the Twelve Apostles. The number twelve also:

> symbolizes the spiritualizing of human nature and of the world by faith . . . or the universal Church. The reason is that three, the number of the Blessed Trinity, figures the Divine nature, and four, the number of the elements, typifies the number of the material world. Twelve is the product of three and four, and it consequently betokens the penetration of matter with spirit.[8]

The three doors of the portal represented the Trinity, and were often inscribed with images of Christ. Forty recalls the days Moses spent on the mountain of God, and Christ's temptation in the wilderness. Many churches and baptisteries were designed on the octagonal plan, recalling the symbolism of the number eight.

Images of animals were used extensively, many taken from biblical images, and including the Lion of Judah and the Lamb of God for Christ, and the lion, man, ox, and eagle for the four evangelists, suggested by the apocalyptic visions of Ezekiel and John the Divine. In addition, medieval bestiaries featured natural and fantastic animals to represent Christ, Satan, the virtues and vices, including the peacock for immortality, and the snake for Satan. Other animals, especially prominent in Romanesque architectural decoration, included dogs, birds, boars, unicorns, griffins, stags, rams, rabbits, and snails. It is noteworthy than the meaning of these symbols could shift: a prime example is the lion itself, used in Scripture to designate both Christ and the devil. E. P. Evans, in *Animal Symbolism in Ecclesiastical Architecture*, demonstrated the extensive use of animals as architectural features, such as using lions as pedestals, as well as the wide variety of animals used as applied decorative elements. Medieval architects, craftsmen, and writers replicated these symbols, intelligible to viewers, to carry emotive weight. As we will see upon closer examination of its worship spaces, the plethora of Catholic symbols were replaced by potent symbols of their own: the pulpit, the Lord's Table, and inscriptions of scriptural texts.

---

8. Thurston, "Symbols," paragraph 9.

MEMORY DEVICES AND CONCEPTUAL SPACE

Another aspect of medieval thought can help us to understand the innovation brought by Protestant conceptions of worship space and the spiritual life. So-called "memory devices," or techniques for augmenting the power of recollection, were well known from classical times through the Middle Ages and into the early modern era. These devices relied on conceptual space as metaphorical architecture that paralleled tangible, material architecture.

Frances Yates, in her work *The Art of Memory*, explains how the Greeks invented what is sometimes known as "mnemotechnics," a method for recalling vast amounts of information by relating that information to places and images using known architectural settings.[9] This was a sub-discipline of rhetoric that enabled an orator to "deliver long speeches from memory with unfailing accuracy."[10] This was done by attaching ideas to specific places, most often built structures. The method's efficacy was tied to the vividness of sight, understood to be "the strongest of all the senses."[11] In this way, ideas are remembered in the proper order, as they are associated with the composition or sequence of parts to a building. Learning the art of memory was indispensable for the educated person. On the importance of memorization, Yates writes,

> In the ancient world, devoid of printing, without paper for note taking or on which to type lectures, the trained memory was of vital importance. And the ancient memories were trained by an art that reflected the art and architecture of the ancient world, which could depend on faculties of intense visual memorization that we have lost.[12]

The Greeks passed the technique on to the Romans, who in turn passed it on to European culture at large in the Middle Ages through Cicero, Quintilian, and *Ad Herennium,* an anonymous first-century work of rhetoric. This lead to what Yates describes as "the great Gothic artificial memories of the Middle Ages."[13] Philosophers and theologians practiced the art as well. Thomas Aquinas, who was well versed in Aristotle and Augustine (who

9. Yates, *Art of Memory*, xi.

10. Ibid., 2.

11. Ibid., 4.

12. Ibid.

13. Ibid., xi.

used spatial configurations to convey theology in *The City of God*) recommended this "art of memory as a part of the cardinal virtue of prudence."[14] The source for understanding Aquinas on the subject is his commentary on Aristotle's *De memoria et reminiscentia* (On Memory and Recollection), which complements Aristotle's work *De Anima* (On the Soul) as a constitutive element of the human being. Aquinas picks up Aristotle's argument that mental images are necessary to the mind as aids to memory.[15]

Memory is connected with the virtue of prudence since it guides as well as restrains foolish risk. Reflection on the past leads to right understanding of the present and future. There are two kinds of memory, natural and artificial. The former takes place simultaneously with thought, and the latter concerns what can be strengthened by training. Artificial memory is concretized in the mind through images. A place, or *locus*, is an imaginative structure easily recalled, such as a house, a column, or an arch. The more information to be retained, the larger the imaginative structure needs to be.

This accords with the medieval sense of the superiority of sight. Certain images have greater power as catalyst for the memory. The classical art of memory systematizes recall by association using vivid and random mental pictures. If memorizing verses rather than ideas, then recalling structures, or even actions taking place within these structures, reinforces the memory as art supplements nature. The device then serves in this way as a set of mnemonic cues to retain words.

Around the time of the fall of Rome in 410, Martianus Capella wrote a treatise on the seven liberal arts (grammar, rhetoric, dialectic, arithmetic, geometry, music, and astronomy.) His section on rhetoric included a description of the art of memory, insuring thereby that the classical art would pass into medieval usage under the tradition of rhetoric. The Latin Church Fathers Augustine and Jerome both knew of *Ad Herennium*, according to Yates, and like educated pagans, were familiar with memory techniques. These techniques continued in the perception of twofold memory, both as natural and artificial.

Yates explains that the memory device serves to recall the coming punishment for evil and the joys of paradise as warning and promise. Lists of virtues and vices serve the purpose of imprinting on the memory of images of Heaven and Hell, in what Yates calls the "pietistic and moralized interpretation of memory." As knowledge increased in the scholastic age,

---

14. Ibid., xii, 20.
15. Caruthers, *Medieval Craft*, 153.

the need for remembering also increased. This was the background for Aquinas's reflections on memory.[16]

For Aquinas, it is both an incarnational truth and a concession to human weakness that people must use images in artificial memory. We easily remember "the images of gross and sensible things," but if we are to remember "subtle and spiritual things," insists Aquinas, we cannot do without an image,[17] following Aristotle's notion that "the soul never thinks without a mental picture" (*De Anima*, 431a 15–20). Aquinas has taken the rules for association and order, and transformed them through medieval piety into "corporeal similitudes"[18] arranged in order. Virtues and vices serve as mental markers, by way of figures in turn grotesque and beautiful, harrowing and poignant, for the evangelistic purpose of helping the reader avoid Hell and gain the heavenly reward. Medieval scholars furthered the classical art of memory a development crucial to the art of the thirteenth century and beyond.

We have seen the connections between visual or literary art and the art of memory. Through the mnemonic device, inner images found their way to outer expression. In parallel fashion, known places and images, including artistic depictions, seemingly found their way into devices for the art of memory.

The design of the Gothic cathedral itself serves as a memory device in its treatment of scriptural themes in two and three-dimensional art, and also in its structuring of liturgical enactment within space. Conversely, inner architecture could be used for didactic or devotional purpose; one example of this is the Benedictine monastery of St. Gall, Switzerland. An architectural rendering of an ideal monastery floor plan dates from the ninth century. Resembling the Cologne cathedral, the plan includes a church, gardens, and a cloister with arcades, columns, and buttresses designed along the proportions of the golden section. The plan reinforced the monks' daily pattern of work and prayer, regimented like the life of a soldier in its arrangement for separate activities. The church is according to a basilican plan alongside a rectangular court that forms the cloister, a space for peaceful contemplation, surrounded by space for purposeful labor.

The practice of making memory devices moved in both directions, from enhancing inner perception by apprehending physical space, as well

16. Yates, *Art of Memory*, 57–61.

17. Ibid,. 72.

18. Ibid., 77.

as the conceiving of experience as metaphorical space. As with pilgrimages and processions, the practice of walking the Stations of the Cross increased spiritual awareness by incarnating in spatial configurations the experience of the saints' lives or of Christ's Passion. Conversely, the strain of imaginative movement through architecture in the manner of the art of memory would prove to have a lasting influence on a wide span of Christian devotional traditions. Teresa of Avila, some three hundred years after Aquinas, would compose her work "Interior Castle" using the same principle to communicate spiritual truth. As the memory device came to be understood as an ethical function, it conveyed power to transform, both in its understanding of space, and in its conception of form and symbol projected upon that space.

Architectural frameworks followed the ancient art of memory, reminding the initiated that the center of the cosmos is God's sovereign love. One place that this is enacted is on the floor of the Cathedral of Chartres (twelfth century), which included the design of a labyrinth for worshipers to walk in a meditative spirit. Symbolic space expresses this with power, insuring that edifices would be both memorable and transforming.

CHAPTER 4

A Reformed Conception of Space

An Analysis of Spatial Sanctity
in Swiss and French Reformed Churches

In Chapter 3, we examined a particularly Catholic way of seeing, exemplified in late medieval and early Renaissance church building. Architectural and artistic forms were seen as channels of grace, mediating the presence of God. The understanding of liturgical space worked its way into civic space, bringing it under the reign of God. Reformed Christians conceived of space differently, because they held a variant understanding of how the divine interpenetrates the world. Did early Swiss and later Huguenots conceive of their worship spaces as special in some way? If so, what did they mean to express through these? Chapter 6 will put forth the argument that the work of Philibert de l'Orme, Jacques-Androuet du Cerceau, Salomon de Brosse, Jacques Perret, and Bernard Palissy together contributes to the formulation of a Protestant architectural aesthetic. For now, we will explore the general idea of sanctity in Reformed churches. Is it oxymoronic to speak of a Reformed understanding of sacred space? Indeed not, and it is in the reformulation of the ancient Catholic Church of St. Pierre and in the refined architectural inventions of de Brosse that we most clearly see a Reformed and Huguenot spirit, in which idolatry is purged and the imagination directed in true worship.

Reformed approaches to worship space come into clearer distinction when compared with an Anglican attitude. The English divine William

Cave wrote in 1672, during the period when Huguenot architecture had coalesced into a coherent pattern of Reformed church design, of the importance, and even the inevitability, of sacred space. Counter-intuitively, he argued in *Primitive Christianity* that even the New Testament church saw the importance of the physical sanctuary.[1] By way of example, he stated that the Upper Room, consecrated by the Holy Spirit and by association with the ministry of Jesus, reflected its holy usage. Reformed Christians had arrived at a different conclusion than that of Cave, an Anglican. For them, a sanctuary for worship had no intrinsic holiness, and yet it did transcend functionality and served to reinforce the sense of a holy calling to a people set apart.

Where and on what period might one begin to focus on the architecture that expresses a Reformed style and state of mind? Zurich converted to Protestantism in 1523 under the leadership of Ulrich Zwingli. The Geneva city council voted in May of 1535 to abolish the Catholic Mass and to adopt the Reform, and the government of Bern ordered a public disputation on the matter in Lausanne in October the same year. Large portions of northern and western Swiss cantons followed the new confession. The "cleansing of churches" in the Protestant territories of Switzerland followed a similar pattern. Examining these developments will help develop conceptual foundations for a Reformed conception of space.

For the first generations of the Reformation in Switzerland, few new churches were built; instead, Protestants adapted existing medieval churches for the purpose of Reformed worship. In France, Protestants grew in number from the 1530s, even with increasing persecution following the Affair of the Placards in 1534; by their 1550s numbers swelled, particularly among city denizens and the nobility. As a minority religion, Protestants in France needed to construct places of worship if they were not to gather in homes or *en plein-air*. Few Reformed churches survived the wars of religion of the second half of the sixteenth century in France before the Edict of Nantes in 1598. In Switzerland, Reformed habits of church interior arrangement had been well established, but new construction lagged behind; although medieval churches were extensively remodeled and enlarged to serve the needs of Protestant congregations (as in Avenches and Moudon,) Heiliggeistkirche, the first purpose-built Protestant church in Bern, would not be erected until 1726; Peterskirche in Zurich in 1706; the Temple de la Fusterie in Geneva, in 1715; and Elisabethenkirche in Basel in 1857. One

1. Cave, *Primitive Christianity*, 78ff.

early example of the first specifically Protestant architecture is the church of Chêne-Pâquier in Vaud, built in 1667; following one common Protestant pattern, the building is oval with a conical roof and a small square tower. In general, however, the strategy of the Swiss Protestant churches in the first generations of reform was to transform Catholic space rather than erect new structures, as Bernard Reymond explores in *Temples de Suisse romande*. He explains, "Considérée sous l'angle de l'architecture, la Réforme a commence par réorganiser les édifices religieux existants, donc ceux du Moyen Age, pour les adapter à la conception du culte qui découlait de sa remise en forme de la foi chrétienne."[2] Andrew Spicer adds, "The adaptation of the existing medieval churches for Reformed worship served the needs of the Genevan congregations until the early eighteenth century."[3] Initially, the architecture of the Reformation in Switzerland reorganized and rebuilt rather than design and build from new foundations.

The manner in which Reformed Christians either adapted existing space or conceived of altogether new space reveals a habit of mind that built on the thinking of Calvin, coalescing from the middle of the sixteenth century and culminating in the work of Salomon de Brosse in the second decade of the seventeenth century.

In *Sacred Space in Early Modern Europe*, Will Coster and Andrew Spicer demonstrate the inseparable link between divine space and the awareness of God for the late medieval and early modern world.[4] They argue against the longstanding paradigm of Emile Durkheim and Mircea Eliade in which a hard and fast line differentiated between the sacred and the profane over the course of the thirteenth to the eighteenth centuries, detecting, rather, an overlapping of the sacred and the secular. There is, in fact, a more complex relationship between sacred, secular, and natural worlds, with interplay between the three. Evidence suggests an overlapping wherein secular commerce infiltrated monastic enclaves and the rites of public civic life. An example of that tendency might be seen in the establishing of market stalls in the bays between the chapels around the nave of the Heiliggeistkirche in Heidelberg, which symbolically put the stamp of clerical approval on the buying and selling of the marketplace. In an example from the Reformation era, the Bernese troops who imposed Reform on the canton of Vaud in the sixteenth century transformed the Romainmôtier

2. Reymond, *Temples*, 17.
3. Spicer, *Calvinist Churches*, 15.
4. Coster and Spicer, *Sacred Space*, 4.

Abbey in Vaud into a grain storage barn, implying that spiritual renewal comprised more than sacred use of venerable ecclesial architecture. The secular intruded into the churchly realm, as well, when city magistrates in Reformed Lausanne processed into the cathedral with church leaders for an annual service of ordination. In Catholic practice, public space had been sanctified through sacred plays, processionals, and pilgrimages that brought theological meaning into the city and the marketplace. This overlapping of sacred and secular can perhaps be seen in Protestant stylistic preferences, as well. For example, while classical architecture is itself often identified as "secular," it would become a favored mode of expression of Reformed architects.

As we shall see, early modern Protestants conceived of space in radically different ways than did Catholics. Whether Protestant places of worship lay in territory recently reclaimed from Catholics or in contested territory, they wanted to eradicate Catholic memorial space. At times, the Protestants did engage in a kind of processional themselves, but as a matter of practical necessity, such as when travelling five leagues outside the city of Paris to their temple at Charenton, which they did while singing psalms. Thus their physical movement was sanctified not by holy objects or relics, but by the Word of God. While the idea of sacredness did enter into Reformed thinking about the church, it related to a holy people and the sanctifying Word of God instead of to space as a receptacle for the heavenly. The previous examples suggest that there was a kind of Reformed understanding of sacred, or perhaps special, space.

Overlapping between the secular and the sacred could also be seen in growing domestic devotion in the late medieval period, wherein believers would express piety in private homes, usually aided by sacred objects such as small scale devotional paintings or altars. In this way, what might have been thought of as secular space was consecrated to holy use. Coster and Spicer point out that "holy spaces defined medieval religious experiences and were fundamental to the geography and social history of medieval and early modern Europe." Late medieval Europe was a place "filled and defined by points of access to the holy,"[5] or, to paraphrase Henri Lefebvre's term, a land haunted by the God's presence.[6] The landscape was dotted with sacred space defined by churches, monasteries, shrines, chapels, and holy wells, where temporal and eternal worlds coincided. The Reformation

5. Ibid., 3.
6. Ibid.

entailed a conflict of competing world views and an ongoing and intense renegotiation of public space.[7] Now the influence of the gospel was seen in abolishing the abbeys and pilgrimage sites as separate spaces cut off from the rhythms of public life, and in radically de-sacralizing places of worship.

The essays in Coster and Spicer's volume explore aspects of sacred space in the context of the Reformation period and question the strict bifurcation of the sacred and secular, but they do not provide a thematic discussion of sacred space. Instead of seeing trends or recurring dimensions, they take an anecdotal approach, examining phenomena as diverse as the Carmelite utilization of the land and the reclaiming of civic culture in France. Overall, they characterize late medieval Catholicism, in all its variations, as "dependent on a highly complex landscape of the sacred."[8] Whether in natural or built environments, sacred space was possible because the divine was embodied, localized, and communities and individuals would impart signification onto specific places.

The sixteenth-century understanding of space is investigated further in *Defining the Holy: Sacred Space in Medieval And Early Modern Europe,* by Andrew Spicer and Sarah Hamilton. The point of departure for the essays there is the division of sacred and secular proposed by Mircea Eliade in *The Sacred and the Profane.* Spicer and Hamilton point out the great body of work on this subject by historians, anthropologists, sociologists, and students of architecture, and note the lack of corresponding reflection on the part of Reformation studies, suggesting a real need in scholarship to address this deficiency. Exploring dimensions of sacred space is a form of cultural history that may enhance appreciation of popular religion and how reformers were able to accomplish a transformation of religious life. The sources for such study include not only theological writings and ecclesiastical documents, but consistory minutes, burial records, cultural objects, and architectural spaces themselves. For Eliade, the division is primordial to human experience, but "to date, however, there has been no serious and

---

7. Indeed, that conflict was not entirely confined to the early modern period. Even as late as 1929, the citizens of the Swiss commune of Marsens in the French-speaking Catholic Canton of Fribourg, an area of intense Jesuit mission activity in the seventeenth century, destroyed a large boulder on a hill within the township. According to town council records, the boulder was discovered to have been a place of Celtic druidic worship in the Iron Age. Even if the syndics did not see themselves as eradicating a pagan idol, at least the needs of city planning trumped those of historical preservation. See Tornare, *Commission.*

8. Ibid., 4.

sustained attempt to investigate this important facet of the period in the variety of contexts that prevailed across the continent of Europe."[9]

But more importantly than arguing for the existence of sacred space in the Catholic world view, or even the definition of liminal points of contact between the metaphysical and the material, is the question of why the idea of sacred space resonated with a Catholic world view. Medieval Catholic thinking focused on images and places, and attributed meaning to these, because in these it found transcendence.[10]

In contrast, Protestants believed that a focus on physical objects or places is self-referential; the only reality in such practices is what takes form in the imagination. This was the nothingness of images, in which the adherent of Catholic devotional practice perceived precisely himself or herself, and projected that image on the divine. Therein lay the danger of Catholic practice, and therein constituted the nature of idolatry. Was the Protestant condemnation of Catholic images in conflict with their own kind of symbolism, such as the pulpit, or the communion table? Perhaps, although in the Protestant usage the symbols were intended to turn the attention to what took place at that locus—to the preaching and hearing of the Word, and to the receiving in community of the bread and wine of communion. For the Reformed, the experience of images was ambiguous, and placing transcendent, salvific potential in the material was useless. Calvin writes, in his explanation of the second commandment in his *1536 Institutes,* that God "is incomprehensible, incorporeal, invisible, and so contains all things that he can be enclosed in no place. Let us then fervently pray against our imagining he can be expressed in any figure, or represented in any idol whatsoever, as if it were God's likeness. Rather, we are to adore God, who is Spirit, in spirit and truth."[11] The solution was to learn to truly see—that is, to discern the difference between one's spiritual longing and the reality of God, who alone can define who he is and how he is to be found.

For the Reformed, therefore, space was largely functional in nature as the backdrop for the worshiping community. "We are not so obstinate as to continue to believe the vain prejudice that one piece of land is holier than another," wrote Huguenot historian Élie Benoist.[12] While Reformed Chris-

---

9. Coster and Spicer, *Sacred Space,* 1.

10. While the idea of transcendence is not limited to medieval Catholic thinking, the term does serve to describe the vivid expectation of an encounter with the divine.

11. Calvin, *Institutes,* 2.8.17.

12. Benoist, *Histoire,* 1:232.

tians did perceive the church as holy, it was not the place but the people who gathered in it, a people sanctified by the Word to be a fit temple for his Spirit. In Switzerland, France, and elsewhere, Protestants in the theological tradition of John Calvin came to see communion itself as metaphorical sacred space, the place where God gave himself to the believing community. Communion was no longer literal and incarnational, as for Aquinas. No longer did church attendees have to conjure artificial memory through "images of gross and sensible things," but rather to remember through a Scripture-shaped imagination the salvific event that became new in the believing heart. Space was indeed important, but first of all as a locus for the true image of God, namely the "icon" of the body of Christ gathered in community for hearing and responding to God's Word through Scripture, preaching, and prayer.

This is not to say space as such had no role to play. Encountering God's holy Word and presence in preaching and the sacrament, worshipers were transformed into a holy people. By nature these encounters could only take place in space and time. And although the physical space in which they met was secondary to what took place there, inevitably it came to be considered a place apart, itself in some manner sanctified by the divine office.

The development of a Protestant culture in Renaissance Europe can be seen as a secularizing movement on account of its suppression of monasteries and divesting of churches.[13] Nonetheless, dimensions of sacred space are perceivable not only in the usage of ecclesiastical structures but also in the bringing Calvinist sensitivities to secular environments. The latter movement, that of sacralizing natural and public space, took place as Reformed services were initially conducted in private homes and estates, in town pubs, or out of doors. At various times, the confused process of reform meant individual Christians did not cleanse themselves of Catholic practices as much as reformers and pastors might have wished. Furthermore, churches, as places distinguished from other physicalities by their religious purpose, were no longer places cut off from the world by their sacred character. Indeed, it was the opposite: reformers intended to etch the reality of spiritual into everyday life, and the place of worship played a significant, albeit secondary role, in witnessing to the presence of God in the specificities of life.

The Reformation could be said to be essentially a doctrinal, verbal, and literary movement, but it nonetheless it relied on visual elements, such

---

13. See Gorski, "Historicizing the Secularization Debate."

as the woodblock or etched print to disseminate its ideas, or the architectural and interior space for worship that emphasized the character of the Reformed community as one set aside, sanctified for the purpose of God. This suggests a polarity, a positive embracing as well as a negation, a formulation of a new aesthetic as well as the repudiation of an old. Bernard Reymond insists that the Reformation placed nearly as much influence on the visual as on the preaching of the Word.[14] The new images it brought into the lives of its adherents included new ways of conceiving Christian piety, no longer tied to statues or icons as a way of apprehending God, who was now conspicuous through his physical absence. While all spatial and liturgical decisions were negotiated, there was a far greater consensus among the Reformed against traditional images of any kind than among German Lutherans, for example, where statues and paintings in the setting of worship were tolerated. In the new Reformed context of the fifteenth and early sixteenth centuries, more than a modified collection of theological canons were needed, however. In order that the new faith might take root and flourish among the laity, new prayers, forms of worship, and a system of pastoral care and discipline were put in place, helping shape confessional identity. The symbolic center was the way of celebrating the Reformed service of worship in a newly configured space. This entailed a new stage for Christian worship, one in which faith was practiced by consecrating the heart, directing the intellect toward the proclamation, and devoting one's life to the service of neighbor, following God in everyday life. The visual element of Reform, it seems, was not neglected after all: table rather than altar; domestic and communal rather than private and mystical; engaged with the world rather than retreating from it; and a sense of God's transcendence rather than immanence.

It may seem, in light of the iconoclastic tendencies of the sixteenth century's Reformed movement, that the power of symbols was entirely overlooked. However, Protestants took real interest in animals and the created order, as can be seen in the zoological treatises of the sixteenth century, such as those by Konrad Gesner's *History of Animals* (1551–1562) and Guillaume Rondelet's *On Marine Fish* (1554). In these works, animals were not only noteworthy as creatures in their own right, but also because of their symbolic value.[15]

14. Reymond, *Le Protestantisme*, 67.
15. Crowther-Heyck, "Wonderful Secrets," 253–56.

At times the removal or destruction of Catholic images was indiscriminate, but often it came under the direction of the authorities, and persons who had donated works to churches or abbeys were invited to take them back for private use. The elimination of images and the alteration of worship space were implemented intentionally. Not all art pieces were proscribed, but just those used as objects of devotion.

CALVIN'S PERSPECTIVE

Calvin, while allowing that the arts, including the visual arts, were a gift of God for human enjoyment[16], was unequivocal when it came to their use in the setting for common worship. One essential criterion for valid worship was found in the second commandment, "You shall make no graven images" (Exod 20:4). In his commentary on the commandment Calvin asserts, "It is wrong for men to seek the presence of God in any visible image, because he cannot be represented to our eyes."[17] The implications of this proscription for Calvin were sweeping, leading to the stripping of altars, paintings, statues, shrines, and reliquaries, as well as many tombs, although the process began with the adoption of the Reformation before Calvin's arrival in the city and would continue after his lifetime. Christian Gross points out that "further whitewashing" of frescoes took place as late as 1643.[18] Although Calvin did not endorse iconoclasm, suspecting it may lead to anarchy, he saw no value in images in the churches. At best, they are ineffective in teaching true doctrine, and at worst, they obscured the majesty of God.

In addition, Calvin looked upon church buildings as incidental realities, secondary to the worship that takes place there. In his commentary on Haggai, which concerns rebuilding the Jerusalem temple, he claims the true temple of God is now spiritual rather than physical,

> As God's temple is spiritual, our fault is the more atrocious [than that of the Jews] when we become thus slothful; since God does

---

16. Calvin remarks, "I am not gripped by the superstition [!] of thinking absolutely no images permissible. But because sculpture and painting are gifts of God, I seek a pure and legitimate use of each, lest those things which the Lord has conferred upon us for his glory and our good be not only polluted by perverse misuse but also turned to our destruction." (*Institutes*, 1.11.12.)

17. Calvin, *Harmony of the Law*.

18. Grosse, "Liturgical Sacrality," 69.

not bid us to collect either wood, or stones, or cement, but to build a celestial temple, in which he may be truly worshipped. When therefore we become thus indifferent, as that people were thus severely reproved, doubtless our sloth is much more detestable.[19]

Calvin appears to have inherited a medieval Platonism here, prioritizing the spiritual over the physical, though it is in the physical realm that the people of God are to demonstrate their faithful obedience. While treating the rebuilding of the ancient Israelite temple, he made no allowance for principles of building new structures.

Randall Zachman, in his book *Image and Word in the Theology of John Calvin*, makes the case that the relationship between seeing and hearing is central for Calvin's theology. He claims, "Indeed, far from making hearing the primary way of knowing, Calvin associated words themselves with visible symbols and images in which unseen reality manifests itself to us. . . . Signs form a veil behind which God conceals his presence in human affairs. They are at the same time focal points for the meeting between God and man."[20] Zachman contradicts the consensus of Calvin scholarship with his insistence that the visual, or manifestation of God in signs, is as central to Calvin as his theology of the revelation of God strictly through Scripture. As Peter Opitz writes in his review of *Image and Word*, Zachman misses the mark when he argues "that for Calvin the 'interdependence of Word and work of God, or proclamation and manifestation, is . . . central of the way he thinks theologically.'"[21] Indeed, Zachman himself sees Calvin as inconsistent on this issue by failing to incorporate symbols into the space for worship.

We come to the conclusion that Calvin is somewhat ambivalent on the relationship between God's Word and works, between his primary revelation in Scripture and God's manifestations in the world and in the gathered community. In another place in the *Institutes*, he does allow for built spaces, and a vestige of sanctity for the space itself, however, when he ruminates,

> When I ponder the intended use of churches, somehow or other it seems to me unworthy of their holiness for them to take on images other than those living and symbolical ones which the Lord has consecrated by his Word. I mean Baptism and the Lord's Supper, together with other rites by which our eyes must be too intensely

19. Calvin, *Habakkuk*, 251.
20. Zachman, *Image and Word*, 7.
21. Opitz, review of Zachman, 117–20.

gripped and too sharply affected to seek other images forged by human ingenuity.[22]

Holiness does not dwell in the churches ["temples"] where worship takes place, but in the very act of corporate worship. Calvin cannot completely remove himself from language that elevates and dignifies the worship space itself, as if a residual sanctity still colors the sanctuary, lest its "holiness" be compromised. Still, what beautifies the space itself is the proclamation of Christ in preaching and in the Sacraments. When persons are transformed by God's Spirit by these means of grace, the interest in counterfeit images of human origin fades away. Calvin is engaged in an epic task, one of re-forming or reconfiguring the individual human soul as well as the collective body politic.

This work of reconfiguring the church, figuratively and literally, became the quintessential work of reform in the city of Geneva. Removing idols was a visible sign that renewal of Christ's church was taking place. For the most part in France, from which Calvin fled as a refugee, the political situation meant that Protestants were not free to construct an ecclesial stage on which to enact their theological concepts. In Geneva, Calvin developed a space from which to construct a public expression of his theological and theoretical understandings. Since the six existing medieval churches of the city were consolidated into three parishes there was not a need for further construction of church buildings during Calvin's time. However, Catherine Randall argues that the idea of architectural space finds conceptual grounding in Calvin:

Calvin wanted to move from an exclusively theological understanding of the dimensions of real space to an insistence on the interrelationships between public, external, empirical space and space typified by an inner, moral spatial dimension. Calvin's *Institution de la religion Chrétienne* can be read as an innovative document concerned with ecclesiology, theology, and the notion of space, because in it Calvin desires to locate the visible church on earth in an approximate conjunction with that of the perfect invisible church. He is also concerned with the right structuring of the human heart.[23]

Randall maintains Calvin's "space, syntax, and significance are superimposed on each other. Space displays the true church, its opposite, and its

---

22. Calvin, *Institutes*, 1.11.13
23. Randall, *Building Codes*, 26–27.

possible correction."[24] Like the Renaissance architects in France, returning from Italy with newfound theoretical discoveries, Calvin understood space as relational and dialectical. Scripture alone is immutable, eternal, authoritative, and yet, inhabiting a sinful world, it resides in disfigured and compromised space. Randall is correct in her observation that Calvin wanted to move beyond "an exclusively theological" perception of real space, which appears to mean a conceptual understanding, seen for example in his corrective of the literalistic and material view of the Latin Mass. Calvin indeed articulates an alternate view, one comprising a network of "interrelationships between public, external, empirical space." But the alternative to a purely theological or spiritual theory of the space had also to include memory, not simply syntax in the sense of use of language or of the study of signs. Calvin, in attempting to mediate a moderate position on communion between Luther and Zwingli, moves beyond Augustine's phrase "sign and signifier." He sees both the memorial aspect and the spiritual aspect of the Supper joining together in time and space to join the believer in faith to God through Christ. From sign and signifier, then, he arrives at meaning.

One way this works itself out is in the administration of the Lord's Supper, the place where the believer experiences most vividly a communion with the cloud of witnesses. Theoretically open to all believers, the Holy Supper is indispensable to the church for connecting it to its Savior. To maintain its integrity, however, those responsible for its administration (the company of pastors) must retain the ability to exclude persons for moral reasons. In *Articles Concerning the Organization of the Church and of Worship* Calvin writes, it

> . . . cannot be said to be well ordered and regulated [two vivid concerns of Calvin] unless in it the Holy Supper of our Lord is always being celebrated and frequented, and this under such good supervision that no one dare presume to present himself unless devoutly, and with genuine reverence for it. For this reason, in order to maintain the church in its integrity, the discipline of excommunication is necessary. . . .[25]

If Calvin can be said to move beyond an exclusively theological understanding of communion, then this movement also entails memory of the signified, the historical event of the cross. The space of communion is a spiritual and "virtual" one, perfect from the divine side, yet also inhabiting

24. Ibid, 28.
25. Calvin, "Organization," 48.

a very human space, which at times risks being compromised by sin, and stands in need of discipline and correction. In 1537, Calvin's *Articles Concerning the Organization of the Church and of Worship* were refused by the Council of Ministers, undermining his hope for both the power of excommunication and for monthly observance of communion. The cardinal rule, insists Calvin, is that the sacrament not be spoiled or polluted by including people who show themselves unworthy by their conduct. As scriptural warrant for this discipline, Calvin uses Matthew 18, 1 Corinthians 5, and 1 Timothy 1, and also passages emphasizing the element of remembering. Thus, Calvin argues for the importance of physically removing members of the community not just from "sacred space" in which the church gathers for worship, but from the sacred community itself. The test for covenant faithfulness, he suggests, is to require each person to "make confession and give reason for their faith."[26] He also insists on the singing of psalms and on the catechizing of children in order to build up the church; it should be noticed that all these practical steps for strengthening the church rest on the foundation of the reading, hearing, and understanding of Scripture. To allow the ungodly in the theological and physical space of communion is to cause the space to degenerate into conflicted space, or no-space.

Transformations of space could become confused as reformers attempted to work out implications of reform (implications that were practical, liturgical, and relational.) The architectural use of the Genevan churches evolved over time as Calvin and others consolidated the Reform.[27] For example, a cross in front of St. Pierre was finally removed in the 1540s. Wall paintings not containing figurative images, which had been overlooked in the iconoclasm of the 1530s, continued to periodically be painted over. People's patterns of using the temple changed over time. This is key—rather than simply use space differently, people were perceiving and talking about space differently. The new look of St. Pierre's interior space from 1535 signaled Protestants' new, non-Catholic identity. Nonetheless, the changes to the space evolved, sometimes awkwardly. For instance, authorities began the practice of melting down the former cathedral's organ pipes to make communion utensils and goblets, but the practice was halted in 1562.[28] Furniture was arranged and rearranged, a gallery added, the pulpit moved, and eventually seating added to fill the entire nave.

26. Calvin, *Theological Treatises*, 53.
27. Guillot, *L'Église de St. Pierre*, 67ff.
28. Ibid.

Tenets of Reformed worship space included the following: the church was not a building but the people of God; the building should enhance the hearing and understanding of Scripture; God is present in the everyday elements of life in the world, and cannot be confined to one place; ostentation is inappropriate, and diverts resources from the work of God. In consequence, the use of space would be relatively simple, though still in the case of St. Pierre that space occupied an architecturally complex and impressive space. But Calvin maintained,

> We must guard against taking them [worship structures] to be God's proper dwelling places, whence he may more readily incline his ear to us—as they began to be regarded some centuries ago—or feigning for them some secret holiness or other, which would render prayer more sacred before God . . . for we have the commandment to call upon the Lord, without distinction of place, "in spirit and in truth."[29]

In addition, in his commentary on Exodus, Calvin writes,

> Thus it is certain that by its external ornaments the excellence of spiritual gifts was designated. On this ground Isaiah, discoursing of the perfect glory of the Church as it would be under the reign of Christ, says, "I will lay thy stones with fair colors, and lay thy foundations with sapphires; and I will make thy windows of agates, and thy gates of carbuncles, and all thy borders of pleasant stones." (Isa 54:11–12)

By these words he plainly signifies that the Church would be adorned with heavenly beauty, since all kinds of graces shone forth in her But the chief excellence of her adornment must be referred to the instruction which renews us into the image of God. Thus David, when he celebrates the beauty of God's house, assigns this honor chiefly to the exercises of faith and piety: "One thing have I desired of the Lord," he says, "that will I seek after, that I may dwell in the house of the Lord all the days of my life, to behold the beauty of the Lord, and to inquire in his temple" (Ps 27:4).

> Was this that he might feed his eyes with empty pictures, with its costly materials, and with the exquisite workmanship of it? Assuredly, he does not speak of gazing inquisitively at it, but thus alludes to its visible workmanship, that with the spiritual eyes of

---

29. Calvin, *Institutes*, 3.20.30.

faith he may "consider the glory more excellent than the whole world, which was there represented."[30]

In this section, Calvin spiritualizes the physical attributes of the Old Testament tabernacle: where the divine directions call for "external ornaments," Calvin explains these typologically, signs pointing to spiritual gifts, especially that of faith. Israel, in its worship, was intended to shine as a foretelling of the Church in its glory. Reflecting on David's contemplation in the house of the Lord, Calvin insists this was not directed to the opacity of human workmanship, but instead to a transcendent vision represented by those works. This mirrors an incarnational dynamic in which physical objects do not draw attention to themselves, but rather points instead to God's revelation to his people. The literal worship space in which the believing heart finds itself cannot be sacred in a sacramental sense, but it can accommodate and make space for an encounter of faith.

THE LATER EVOLUTION OF CALVIN'S INFLUENCE IN FRANCE

The Italian campaigns of Charles VIII, Louis XII, and Francis I in the first quarter of the sixteenth century brought an influx of new artistic ideas to France. Other ideas infiltrated the culture at the same time. The Meaux circle, a humanistic theological movement following the teachings of Martin Luther, worked for reform in France in the 1520s with the work of scholars like Lefèvre d'Étaples and his protégées. Although humanistic studies flourished in Paris, the Sorbonne condemned Luther and his writings in 1521. In 1534, in what became known as "the Affair of the Placards," messages denouncing the Catholic Mass were posted around Paris, even in the king's chambers.[31] The placards may be seen as a kind of "anti-icon," not simply a polemic but a visual cue that Protestants intended to reclaim Catholic devotional and political space. In response, the French crown asserted its authority more severely, making widespread arrests.

It was during this period that Calvin fled from Paris, eventually settling in Geneva. By 1540, the French government subjected Calvinists to the Inquisition, and by 1542, the Huguenot Diaspora from France had already begun. Thousands of Huguenots fled to Geneva within the next decade.

---

30. Calvin, *Harmony of the Law*, Exod 26:1–37.
31. McGrath, *Life of John Calvin*, 15.

The cause for this was persecutions launched by Henry II and his creation of the Chambre Ardente, whose task it was to enforce religious compliance within the jurisdiction of the Parliament of Paris. Calvin worried about the religious pressures on his French compatriots, writing "the cause of the gospel in France, object of [my] constant preoccupation, seems ever more compromised."[32] He had an especial anxiety for Reformed churches under threat, and composed his French Confession of Faith to address their needs in 1559.[33] He expressed this concern and protested the Protestants' innocence of the crime of sedition, in his preface to Francis II from his French Confession:

> We humbly beg, Sire, that we may sometimes be permitted to gather together, to be exhorted to the fear of God by his Word, as well as to be confirmed by the administration of the Sacraments which the Lord Jesus Christ instituted in his Church. And if it should please your Majesty to give us a place where any one may see what passes in our assemblies, we shall thereby be absolved from the charge of the enormous crimes with which these same assemblies have been defamed. For nothing will be seen but what is decent and well ordered, and nothing will be heard but the praise of God, exhortations to his service, and prayers for the preservation of your Majesty and of your kingdom. And if it do not please you to grant us this favor, at least let it be permitted us to follow the established order in private among ourselves.[34]

In addition, Calvin dispatched Théodore de Bèze to the Colloquy at Poissy near Paris in 1562 in a failed attempt to secure a détente with Catholic imperial power. The decade would prove to be a confusing time of agonizing religious strife, but nonetheless French Protestantism flourished. In such an incendiary climate, reforming religious ideas, including worship centered on Scripture read and exposited in the vernacular, were revolutionary. French Calvinism was essentially militant in that it sought an altogether new ecclesiastical order, reformed according to the purity of God's Word, which implied to Catholic royal authority a new societal order. Diefendorf shows that popular Catholic resistance to Reform, especially vehement in France, was in part reaction to Protestant attacks on the Eucharist and destruction of religious relics and images. In addition,

32. Ibid.

33. Schaff, *Creeds of Christendom*, 356–59.

34. Ibid., 358.

the Protestant cause in France came to be identified with sedition, as Calvin's preface his French Confession reveals. Increasingly, it became difficult to find a mediating position. The massacre of one hundred Huguenots at Vassy in Champagne in 1562 sparked religious war across the country. The Peace of Saint-Germain-en-Laye in 1570 accorded religious freedom to Huguenots within their own territories and allowed them to fortify their cities. However, the treaty did not fully satisfy either party, and both sides continued to vie for advantage, culminating with the St. Bartholomew's Day Massacre in 1572.

As a result, civil war would last, intermittently, another twenty-six years, until exhaustion pressed both sides to move toward truce. The Edict of Nantes, signed by Henry IV in 1598, allowed for some degree of freedom of conscience, granted the right of Protestants to attend university, and the right to maintain fortress towns in the territory they currently held.[35] These reluctantly-given rights brought respite from outright armed conflict, and relief to beleaguered Protestants, while at the same time confining them to specified areas and establishing their minority status.

In the eighty-seven years the edict was in effect, civil rights for Huguenots would increasingly erode, with civil pressure building in particular under Cardinals Richelieu and Mazarin. Calvin had disparaged what he called "Nicodemites," or secret Protestants, after the man who went to speak to Jesus at night out of fear for his peers. Nevertheless, it was unavoidable that many second- and third-generation Reformed Christians in France, already marginalized, would respond to increasing pressure by moving underground. Increasingly, to live openly as a Protestant in imperial France was to court persecution, imprisonment, and potentially martyrdom. In the 1680s, Louis XIV harassed the Huguenots from public office and barred them from certain professions. In 1685, he revoked the Edict of Nantes altogether, ordering the destruction of Protestant church buildings; banning of Protestant preaching and worship, including in private homes; the banishment of pastors; the forced rebaptism of Protestant children; the closing of parochial schools; and the prohibition of leaving the country. Other persecutions included the prohibition of singing of psalms, the obligatory billeting of government dragoons, and the removal of their children from Protestant parents who refused to convert. The edict eliminated the Protestant faith in France apart from the "church of the desert," a remnant, illegal,

35. Guicharnaud, "Architecture," 134.

and clandestine movement, until the time of the French Revolution more than a century later.

Although the influence of Calvin on the theology and ethos of the French churches was incalculable, it was not absolute. Indeed "pour les églises de France, l'Église Mère n'est pas celle de Genève. C'est l'église de Strasbourg à la façon 1540–1542."[36] ("For the churches of France, the mother church isn't that of Geneva, but rather of Strasbourg as she was in 1540–1542.") That is, French Protestant churches tended to look not to Geneva but to Strasbourg as their "mother church." Nevertheless, from the time of Calvin's French Catechism and the first French Synod in 1559, to the Revocation in 1685, the practices of the Reformed church in France generally followed closely those of Geneva in liturgy and polity, although some distinctions emerged. Following Calvin, they believed the church was founded on preaching, sacraments, and discipline. The order of worship focused on the preaching, the reading of Scripture (including the Gospel, the Law, the Psalms, and the Epistles), corporate confession of sin, prayers, and the singing of psalms. The polity of the local church closely followed the Genevan model, including four ordained offices of pastor, elder, doctor, and deacon, organized in each local parish around a strong consistory, and subject to the higher governing body of synod and national assembly. Every consistory included one or more pastors and perhaps a dozen elders, meeting weekly to administer the affairs of the congregation, to supervise its moral life, and insure the collective interests of its members.[37]

Calvin deeply influenced French Protestantism through the *Institutes* and his *French Confession*; through de Bèze's teaching in France and representation in colloquies such as that at Poissy in 1560; and through missionary pastors trained in Geneva. One estimate figures some 1,240 churches were organized in France between 1555 and 1570.[38] Consistory records from Geneva show that church sent over two hundred pastors to France, and the other francophone cantons of Vaud and Neuchâtel were sending pastors as well. It was natural, then, Genevan or Vaudois church organizational models would have exerted some influence on the churches of France. Even as they developed independently, many French Reformed churches followed Strasbourg or the French-speaking Swiss churches in

---

36. Vassaux and Messner, *Églises réformées*, 44.

37. Guicharnaud, "Architecture," 203.

38. Garrisson-Estèbe, *Protestants du Midi*, 83.

liturgy, catechism, and in much of church order, including local congregations administered by a local consistory of elders.[39]

The French order was not identical to Swiss model in Romandie, however. Its particular forms had to work as a minority church, and as such were newly developed in the sixteenth century. This contrasted with the Swiss magisterial reform, "where the reformers tended to retain and adapt pre-Reformation civic forms, ecclesiastical buildings, and parish arrangements, including parish boundaries."[40] In spite of the French Reformed churches' indebtedness to Calvinist teaching, they were forced to adapt to local conditions, and there were significant differences as the French Calvinists applied reforming principles to their own context. Instead of reform supported by local magistrates and city councils, they functioned in a state of uneasy détente at best, and for years under open conflict, with Catholic imperial power. As a minority population, Huguenots were compelled to translate confessional identity into an organizational shape that would meet the practical needs of the church. Though the Swiss remained divided along the lines of language and cantonal government, the French organized into a national synod as early as 1559. In particular, early Protestant communities in France often had to do without regular pastoral leadership, and the elders of the church in such cases would be forced to assume responsibility for teaching and insuring stability.[41] Consistories played a key role in shaping Reformed identity by regulating worship, administration, and morality of Protestant believers' lives. They maintained "accounts of worthy communicants, members of the congregation whose good character, correct behavior, and satisfactory understanding of the faith as verified by the elders entitled them to share in the Lord's Supper."[42]

The religio-political situation in France made an impact on the relationship of Protestant houses of worship, where they were permitted by civil authorities, to build churches in urban space. Under the peace accord of 1563 and later under the Edict of Nantes in 1598, the Reformed had the right to build churches, but only outside of cities, a situation opposite to the places where Protestants controlled the government, as in Switzerland (or, sporadically and in limited areas, in France.) This meant that that Protestants had to leave the urban center and move to liminal space in order

39. Benedict, *Christ's Churches*, 134ff.

40 Garrisson-Estèbe, *Protestants du Midi*, 202.

41. Mentzer, *La Construction*, 3.

42. Mentzer, *Sin and the Calvinists*, 98.

to worship. It also reinforced Reformed identity as a marginal and oppo-
sitional minority among the Catholic imperial majority, and also the Reformed self-understanding as a people defined by the Word of God rather
than by tradition or stable location, creating a new kind of threatened and
yet dynamic space. Ironically, it also freed them from the weight of sacred
associations in their former places of worship, bringing to mind worship as
a response to and movement toward God, as seen in the opening of Psalm
122: "A song of ascents. Of David. I rejoiced with those who said to me, "Let
us go to the house of the LORD.""

Other factors led to French Protestantism's distinct form from that
of the Genevan model. Although the Protestants saw Catholic devotional
practices as superstitious or idolatrous, Protestant leaders were unable to
expunge all traces of medieval spiritual practices. Not surprisingly, this
was the case where Catholics held power. In many rural areas, Protestants
lacked instruction available in Protestant urban centers. In such cases,
familiar practices and symbols proved resilient for many when religious
and social change to the Reformed religion came with bewilderingly speed.
Some traditional tactics proved useful for the new religion: much of the
French Reformed church continued in the use of catechism for instruction
in the faith, and the elders took the lead in teaching it.

As reform waxed and waned in French society, practice sometimes
deviated in face of practical need and changing political climate. Indeed,
as Thierry Wanegffelen has shown in his work *Ni Rome ni Genève*,[43] there
existed a practical blurring of confessional lines between Catholic and Reformed. In this history of the individual believer ("une histoire de la per-
sonne croyante"), he demonstrates that confessional choice in the midst
of Catholic-Protestant violence was far from consistent, and distinguishes
between categories of church doctrine and membership on one hand, and
"religious sensibilities" on the other. Confessional accommodations were
negotiated formally, as well as de facto accommodations made in individual practice.

In this confused situation, members of the French Reformed church
in the seventeenth century participated in the wider Catholic society in
varying degrees; according to Randall, most of the royal artists, artisans,
and architects of this period were either outright Calvinists, or were at
least sympathetic to the Calvinist cause.[44] For example, the architects who

43. Wanegffelen, *Ni Rome ni Genève*, 56.
44. Randall, *Building Codes*, 2.

designed Marie de Médici's Luxembourg Palace, the modifications on the Louvre, and several Catholic Churches in Paris were all Protestant. Randall posits that they imposed a visual code of subterfuge, intelligible only to those within their community of faith, intended to conceptually undermine the imperial Catholic power they ostensibly supported.[45] Randall is no doubt correct in this with cases of Huguenot architects commissioned to design and build for Catholics. In the case of purpose-built Reformed worship space, however, the case was more clear-cut. In those cases, the Huguenots built spaces that stated unambiguously who they were and what they believed, and the larger Catholic community did not fail to understand the churches' meaning, which came through in building forms such as round, octagonal, or basilican forms lacking transepts, or in the plainness of the structures themselves. Evidence that Catholics perceived Reformed theological convictions to be expressed in their churches may be seen in the burning of Protestant churches in riots, and without a doubt in the fact that the Edict of Fontainebleau ordered the destruction of these churches rather than their re-use.

In the succeeding years the situation became infinitely more confused as both Catholics and Protestants struggled for supremacy in the public realm. When they came into possession of formerly Catholic space, as in Lyons, Orange, Navarre, Montauban, and many independent cities in France, Protestants would eliminate all physical evidence of Catholic "idolatry." In the places where Catholics repossessed churches formerly taken by Protestants, they were cleansed of the contagion of heresy and re-consecrated. These events were part of a contest to assert spatial meaning and establish rival claims through "hierarchies of religious space within the city."[46] Amanda Eurich describes one such battleground in the city of Orange in Southern France, where Calvinists attempted to:

> demystify the sacred 'hot spots' of the local Catholic community . . . with each new wave of sectarian violence. During the 1560s and 1570s the Cathedral of Notre Dame and the chapel of St. Eutrope were subjected to repeated iconoclastic attacks. The intensity and frequency of these hostilities certainly owe more to mere opportunity and can be clearly linked to the central importance of these churches within the sacred geography of local Catholicism.[47]

45. Ibid.
46. Eurich, "Sacralising Space," 265.
47. Coster and Spicer, *Sacred Space*, 265.

On one occasion Protestants climbed into the bell tower and cut loose the massive church bells, which fell from the tower and through the roof below. Eurich remarks that this action silenced the bells that served to announce the space as belonging to the Catholic faith and "laid claim to the acoustic landscape."[48] The Protestants' destructive act was not simply random; it was a repudiation of Catholic claims and ritual markers both temporal and lateral.

During the years of the civil wars and the supposed period of toleration, then, a period of some 125 years, Catholic political powers worked to convert or contain their religious adversaries. The unique Protestant architectural language was not so easily controlled, however, and in spite of all its similarities to that of their co-religionists in the Swiss territories, Huguenots developed and retained a distinctive visual language for their churches.

THE COMMUNION AS SACRED SPACE

Protestants of the sixteenth and seventeenth centuries were suspicious of visualization techniques for fear that worshipers might replace "idols" of wood and stone with idols of the mind. The Huguenots of France followed Calvin in this thinking, preferring to allow Scripture exclusive rights to suggest images for reflection and recollection. On its own, human intellect is suspect: "From this we may gather that man's nature, so to speak, is a perpetual factory of idols," as Calvin insisted.[49] The sixteenth- and seventeenth-century followers Calvin did possess one powerful memory device however—the Eucharist itself. The Holy Supper was the place where believers were reconfigured and taken into a past event, the Crucifixion, and by faith lifted to heaven, participating already in the reality of the kingdom of God. In the complicated process of both connecting to the past and repudiating the past, "intertext" revealed itself especially in relation to communion, as the Latin Mass gave way to the Lord's Supper, and the sacrificial understanding of the medieval Mass changed to a shared understanding of the Eucharistic observance.

For Reformed Christians, sacred space was often experienced in the midst of the profane. In order to grasp their understanding of change and continuity, we must begin by scrutinizing their sense of the holy. Documents

48. Ibid., 267.
49. Calvin, *Institutes*, 1.11.8.

for the spiritual formation of adherents to the new faith provide some direction. Christian Grosse analyzes the *Form of Prayers and Ecclesiastical Songs* (1542) and the *Catechism of the Church of Geneva* (1542) to understand what meaning "sacred" might have had for sixteenth-century Genevans.[50] Grosse points out that the words "sacred" and "holy," used interchangeably, nearly always appear as adjectives, such as in "the holy gospel." Of the two terms, "holy" was more commonly used, and referred to the Persons of the Trinity as well as to that which came from God, as the divine Word ("commandments," "holy doctrine," "thy holy gospel," "his holy promises") and the sacraments. Calvin expressed a vivid concern for protecting the sanctity of divine worship through excommunication: the communion table must be protected from pollution by wrong belief or behavior.

This is made clear in the warnings to fence the Lord's Table in the Geneva Catechism:

> P[upil]: In the Supper, however, the minister should take care lest he offer it to someone who is publicly well known to be unworthy of it.
>
> M[aster]: Why?
>
> P: Because that would involve contempt and profanation of the Sacrament.
>
> M: So has it been a good thing that a defined order of government has been set up in the churches?
>
> P: Certainly, for otherwise they are not well constituted or suitably established. That is the reason why Elders are chosen who are guardians of morality and watch over and warn offenders. When they know that some persons are not in a state to receive the Supper and cannot be admitted without the sacrament being thereby polluted, they exclude them from communion.

The resulting sense of holiness is associated with God and is thus separated from the temporal world. However, although this suggests a distinction from the profane, it also lifts up the possibility of a point of contact with the divine in the sacrament and in the preaching of the Word. Ritual protection of Holy Communion suggests a possible connection with God's holiness, and thus "establishes a link between the believers and the sacred."[51]

---

50. Coster and Spicer, *Sacred Space*, 61.

51. Ibid., 62.

The tendency to removing the element of mystery can be seen in Calvin. His hermeneutical principles, according to Ward Holder[52], include the authority of Scripture, understanding the mind of the author, hermeneutical circles, and edification, which tend toward a spare interpretation of liturgy and church life. But these principles can cut both ways. Calvin allows for God's accommodation of human weakness, and for latitude on secondary things. The possibility exists that in deference to local practices or to human weakness elements could be permitted that would in the best of circumstances be eschewed. An example might be the use of art, in theory at least: though Calvin was adamant that it had no place in worship, art in another context could be seen as a gift of God. Calvin emphasizes God's work in creation and redemption because of the seriousness with which he takes the Fall and its consequences for humanity.

The transgression of representative Adam corrupted all subsequent humanity. Humans are now incapable of any spiritual good and are inclined only to evil, and deserving of eternal judgment. This condition of total depravity precludes optimism and suggests human propensity to corrupt even worship.

It is not, however, where God leaves humanity; instead, his grace reaches out to save us in our wretched condition. God's salvation is based not on any human virtue, but on his mercies, expressed in the covenants of the Old and New Testaments. God's plan of salvation is willed by the Father, accomplished by the Son, and applied to the elect by the Holy Spirit. Many of Calvin's exegetical practices, including paraphrase, contextual interpretation, the importance of humility, fuller meaning, and tradition's possibilities, could be seen as opening the door to visual expression and spatial dimensions of holiness, at least in the hands of other interpreters. In addition, his view of God's accommodation to our human way of thinking would make some leeway for visual and architectural artistry.

Calvin's doctrine of the sacrament of communion reveals his understanding of its meaning, and reveals how he understood the concept of holiness. In his 1541 work *Petit traicté de la saincte Cène du nostre Seigneur Jésus-Christ,* Calvin laid out his understanding of the sacrament. The treatise was intended as a clear and comprehensive explanation in French of his views on the Eucharist.[53] It was written to appeal to readers with no particular training in theology or Latin, and was popular enough to appear in

52. Holder, *John Calvin*, 29ff.
53. Elwood, *Body Broken*, 61.

several editions within ten years. As such, the work contributed to the propaganda struggle of the 1530s. During the 1540s the Sorbonne, concerned
about the propagation of heresy, compiled lists of prohibited books. Genevan writings regularly appeared, and the list from 1542 included Calvin's
Institution, Formes des prières, Catéchisme, and the *Petit traicté de la saincte
Cène*.[54] The list suggests the availability of writings for those attracted to the
Reformed faith. On the basis on the list of banned works as well as letters
from his correspondents, Calvin's ideas seem to have circulated widely as
he had hoped in his native France.

Calvin offered a definition of a sacrament in his Geneva Catechism:

> M[aster]: What is a sacrament?
>
> P[upil]: An outward testimony of the grace of God who by a vis-
> ible sign shows us things spiritual, to inscribe his promises in our
> hearts and to make us more certain of their truth.
>
> M: Does so much power exist under a visible sign that it can se-
> cure conscience in the assurance of salvation?
>
> P: It does not have this of itself, but by God's will because it is
> instituted to this end.[55]

In this definition, distance is drawn between the sacrament, or sign,
and the thing signified, the grace of God. The sacrament is not said to
convey the grace of God, but to testify to it, and yet it is more than a bar-
ren sign; it has real power in the life of the Christian—it inscribes God's
promises on the heart, and makes the believer more certain of the truth of
God's promises, or words. While it has no magic or intrinsic power, but real
power nonetheless as ordained by God to accomplish his purpose. Calvin's
conceptualization of the tension between matter and the spiritual world is
a complicated one. He writes,

> For this reason, the apostle, in that very passage where he calls the
> worlds the images of things invisible, adds that by faith we under-
> stand that they have been fashioned by God's Word [Heb 11:3]. He
> means by this that the invisible divinity is made manifest in such
> spectacles, but that we have not the eyes to see this unless they be
> illuminated by the inner revelation of God through faith.[56]

54. Ibid.

55. Calvin, "Catechism of the Church," 83–84.

56. Calvin, *Institutes*, 1.5.24.

Calvin posited a notion of "sign," explicitly taking up Augustine's term. He came to his notion in the *Institutes* after he had laid out his understanding of human perception, most centrally to his conceptualization of "sign," his argument that human eyes were enabled to see revelation in the physical and material world through God-given faith. That sense of being able to see God where others could not, which became so central to Reformed Christians' sense of themselves in the world, informed Calvin's approach to signs.[57]

In his *Institutes*, Calvin defined a sacrament as "a testimony of the divine favor toward us, confirmed by an external sign, with a corresponding attestation of our faith towards Him."[58] He described it as akin to the preaching of the gospel, a help to our faith through an external sign by which God seals his grace on the believer. Calvin understood a sacrament as help to sustain us in our weakness, and his explanation of it was consistent with Augustine's definition of a visible sign of a sacred, invisible grace. Through it, God "provides first for our ignorance and sluggishness, and secondly, for our infirmity; and yet properly speaking, it does not so much confirm his Word as establish us in the faith of it."[59] The term *sacramentum* is used for Paul's term "mystery," especially when it refers to divine things, as in Eph 1:9, "Having made known unto us the mystery (*sacramentum*) of his will." The mystery is the grace of God revealed through his Word in Christ. Calvin was expressing the dynamic between objective reality in the Word of God, and our subjective experience of it through an outward sign. What makes the Holy Supper holy is the Word of God, not the outward sign. The sacrament corresponds to "an antecedent promise," a kind of "appendix" that confirms and seals, or attests to the promise, in order to enhance our experience of it. At this point Calvin quoted Chrysostom, "Were we incorporeal, he would give us these things in a naked and incorporeal form. Now because our souls are implanted in bodies, he delivers spiritual things under things visible. Not that the qualities which are set before us in the sacraments are inherent in the nature of the things, but God gives them this signification." He went on, "It does not so much confirm his Word as establish us in the faith of it."[60] He argued the same point in *A Short Treatise*

---

57. Wandel, *Reformation*, 245.

58. Calvin, *Institutes*, 4.14.1

59. Ibid., 4.14.3

60. Ibid., 4.15.3

on the Lord's Supper (1541.)[61] "We must confess, then, that if the representation which God gives us in the Supper is true, the internal substance of the sacrament is conjoined with the visible signs." Thomas J. Davis helps us see Calvin's major theme in his view of the Supper: that the elements serve as elements wherein the believing community receives the body and blood of Christ, not simply for the benefits they impart but as a communion with Christ. Davis sees a development in Calvin's thought on the Supper, moving from the Supper as an impartation of religious knowledge, to experiencing in it the "real presence" and "substantial partaking," to the Supper as the way in which God accommodates believers and gives a "means of grace."[62]

The benefit of the Supper is not physical, but something spiritual. It permits fellowship with Christ's body and blood, and yet does not warrant confusing the real presence of Christ, the substance, with the signs. It also entails a memory space, because the Eucharist celebrates the past, present, and future saving work of Christ. The communion remembers the historic event of Christ's atoning death, his presence with the church through his Holy Spirit, and his eschatological return to complete the redemption of his body, the Church. In communion, the Church is cleansed from sin, renewed in faith, and empowered for godly service.

The language is that of signification and outward signs. Word is inseparable from sacrament as external sign, not merely as an incantation which consecrates the elements, but as a preached Word that "makes us understand what the visible sign means."[63] Quoting St. Augustine, Calvin insists on the Word "not as pronounced, but understood."[64] Sacraments are not worthy of the name without an intelligible explication for the gathered worshiping community.

Christopher Elwood, in *The Body Broken: The Calvinist Doctrine of the Eucharist and the Symbolization of Power in Sixteenth-century France*, points out that in articulating thus the meaning of the Eucharist, Calvin, along with his Reformed predecessors Zwingli, Oecolampadius, and Farel, subverted the Catholic order wherein signs were stable and referents did not depend on their proper interpretation. He wrote, "This critical assault of the Reformed thus called into question the entire medieval Catholic symbolic

---

61. Calvin, *Writings on Pastoral Piety*, 17.

62. Davis, *Clearest Promises*, 147ff., 167ff., 180ff.

63. Calvin, *Institutes*, 4.15.3

64. Calvin, *Writings on Pastoral Piety*, 48.

structure that posited a stable relation of correspondence between material signs and spiritual realities and between temporal and divine orders."[65]

The ascension of Christ himself served as a model and interpretive lens for the Christian life, lifting up the goal of union with God through Christ. His purpose in descending to earth was to lift us to the Father, and also to him insofar as he is in communion with the Father. Julie Canlis fleshes out some of the implications for worship space of this view of the believer's *koinonia* with God:

> This calls for a spirituality that, in Calvin's (and Paul's) language, is oriented "toward the goal of the upward call." (3.25.1) Because our "hope rests in heaven," Calvin exhorts "the godly . . . with eyes fast fixed on Christ [to] wait upon heaven," thus displaying the truth that "where our treasure is, our heart is" (3.25.1). "Heaven" is to be understood in terms of the fulfillment of our communion with Christ; for even Plato, Calvin notes, understood union to be man's highest good! (3.25.2)[66]

Simultaneously, Calvin recognizes that the key to God's communion with humanity is God's transcendent freedom. It is in this second sense that Calvin's emphasis on heaven and ascent must be understood. If "people dare limit the operations of God, according to their own pleasure, [to render him], as it were, shut up within bars of wood or iron," then Calvin would combat this with a resurrection of the biblical imagery of heaven. "When they place God in heaven, they do not confine him to a certain locality. . . . In short, they put the universe under his control; and, being superior to every obstruction, he does freely everything that may seem good to him."[67]

As important as the metaphorical space of the Eucharistic celebration was to Calvin, and in spite of the fact that he wanted to celebrate the communion more frequently, he was not to win this argument with the city council. Therefore, preaching and not communion would be the major focus of worship, although, given Calvin's other remarks, this may have been his preference in any case. Under regulation of the city council, communion was to be celebrated only four times a year during Christmastide, Easter, Pentecost, and in mid-September. Even in those times, the Supper was a part of a larger liturgy which focused on the sermon.

65. Elwood, *Body Broken*, 168.

66. Canlis, *Calvin's Ladder*, 118.

67. Ibid., 119.

Calvin argues that Scripture itself, "in accommodation to the rude and gross intellect of man, usually speaks in popular terms." "God himself being the only fit witness to himself"; although humans long for images, as depictions of the divinity, these can only corrupt or diminish the glory of God. This notion is central for Calvin, founded on his interpretation of the second commandment. Only God can define God, and therefore humans are forbidden to construct images to represent him. Nonetheless, the human authors of Scripture, directed by the Holy Spirit, used a great multiplicity of images as signs—God's manner of speaking for himself. When God occasionally manifested himself through physical signs, these made clear his teaching ("doctrine"), and at the same time remained ephemeral to give "intimation of his incomprehensible essence."

However, Calvin frequently speaks of God in terms which emphasize seeing, with words such as "sign," "beauty," "mirror," "image," seemingly attempting to apprehend the reality of God in artistic form, through the medium of rhetoric. In his commentary on Psalm 104 Calvin writes that God is "inaccessible" and "hidden in himself," but that he "irradiates the whole world with his splendor" and "appears in a manner accessible to us." This way of apprehending the glory of God is a secondary one: we cannot search to know him in his essence, but can perceive true echoes of him in nature. In consequence, he explains that humans are invited to "contemplate" God or to seek "the face of God." Jesus Christ is the true image (and Word) of God; we perceive God's glory, indirectly, in creation. In this way his divinity is seen through the created world, and yet unaided human eyes, corrupted by sin, are unable to perceive this revelation apart from the Spirit's illumination. In addition, the sacraments present a picture of salvation to the church, a necessary visual metaphor that evokes a spiritual reality. Calvin is using visual language and a vocabulary of seeing to speak of the place where the material connects with and conveys the spiritual. The image of the Supper has indeed become an object of contemplation, not simply material and optical, but spiritual, through faith enabling us to lift our hearts to heaven and to see God. In Book IV of the *Institutes*, Calvin utilizes architectural and visual metaphors to underscore the purpose of the sacraments:

> For just as a building stands and leans on its foundation, and yet is rendered more stable when supported by pillars, so faith leans on the Word of God as its proper foundation, and yet when sacraments are added leans more firmly, as if resting on pillars. Or we

may call them mirrors, in which we may contemplate the riches of
the grace which God bestows upon us. For then, as has been said,
he manifests himself to us in as far as our dullness can enable us
to recognize him, and testifies his love and kindness to us more
expressly than by word. (4.14.6)

The right foundation for faith is the Word of God spoken in Scripture,
yet Calvin articulates a distinct purpose in the sacraments as "supports" for
the Word. They are not the source of grace, but aids, capable of speaking to
us through our weakness, to perceiving the grace already given.

This meant that the space required in which the sacred rites would
be performed would be streamlined, simple, not distracting the sanctified
and believing imagination with ostentatious ornamentation that pointed to
itself rather than beyond to the spiritual realities the sacraments recalled.
Space needed to envelop worshipers, yet remain empty enough to refuse
attention for itself. Various Reformed churches handled this need differently; some brought in multiple tables for the occasion of the Lord's Supper.
Others placed a stationary table in the choir or transept, the visual center of
the church. The abbey church of Romainmôtier in Vaud altered the Gothic
vaulted ceiling in the eighteenth century for the needs of Reformed worship, constructing a flat wooden suspended ceiling over the nave in order
to improve audio quality. Demonstrating sensitivity to visual and symbolic
dynamics as well, builders designed a large circle above the place where
communion was served.

The principal practical consequence of Calvin's theology of communion was the need for space for worshipers, to gather together at the table,
emphasizing community and allowing for maximum sight and sound, and
thus comprehension. Calvin did not discuss particular styles of architecture
which might be appropriate for worship space, and though he did not label
church architecture as a matter of indifference, we may place the subject
into Calvin's understanding of *adiaphora* as it is developed in a disserta-
tion by David Anderson Bowen.[68] Bowen argues that Calvin had a triplex
understanding of the doctrine, which was widely discussed in the Reformation as a component of the debates on the nature of the church. Rather
than classifying controversies in worship, polity, or the life of the church as
simply a matter of good and evil, the idea of *adiaphora* allowed that some
things are not essential to salvation and therefore some deviations may be
viewed with a level of tolerance in the church. Bowen, who sees Calvin as

68. Bowen, *John Calvin's Ecclesiological Adiaphorism.*

a unique voice on the subject in the sixteenth century; rather than simply essential matters and indifferent matters, Calvin saw a middle category of "important," though non-essential for salvation.[69]

This is to suggest that Calvin, while he did not articulate a theory of ecclesiastical architecture, had the vocabulary to do so had he understood the subject to be of particular concern. While he touched upon appropriate appointments for worship in the *Institutes* and in his commentaries, he eschews specific instructions. It is therefore reasonable to conclude that he considered architectural style as a matter of *adiaphora*—important insofar as removing obstacles to pure worship, but indifferent as to one expression being holier than another, or an avenue into union with God.

REFORMED USE OF SPACE: ARE CEMETERIES SACRED?

Theoretically, this seems to leave open the possibility of object as means of grace, at least if the sacrament is rightly understood and received by the faithful. In practice, the church was emptied of altars, reliquaries, paintings, rood screens, and even tombs. New objects were introduced sparingly: communion table, pulpit for preaching. Grosse points out that burial niches were re-introduced in Geneva only in the seventeenth century when the need for conferring special honor on citizens of status became clear, and this was not unproblematic: after churchgoers began praying at the tomb, authorities installed a wall around it. As Pierre Viret, Swiss reformer, theologian, and pastor of the church in Lausanne who also preached extensively in France, said, "It is both a great superstition and idolatry to think that the ground itself confers some sort of sanctity on the dead."[70]

Reformers purposely undermined, then, a sense that one place was holier than another. Keith Luria, in a study on the complexities of Reformed and Catholic living together in seventeenth-century France, quotes Élie Benoist, author of a 1693 history of the Edict of Nantes. In a helpful study of the differing confessions' views of burial space, he writes,

> For Calvinists, the notion that cemeteries were sacred ground, hallowed by the bones of the faithful, was just another example of Catholic superstition. The Huguenot historian Élie Benoist wrote

69. Ibid.
70. Viret, *L'office des mortz.*

that we are "not so obstinate as to continue to believe the vain prejudice that one piece of land is holier than another."[71]

Luria contends that Reformed Christians were less troubled than Catholics in burying their dead alongside their confessional rivals, for whom the Protestants' beliefs made them unworthy of Christian burial. One explanation for this is that the Protestants desired access to the graves of their forebears, suggesting it was difficult to entirely eradicate a sense that some land possessed greater meaning.

The use of burial space by both Reformed and Catholics shows the two confessions had different understandings of the sacredness of the same space. Protestants counted the land as of no special consequence, yet still, they would not willingly neglect the place they had buried their dead.[72] Calvin simply advocates freedom of custom, so long as burial is done fittingly: "In those matters the custom and institutions of the country, in short, humanity and the rules of modesty itself, declare what is to be done or avoided" (*Institutes* 4.10.31). Further, French Reformed Protestants buried their dead with what Catholics found to be scandalous lack of ceremony, wordlessly lowering the bodies of their dead to the ground.[73] Their funerary practices are linked to baptism in that the recipients of the elements are called to die to themselves and the world, and to live to Christ. Bernard Roussel sees an understandable paradox in this juxtaposition:

> Reformed Protestants existed in a world that they had disenchanted more thoroughly than had other Christians and in which they actively intervened. This disenchantment occurred precisely at the moment of the Lord's Supper by demonstrating that there is nothing "divine" here below, even in the Eucharistic elements. At the same time, and for the best reasons, they appeared to turn away from earthly concerns to attain, as soon as possible, "true life." The paradox in this is not difficult to comprehend, and the Lord's Supper along with funerary practices allow the believer to come to terms with it.[74]

There was no place, then, for either objects or places to access God apart from the means established by Christ. Yet it was not as though there was no care given to the setting of worship, no reverence in conducting

71. Luria, "Separated by Death?," 185–222.

72. Ibid., 190.

73. Roussel, "Ensevelir honnestement," 201.

74. Ibid.

last rites for the dead, no artistry in assembling necessary supports for the worshiping life of the faithful. The community's values were communicated through architecture; church interiors were done thoughtfully and pleasingly; even tokens to admit congregants to the Lord's Supper (used in Nîmes, Montauban, and La Rochelle,) were designed with care.[75] The Protestant churches endeavored to create a new culture based on the Word of God that would replace superstition and prove that idols had no power. In time, a new form of art developed in the Reformed churches: the painting of scriptural texts on panels, an art form less emotional, more didactic and intellectual, and one that embodied the value of worship space sanctified by the Word.

HOW DID REFORMED CHRISTIANS UNDERSTAND THE HOLY?

In seeking to understand Reformed sense of sacred space, it is instructive to consider how a reformer such as Pierre Viret employs forms of the word "holy." Viret was a Swiss reformer, theologian, and pastor of the church in Lausanne who also preached extensively in France. He was, along with Calvin, Théodore De Bèze, and William Farel, one of the most important reformers of his generation. Further, he was the only native Swiss of this company, born near Lausanne in the French-speaking city of Orbe. In his *Instruction Chrétienne En La Doctrine De La Loi Et De L'Évangile* (1564), a word count reveals he used the masculine or feminine form of the word "holy" (*saint* and *sainte*) a total of 2311 times, and variant spellings of the words another thirty-four times,[76] used for the development of a distinctively Reformed doctrine of human nature, reveals that Viret consistently uses the term holy or divine as an adjective, and almost never as a noun. The most common referents are *Saint Esprit*, "Holy Spirit" (twenty-four times), *saintes écritures*, "Scripture" (twenty-two times), and the *sainte bible* another time; *sainte volonté*, [God's] "holy will" (fourteen times), and *saint sacrament*, "holy sacrament" (thirteen times). Less common uses of the term refer to the Apostle Paul (seven times), the Evangelists Matthew

75. Wandel, *Eucharist in the Reformation*, 181. See also Mentzer, "Edict of Nantes and Its Institutions," in *Society and Culture*.

76. From my examination of the catechism section ("Sommaire de la Doctrine Chrétienne, Fait en Forme de dialogue et de Catéchisme, de la Principale Cause et Fin de la Création de l'Homme").

and Luke (two times each), the communion table (six times), Hannah the mother of Samuel, the ministry of the gospel, the Christian life, the mouth of God, the doctrine of the Church, the company of Jesus, and God's *garde et protection* (one time each.) The company of saints or the individual believer as saint are referred to nine times, and the church another four.

Overwhelmingly, Viret understood holiness in relation to the person of God as he is apprehended through his Spirit and Word, which is coterminous with the words of the canon of Scripture. The attribute of holiness in the sacrament is in accordance with its sanctification by the Word of God. In similar fashion, the human ministry of the gospel is also divine insofar as it is the proclamation of the good news of the kingdom and the covenant of grace. The community of saints, the church, is holy because it is redeemed by Christ's blood and sanctified by the Word. Notable is the absence of any attribute of holiness to objects of the cultic apparatus of Catholicism: not furniture or relics or places of worship or pilgrimage. As Viret explains in his *Bref Sommaire* (under "Sacrements de l'Église" in his *Instruction*): "The manner of [Christ's] presence is not carnal and material, but spiritual and divine." It is not the elements of bread and wine that are holy, but the sacrament of the Lord's Supper itself.

Coster and Spicer acknowledge the work of Lionel Rothkrug, who notes the preponderance of sacred sites in late medieval Germany, while France was notable for the greater significance of holy objects. He suggests a correlation with the greater success of the Reformation in Germany and its ultimate failure in France to the areas with higher density of sacred sites[77], seeing a relationship between sacred space and the rate of religious change. Rothkrug concludes that spiritual climate linked to local geography may influence public consciousness, and conversely, is likely to be susceptible to change if the map is redrawn. In disputing the efficacy of sacred sites, the Protestant movement, it is widely held, broke down barriers between sacred and secular as well as clergy and laity. The movement's polemic against sacred space and its attempt to redefine it may have been necessary to capturing the popular imagination. As we will see, the newly-defined worship space did possess a power to persuade and capture the imagination with its dimensions, sharp focus, and spatial dynamics. At least with some reformers—and with some designers of worship space—the redefinition of space was argued with intentionality.

---

77. Coster and Spicer, *Sacred Space*, 4.

HUGUENOTS AND THE SHAPING OF WORSHIP SPACE

How, then, did French Reformed believers construe the space in which they met for worship? Their configuration of space followed a typical pattern, according to Hélène Guicharnaud in her essay "An Introduction to the Architecture of Protestant Temples Constructed in France before the Revocation of the Edict of Nantes."[78] The earliest groups of Reformed believers met in private homes, which afforded both necessary shelter and privacy for their clandestine gatherings. As Protestants grew in numbers and influence, they acquired public buildings and churches in places such as Montauban, Nîmes, Agen, La Rochelle, Gap, Cen, Lyons, and Montpellier.[79]

With newly-gained freedom of conscience under the Edict of Nantes in 1598, Protestants were free to build churches in the areas they had controlled in the two preceding years. They designated these churches "temples," which both indicated their understanding of the church as the people of God, and differentiated their places of worship from those of their Catholic counterparts.[80] In their own established territories and cities Protestant worship was tolerated within limits. Extant evidence of the rationale behind particular architectural design is scant, however; temples constructed prior to 1598 were mostly demolished during the Wars of Religion, and the churches of the seventeenth century, over eight hundred across France, were destroyed with the revoking of the edict of toleration in 1685. Direct study of these structures is thus impossible, and we must rely on consistory records and contracts for our knowledge of them. Guicharnaud points out that some of the existing evidence is unreliable, however, and must be read critically: Catholics disparaged Protestant places of worship for their impoverishment or their intentional artlessness, and Protestants tended to exaggerate numbers of worshipers to suggest greater influence than they had. For instance, in his *Histoire de la ville de Rouen* François Farin maintains that the temple of Quevilly could seat 11,000 worshipers for its services.[81] In any case, the term "temples" is another indication that the Protestants understood space differently than Catholics; the ecclesiology of the former underscored the reality not of a holy place, but a holy

---

78. Guicharnaud, "Architecture," 133.

79. Ibid.

80. Ibid., 134.

81. Ibid.

people elected for their salvation and God's glory. The Huguenots viewed the spaces in which they worshiped not as holy realms in themselves, and not adorned with outward display as in Catholic churches, but as structures of convenience—places to facilitate the pure preaching of God's Word and the right administration of the sacraments.

A HOLY PLACE, OR A HOLY PEOPLE?

Certainly, much of Reformed understanding of space came from their reading of Scripture, one which emphasized the prohibition of image making. This becomes clear in Viret as well as Calvin, who treats the issue in his extended discussion on the second commandment, "You shall make no graven image."

Calvin addressed the issue in the *Institutes*, "We must hold it as a first principle, that as often as any form is assigned to God, his glory is corrupted by an impious lie."[82] This formed Calvin's interpretive framework for all images in the context of the church. God has reserved his glory for himself alone, and forbidden the use of any object to represent him "by a visible shape," and further, any object or depiction that may cause the superstitious to believe it helps apprehend the divinity. Calvin allowed that God manifested himself through certain theophanies such as fire, smoke, or a man,[83] but insisted on the transitory nature of these symbols so that they might not become fixed in the imagination. One might see the same guard in the Scriptures' use of various metaphors, including shepherd, dove, mother, and warrior. Even in the cherubim that covered the mercy seat were not, for Calvin a positive image for God, but rather, with outstretched wings covering the mercy seat, a means of depicting his ineffable supernatural wings. Finally, Calvin took up the question of whether any images could be permissible in the church. He wrote, "Let us remember, that for five hundred years, during which religion was in a more prosperous condition, and a purer doctrine flourished, Christian churches were completely free from visible representations."[84] This claim on the part of Calvin is striking, stating emphatically the relationship between unadorned space and the purity of the church's teaching. Here, the value of simplicity is implied, or preferred. The reformer is categorical: the church is to be adorned by

82. Calvin, *Institutes*, 1.11.1.
83. Ibid., 1.11.3.
84. Ibid., 1.11.13.

the Word of Christ and his sacraments alone. Furthermore, he does not simply claim the New Testament church as his authority on the manner, but the church of the Fathers as late as the sixth century. God may express his reality through natural signs and manifestations, but not through human-made ones, and not in the sanctuary for worship.

In the same vein, French reformer Lambert Daneau, in his commentary on the Minor Prophets, wrote on the rebuilding of the temple. He commented on Hag 2:14 (15), "Haggai then said, 'So it is with this people, and with this nation before me,' says the LORD; 'and so with every work of their hands; and what they offer there is unclean.'"[85] Daneau observed, "The answering of an objection, least that therefore they should leave off from the work of the Temple, because they are not sanctified or made holy by that same heap of stones, and outward frame and building of the Temple."[86] The physical setting of worship does not sanctify the worshiper, but rather the inverse: if there is any sanctity to the physical place, it is conveyed by the obedient worshiper. A sanctified object, such as meat, will not convey its sanctity to another object by touching it (Hag 2:12), and yet "you are holy, O you who are enthroned upon the praises of Israel." (Ps 22:3)

Calvin articulated how it is and for what purpose God sanctified particular objects when he commented on the construction of the tabernacle in Exodus.[87] In particular, he examined the use of oil to anoint objects in the sacred enclosure, insisting there was nothing in the oil itself that sanctified "except in so far as it was a type of the Spirit, from whom all holiness emanates." Yet in the scriptural pattern wherein the oil symbolized the gifts of the Holy Spirit, Calvin saw the principle that "nothing is pure or holy in His sight, except what has been purged, and duly consecrated by the influence and grace of the Holy Spirit." Calvin was representative of many reformers in their changing attitudes that helped desacralize the liturgical apparatus of the late medieval church. Edward Muir points out in *Ritual in Early Modern Europe* that some reformers were in fact reluctant to anoint the sick with oil, lest people ascribe healing power to the oil rather than to God. About the changing perspective on "sacramentals," rites, and sacred objects, he writes,

> The ritual dispute in the sixteenth century took the form of a debate about whether rituals presented something, such as the body

85. Daneau, *Commentary*, 3ff.

86. Ibid.

87. Calvin, *Harmony of the Law*, vol. 3, Exod 40:9.

of Christ or the king, or merely represented the eternal God or the perfect King, a debate that sets off the "long Reformation" as the most crucial epoch in Western history for transforming the understanding of ritual.[88]

For Muir, "The question for [the reformers] became less how the Word assumed flesh, as it did in the Mass, than how the Word assumed meaning as it did through preaching, prayer, and study."[89] For Protestants, rituals, sacred objects, and places did not "present," or mediate God. Preaching the Word of God did, and God was to be found in the worshiping community itself. Meaning emerged from knowledge of and engaging with Scripture in the community, using the tools of scholarship and guided by God's Spirit.

On the spectrum between presentation and representation as it applies to interior decoration, Calvin stands far toward the side of decoration. He argues that God would have all the vessels of the sanctuary set apart by this sacred anointing from common use in order that the Israelites might distinguish between things sacred and profane, and thus that God's service might receive its due reverence, so that none should intrude the pollutions of the flesh into that place, the purity of which had been signalized by that sacred symbol.[90]

The oil was a means of signifying God's holiness through the utensils, furniture, and physical space of the cult. Calvin then asked why the altar for burnt offerings was endowed with further holiness, and called the "holy of holies" (the *sacrosanctum*), quoting Lev 6:25: "Speak unto Aaron and to his sons, saying, This is the law of the sin offering: in the place where the burnt-offering is killed shall the sin offering be killed before Jehovah: it is most holy." Calvin concluded that the holiness of the place derived from the expiation for sin through the sacrifices offered there; since God had so established the means for reconciling Israel to himself, so the his holiness was most clearly seen "on the altar itself."

This concern for holiness as represented by the place where God atones for his people's sin translates into an ethical mandate. Calvin commented on Lev 19:1 "You shall be holy, for I the LORD your God am holy," maintaining that Christian obedience is not to be measured against one's own untrustworthy assessment of moral purity, but against the character of God; this makes one aware of the need for purification from sin. In a

88. Muir, *Ritual in Early Modern Europe*, 270.

89. Ibid., 150.

90. Calvin, *Harmony of the Law*.

vivid image of pathetic porcine contentment, Calvin wrote, "For nothing is harder than for men to divest themselves of their carnal affections to prepare for imitating God. Besides, they willingly lie slumbering in their own filthiness, and seek to cloak it by the outward appearance of religion."

Calvin was not unambiguously opposed to the visual arts. In Book I of his *Institutes* he writes,

> I am not, however, so superstitious as to think that all visible representations of every kind are unlawful. But as sculpture and painting are gifts of God, what I insist for is, that both shall be used purely and lawfully,—that gifts which the Lord has bestowed upon us, for his glory and our good, shall not be preposterously abused, nay, shall not be perverted to our destruction.[91]

What strikes one in the opening words of this section of the *Institutes* is the surprisingly (given Calvin's reputation of hostility toward the arts) positive resonance of his instruction. He allows that the visual arts "are gifts of God," unremarkably cautioning they must be utilized appropriately ("purely and lawfully.") He uses the term "gift" (*donum,* French "*don.*") At this point he explains precisely the nature of "unlawful" use, namely, giving "visible shape to God." This use of art is proscribed because God has forbidden it, as Calvin explains elsewhere, in the second commandment. More precisely, "it cannot be done . . . without tarnishing his glory." Rightly used, the gift of art brings glory to God and good to human beings. Corrupt use of the gift does the opposite. Unlawful use of art includes "any corporeal representation of God," and tends to distort worship itself, leading the viewer of the image to "worship such a representation instead of God, or to worship God in it." At this point, Calvin concludes that "the only things, therefore, which ought to be painted or sculpted, are things which can be presented to the eye; the majesty of God, which is far beyond the reach of any eye, must not be dishonored by unbecoming representations." Two categories of images are possible, Calvin concludes: "historical," which is potentially valuable for instruction or admonition, and "pictorial," which Calvin means to "merely exhibit bodily shapes and figures." The latter only encourages frivolous amusement and has no place in Christian churches as they "could not be of any utility in teaching." Certainly the reformer's attitude toward the visual arts would not have been received by artists themselves as unadulterated encouragement—we can imagine that many

---

91. Calvin, *Institutes,* 1.11.12.

of their number would have been out of their source of income once the purges of the reforms had taken place in Geneva.

It appears therefore that Calvin has a somewhat nuanced view of the visual arts. Although he condemns the use of imagistic art for its own sake, he does make allowance for the possibility of art for the purpose of instructing in the faith. The Roman Catholic church of the Middle Ages claimed that works of art, including images and physical relics, claimed to serve a salvific purpose as a means of grace, which Calvin repudiates. Calvin's stance would strongly color Huguenot approaches to visual art within worship space, and Calvin himself states his preference for the undecorated churches of the first centuries, when "churches were completely free of visible representations."[92] Nonetheless, Calvin does leave some margin for the idea that art can edify, or help facilitate the process of sanctification. For Huguenot builders, this would channel their energies away from representational art and into the formal and purely decorative aspects of church design.

In short, Calvin's attitude toward the arts in general and toward church building in particular seems utilitarian. When he considers the Temple of Solomon in the Old Testament, he resolves that it serves as a metaphor or spiritual model for believers rather than as an exemplar for suitable worship space. His instructions on religious imagery are clear—none are to be allowed in churches lest they detract from God's glory or distract from hearing his Word. On architecture, however, he was less unambiguous. Churches were to reflect stewardship of resources and lack of excess, and yet various stylistic approaches could theoretically fit his theology. Bullinger would contradict Calvin when he attributed some element of sacredness to worship space, but even within the parameters of Calvin's thought, it can be argued that there is a distinctive place for Reformed architecture. Reformed architects of the next generation would experiment with these possibilities, both in Switzerland and in France.

An ideology of sacredness would evolve within Reformed thinking about architectural space, but it would turn in a new direction, relating space to the ideal of a holy people and the sanctifying Word of God. Memory would shape the built structures of the sixteenth- and seventeenth-century Huguenots, but in innovative ways. Instead of memory devises per se, memory became enshrined in the Huguenot narrative itself; events such as persecutions, wars of religion, and the massacres of Vassy and St.

92. Ibid., 1.11.13.

Bartholomew's Day shaped conceptual space as Huguenots sought theological and psychological room to practice their faith. Evidence of this is seen in the hypothetical fortresses of Jacques Perret and Bernard Palissy, as well as the communal housing designs of Serlio and others.

Finally, the communion itself became a memory space rather than a literal transubstantiation as the Catholics taught. The act of baptism did this as well, evoking memories of God's deliverance of Israel through the waters of the sea; this was visually enhanced by the baptismal font, usually placed prominently before the congregation. These reconstituted imaginative spaces found expression in buildings meant to accommodate Reformed worship. In addition, they would come to shape the people who gathered there and their devotional practices. Protestant architecture as well as solidifying patterns of church government would lead in two directions: in a communitarian one, represented by the active Protestant congregation, and also to an individual experience of scriptural devotion, but one that led to an active vocation for the whole people of God. These patterns helped develop a distinctively Protestant and Reformed visual language—buildings, decorative arts, didactic or polemical prints—and in turn were shaped by the Protestant experience. Huguenot architecture was so different from medieval Catholic conceptions of space because it needed to be in order to differentiate Protestants in a time of war and given the deep emotional and political meanings attached to being Catholic or Protestant. Visual elements reflected, and had to reflect, these theological differences.

We now turn to some background to developments in sixteenth-century architecture. Our next chapter will explore the reasons behind architecture's elasticity and ability to communicate Protestant values, examining architect Sebastiano Serlio's utilization of the principles of Vitruvius.

PART TWO

PART TWO

CHAPTER 5

Vitruvius, Serlio, and the Sixteenth-Century Architectural Treatise

PROLIFERATION OF THE ARCHITECTURAL TREATISE

THE WRITING AND PUBLICATION of architectural treaties came into its own as a genre in sixteenth and seventeenth centuries. Over one-hundred and forty such works were written in France, translated into French, or were published in France during that time period.[1] Serlio's treatises fit the pattern of this blossoming of architectural writings. This chapter will argue that the writings of Vitruvius were of seminal importance to Serlio, yet not as a strict design template. Indeed, Vitruvian ideas were elastic enough to permit broad interpretation among those who claimed him as inspiration. We will seek to make the case that Serlio (and others) acquired what may be called a spiritual affinity with the classical architect by claiming his core values of *firmitas, utilitas, and venustas,* of proportion and harmony, rather than through slavish imitation. This will allow us to better understand Vitruvian influences on Huguenot architecture, and also pinpoint the unique ways in which sixteenth-century French architects appropriate and adapted this material.

1. Lemerle and Pauwels, "Architecture, Textes, et Images."

The Renaissance and the revival of humanism in the early fifteenth and sixteenth centuries was a diverse phenomenon, internally complex, and as difficult to describe as the Reformation, and the relationship between these movements even more so. Vitruvius was one of a number of the ancients favored by the humanists, referred to repeatedly by Sebastiano Serlio, Philibert de l'Orme, and others, remaining relevant into the seventeenth century. Salomon de Caus was a French Calvinist, an artist and theorist born in Normandy in 1576, whose writing demonstrated a familiarity with Vitruvius, along with Pliny, Euclid, and Boethius. The basic understanding of Vitruvius as setting the stylistic categories through his Orders was widespread.

Men and women in fifteenth-century Italy were intrigued by the traces of ancient Greek and Roman civilization, and the rediscovery of Vitruvius provided a way of seeing and interpreting the structures they saw. In addition, it was clear to architects and those who commissioned them that architecture had power to impress and persuade, which fit into the context of the sixteenth century's renewed interest in rhetoric, also based on reappropriating the writings of the ancients. Desley Luscombe maintains that Renaissance writings on architecture portrayed the architect as not only a practitioner of theory and of technical conventions, but also as "a master of rhetoric skilled at influencing the public life of the city."[2] This appreciation for the art of persuasion fit the larger classical revival and humanist agenda.

Architects of the sixteenth century, in appropriating the language of classicism, were learning new ways of seeing. Contemporary translations and appropriations of Vitruvius will also allow us to better understand the guiding frameworks through which Protestant architects and builders operated. In tracing what they prioritized and rejected from ancient texts, we can better understand their goals and intentions. In the churches they designed the link between visual perception and spirituality was especially evident, and yet the same dynamic showed itself in domestic and civic building as well. Protestants, in differentiating from Catholic design, focused not on forms seen as intrinsically sacred, but as proportional, balanced, and fitting. To contemplate a church's formal elements was not to receive grace directly, but be reminded of the claims of the gospel and through it of the God it announced.

The vestiges of Greco-Roman antiquity fascinated thinking persons in fifteenth-century Italy, who held that the arts had seriously declined

2. Luscombe, "Architect and the Representation."

through the period that would later become known as the Middle Ages, but could be restored by returning to the instruction of the ancients. Niccolò Machiavelli shows the hunger for classical learning of one Renaissance humanist when he writes,

> When evening comes, I return to my house, and I return to my study; and on the threshold I take off my everyday clothes, which are covered in mud and mire, and I put on regal and curial robes; and dressed in a more appropriate manner I enter into the ancient courts of ancient men and am welcomed by them kindly, and there I taste the food that alone is mine, and for which I was born; and there I am not ashamed to speak to them, to ask them for the reasons for their actions, and they in their humanity, answer me; and for four hours I feel no boredom, I dismiss every affliction, I no longer fear poverty nor do I tremble at the thought of death: I become completely part of them.[3]

The Renaissance as a rebirth of classical culture developed in fifteenth-century Florence, spreading across the Italian peninsula before being transmitted across Europe and replacing the Gothic style. It revived naturalism and interest in the column, the rounded arch, and the dome, encompassing architecture, painting, literature, and the decorative arts. Acquaintance with classic architectural works originated from Greco-Roman ruins, and from the treatise *De Architettura* by the first-century BC Roman architect, writer and engineer Marcus Vitruvius Pollio, known as Vitruvius.

VITRUVIAN PROTOTYPE FOR THE ARCHITECTURAL MANUAL

Concerned about what he saw as widespread lack of professionalism and academic seriousness in the trade, Vitruvius wrote *De Architectura,* also known today as *The Ten Books on Architecture,* "synthesizing Greek treatises [written] between 350 and 100 BC and adding lessons from personal experience."[4] His work is the only extant major treatise on architecture from classical antiquity, and is therefore essential to our understanding of the influence of classical architecture on Huguenot church building.

Vitruvius held that Roman designers had much to gain through a thorough study of Anatolian Ionic design, and that knowledge of the

3. Machiavelli, "Letter to Francesco Guicciardini."
4. Smith, *Vitruvius on Architecture,* 9.

ancient Hellenistic builders would renew the architectural profession of his own day. Such a study would even serve as a kind of touchstone for the quality of other areas of endeavor: "The architect would be equipped with knowledge of many branches of study and varied kinds of learning, for it is by his judgment that all work done by the other arts is put to test." (*De Architectura* 1.1.1.). Vitruvius then remarks on the necessity of both reasoning and manual, or theoretical and practical faculties:

> Architects who sought to be skilled with their hands without formal education have never been able to reach a position of authority in return for their labors, while those who relied upon reasoning and scholarship were clearly pursuing the shadow not the substance. But those who have a thorough knowledge of both like men fully armed have more quickly attained their goal with authority.[5]

Vitruvius's object was to renew the ideals of the ancients, Hellenistic builders of Ionic temples in western Anatolia, and he did it by explicating their ideals and incorporating what he had learned through his own experience. In Book I, he addresses the issues of architectural training, fundamental aesthetic principles, and methods of constructing cities and fortifications. In Book II, he discusses the origin of the dwelling, construction materials, and the technology of building walls. Books III and IV elucidate the construction of temples, Orders (styles or units of architecture), and the making of columns, drawing parallels to the symmetry and proportions of the human body. Book V discusses design of public buildings such as markets, forums, basilicas, and theaters. Book VI treats private buildings and the effects of climate, and Book VII interior decoration, color, and the nature of plaster and wall treatments. Book VIII presents water works and aqueducts; Book IX continues with the properties of the constellations, as well as with the construction of sundials and water clocks. Book X concludes with mechanical engineering and machines for hoisting water. Vitruvius's description of the ancient Orders and his theory of proportion became standard components of Renaissance architectural theory, though given the ambiguity of his writing, it is difficult to ascertain whether Vitruvius's ideas of proportion were actually followed. However, this made possible multiple interpretations of his ideas, which adapted themselves to a multiplicity of contexts and needs. With his actual text available by the sixteenth century, and subsequently mediated by various writers, the

5. Vitruvius, *Ten Books*, I.I.2.

aesthetic and architectural theories of the ancients diffused in this way into the contemporary discussions of the Renaissance.

Vitruvius defined architecture's technical aspect or materiality, its function or purpose, or the emotional experience of those who utilize the finished space. Vitruvius expressed architecture's concerns with the apothegm of *firmitas, utilitas, and venustas*[6] or firmness, commodity, and delight, as Henry Wotton translated the terms in his work *The Elements of Architecture* (1624), or variously, strength, function, and beauty. In addition, he lifted up the classical Greek Orders of Doric, Ionic, and Corinthian, and defined six principles or methods of theory and practice necessary to approach problems of design: *ordinatio* and *symmetria,* modules and their relationship to the whole; *dispositio,* the design and representation of buildings; *eurythmia,* the inventive modification of conventions; *decor,* the subjective or expressive selection of elements appropriate for a particular situation; and *distributio,* the organizational decisions appropriate to the purpose of a building. Within these principles he discusses the first architects; he defines architecture and its constituent parts.

Firmitas means firmness, steadfastness, endurance, constancy. This suggests that the first concern of the builder or engineer is structural stability; a building must hold together and endure the elements. This quality may be seen as taking priority among the three, since architecture is the art of building. The use of a building may change over time, and therefore the structures fulfilling these purposes take priority. In any case, the foundational quality must be sustainability, the integrity and security of the building itself, indicated by strength and suitability, entailing materials and methods of construction, and decisions about foundations, walls, floors, apertures, and entrances. Attention must be given to materials, and Vitruvius discusses the advantages and liabilities of stone, bricks, and various kinds of wood, lime, sand, and gravel.

Utilitas connotes a structure's usefulness. In this, an architect or designer must work in collaboration with the patron or client as a competent authority to meet needs of gathering, storage, and administration. A building must function well according to its purpose. This encompasses whether the built space achieves its particular intention. An apartment or a country house must allow for shelter and the human activities associated with daily living such as eating, sleeping, or playing. A theater must accommodate the passage of large numbers of people, comfortable seating, and good lines

6. Ibid., I.III.2.

of sight for performance. A factory must allow sufficient light, maneuverability, and work space. A meeting hall must allow for social interaction, and enjoy clear acoustics. All buildings need to be convenient, accessible, on firm ground, not placed on marshes or lowlands, advantageously oriented toward sunlight and prevailing wind. These qualities define whether a building fulfills its function, entailing "commodity." An edifice is defective unless its spaces are adequate and appropriate for their intended usage.

Venustas is the aesthetic quality of a building. The term indicates loveliness, charm, attractiveness, beauty, grace of appearance, literally, the qualities exemplified in the goddess Venus, implying that architecture should possess a visual quality that will elicit emotion and love. A building's utilitarian requirements take precedence, but beyond quality of construction and efficacy of functioning, construction must please the senses, embrace, inspire, and instruct. A building's utilitarian purpose is convenience and suitability, but its architectural and aesthetic purpose is unity, power, and beauty. It achieves this through the sensitive employment of harmony, proportion, symmetry, ornament, and color.

Vitruvius explains what constitutes beauty in a building, elucidating both "positive" and "arbitrary" beauty. Positive beauty consists largely in materials and symmetry, arbitrary in prudence and regularity, or adhering to the rules of proportion. Beauty is seen mainly in rightly proportioned pillars and pediments, and in the proper relation of their parts. The disposition, form, and proportion of the parts reflect the gender binary, a subjective sense of whether a building is male or female, determined by the thickness or of pillars and the space between them. Vitruvius writes,

> Just so afterwards, when they desired to construct a temple in a new style of beauty, they translated these footprints into terms characteristic of the slenderness of women, and thus first made a column the thickness of which was only one eighth of its height, so that it might have a taller look. At the foot they substituted the base in place of a shoe; in the capital they placed the volutes, hanging down at the right and left like curly ringlets, and ornamented its front with cymatia and with festoons of fruit arranged in place of hair, while they brought the flutes down the whole shaft, falling like the folds in the robes worn by matrons. Thus in the invention of the two different kinds of columns, they borrowed manly beauty, naked and unadorned, for the one, and for the other the delicacy, adornment, and proportion characteristic of women.[7]

7. Ibid., IV.I.7.

Beauty results from fittingness and pleasantness of proportion, and corresponds to the human form.

Pythius's Temple of Athena from the middle of the fourth century BC was valued in the ancient world not only for the manner in which it fit the purpose for which it was built, but also because it best exemplified a pure Ionic style. It seemed to capture the imagination and elevate the spirit, appearing both proportionate and harmonious.

For Vitruvius, beauty has to do with proportion of the parts to the whole. We observe in nature a basic proportion, the geometry of the human body, a kind of metric correspondence which is pleasing to the aesthetic sense and reflected in the built space, especially the temple. This is called symmetry, and buildings are to be ordered analogically to this relationship. Robert E. Proctor, in his article "Beauty as Symmetry: The Education of Vitruvius's Architect and Raphael's Stanza Della Segnatura," comments that art critics in the ancient world normally used the word *pulchritudo* instead of the word *venustas*. The former, more common term connotes a Platonic ideal, while *venustas* suggested a more embodied reality through the experience of seeing and perceiving. The word *pulchitrudo* does not appear at all in *The Ten Books*.

Architecture is connected to the elemental design and order of the universe. The human person seeks such order, and the eye looks for it. Therefore Vitruvius's understanding of beauty is that its appearance relates to mathematical proportions, such as capitals and bases to the height of columns, or the number of columns to a temple, a fusion of philosophy and art. Proctor writes,

> In anchoring his understanding of beauty in the concept of modular symmetries, symmetries based upon precise units of measurement, Vitruvius links the art of architecture to the powerful tradition of ancient thought, beginning with Pythagoras and exemplified in the writings of Plato, that being is number, and that the truth is most closely approached through mathematics and geometry. Plato argues in the Republic that the true motions of the heavens are to be found in true numbers and in true geometric forms, which are grasped by reason and thought, not by sight. The motions astronomers observe are connected to bodies and are visible; it is thus impossible to believe they are always the same and never deviate. In the "Sophist," Plato points out that, in very large statues and paintings, we do not see true proportions; otherwise the upper parts would seem smaller. He then asks if, in order to

produce the illusion of beauty, "craftsmen say goodbye to truth and produce in their images the proportions that seem to be beautiful instead of the real ones?"

Vitruvius's *De Architettura* embodies a creative tension between unchanging number and changeable matter. As a practicing architect, Vitruvius knows that art cannot be "Platonic" because all art, even music, is perceived by the body as well as the mind. Vitruvius can thus speak of numbers as ontological entities and, at the same time, argue that that "our vision always pursues beauty (*venustas*)" and that we must "flatter its pleasure (*voluptas*) with proportion and the addition of modules."[8]

Proctor maintains that the principal contribution of Vitruvius is his "discovery" of beauty's foundational "symmetries in nature, notably in the human body." He has taken the "pre-Platonic tradition of classical Greek sculpture, which visualized Homer's image of a world made radiant by the presence of the gods,"[9] thereby synthesizing practice and philosophical speculation, enabling beauty to be described mathematically, aligned to the proportions of an ideal human body. If architectural designs echoed the laws of nature, embodied in the geometry of the human form, they are able to achieve a sense of *eurythmia*, grace and harmony.

Different mathematical conceptions for perfection, and therefore beauty, have been proposed from Plato to Da Vinci. The search for an ideal is itself evidence of the universal value of beauty, or delight. The concept of the Renaissance, whose goal was the rebirth or re-creation of ancient classical culture, would originate in Florence in the early fifteenth century and thence spread throughout most of the Italian peninsula. By the end of the sixteenth century the new style pervaded almost all of Europe, gradually replacing the Gothic style of the late Middle Ages. It encouraged a revival of naturalism, seen in Italian fifteenth-century painting and sculpture, and of classical forms and ornament in architecture, such as the column and round arch, the tunnel vault, and the dome.

REVIVING CLASSICAL ANTIQUITY

While Calvin does not refer to Vitruvius in his writings, his training was deeply rooted in the humanist tradition. His first published work was a

8. Proctor, "Beauty as Symmetry."
9. Ibid.

commentary on *De Clementia* by the Roman rhetorician Seneca, and it exhibited the skills of philology and textual criticism necessary to sixteenth-century classical scholarship. This demonstrates that Calvin had mastered the art of rhetoric as practiced in the classical world, and practiced in Renaissance humanism.

Perhaps ironically, given Calvin's reticence about visual forms, his character as a rhetorician made him an artist, one skilled in the power of words to convince and persuade. Olivier Millet points out that Calvin regularly employed, for example, rhetorical devices such as the *hysteron proteron*, or placing the most important part of a verbal construction out of sequence in the beginning of the phrase, inversing the order of ideas for maximum impact.[10] Serene Jones, in *Calvin and the Rhetoric of Piety*, also traces the importance of classical rhetoric on Calvin, seeing him as one of the premier rhetoricians of his era.[11] In addition to his time in university at Orleans and Bourges, Calvin spent time as a refugee in the city of Basel, a time which would prove key in his development. The city was throbbing with intense discussion between French exiles and humanist scholars. Jones writes,

> The rhetoric of radical ecclesiastical reform was even stronger, and Calvin soon became acquainted with some of the most famous and controversial figures of the Reformation, men such as his cousin, Pierre Olivétan; Simon Grynaeus, the Greek scholar; Wolfgang Capito, a colleague of Martin Bucer; Henri Bullinger, the powerful reformer who had succeeded Zwingli as the head of the Zurich church; and Pierre Viret and Guillaume Farel, former students of theology in Paris who had been following closely the reform of the French speaking Cantons in Switzerland.[12]

10. Millet, *Calvin et la dynamique de la parole*.

11. Jones's work on the rhetoric of Calvin has been criticized (see D. F. Wright and Richard A. Muller) for claiming too much. Her critics insist that caution is called for in applying a new, rhetorical interpretive framework to Calvin. Indeed, Muller writes in his review of Jones's book, "Thus, if the notion of a 'rhetoric of piety' serves as a potentially useful corrective to the tendency, for example, of Barthian writers to present an ahistorical dogmatic view of Calvin's work, it also has the danger, witnessed by Jones's work, of abstracting Calvin from his historical context and pressing off in yet another direction toward contemporary self-understanding rather than the understanding of history." (Muller, Review of *Calvin and the Rhetoric*, 582–83.) Nevertheless Jones helps us see both that Calvin inherited a rhetorical tradition with a debt to both classical antiquity and Renaissance humanism, and that attention should be paid not only to what he said as a coherent theological system, but also how he said it as an example of persuasive artistry.

12. Jones, *Calvin and the Rhetoric*, 17.

It was during this period Calvin grew into the full stature of a theologian, yet his foundation was humanism, the law, and the art of rhetoric. Because of this, Calvin, like other humanists, saw "the value of the vernacular, the art of translation, the role of social context in determining a word's meaning, and the playful extravagances of discursive ornamentation."[13] These skills were crucial for Calvin's effectiveness as a theologian writing for various readerships: polemic against his adversaries, pedagogy for the instruction of his students, and pastoral encouragement for Reformed believers suffering persecution in Calvin's French homeland, writing in order to move his readers to fitting piety and knowledge of God. However, Millet helps us see that as Calvin matured, his primary concern was no longer for his role as a humanistic rhetorician, but as a biblical teacher in the prophetic mode with the calling and responsibility of writing what was not just pleasing but also useful. Millet concludes, in his analysis of Calvin's "authorial self-assertion,"

> Finally, if Calvin continued throughout his life to use certain distinct literary conventions, depending on whether he was writing in Latin or French, these differences became blurred or secondary over time, as his writings in both languages increasingly were composed of texts also published in the other language, fused into a single œuvre with an overarching structural coherence.[14]

His rhetorical as well as theological skills arguably gave Calvin the capacity to think in spatial terms that provided a conceptual framework for later Huguenot architects designing tangible space for a gathered worshiping community of faith. As Catharine Randall writes, "This structural aesthetics is extrapolated from John Calvin's discussion of space in the *Institution de la religion chrestienne*. Indeed, Calvin has been called a 'church Architect,' and an 'architect of reconstruction.'"[15] Calvin's commentaries on the Pentateuch and Ezekiel also suggest the reformer is thinking in spatial terms. Armed with his insights, Calvinist architects pursued a visual rhetoric that they felt best reflected the ordering role of the gospel. We will pursue this line of thought further in chapter 6.

---

13. Ibid., 15.

14. Millet, "Calvin's Self-Awareness as Author," in Backus and Benedict., *Calvin and His Influence*, 98.

15. Randall, "Structuring Protestant" 341–52.

SERLIO'S APPROPRIATION OF VITRUVIUS

With the appropriation of Vitruvius by Renaissance architects, his ideas were to be diffused to Protestants looking for a new manner of expression, one differentiated from the Gothic style identified with the Catholic Church. This process unfolded in a period of over a century. A manuscript of Vitruvius's *De Architectura* was discovered in a library in Switzerland in 1414. Handmade copies began to circulate, augmenting interest in the work.[16] Increasingly, architecture was becoming more than simply a practical art, but also a subject for theoretical discussion, especially as printing disseminated its ideas beginning with the first architectural treatise since antiquity, and then with the work of Vitruvius himself.

De Architectura became known as copies circulated among the cultural elite. Its publication in Rome around 1486[17] insured a broader audience and made it the chief resource for Quattrocento architects and artists, and did much to revive interest in Greek and Roman architectural principles in Western Europe. Thomas Gordon Smith echoes the consensus when he states that *De Architectura* "remains the most complete and authentic source for cataloging the elements, proportioning systems, and ideas underlying the classical architectural system."[18] Numerous sixteenth-century editions of the work followed, with their own commentary and illustrations, which served to codify the interpretation of Vitruvius's ideas.

Theoretical writing on architecture flourished in the Renaissance as never before or since, with publications on theory, aesthetics, and design. The purpose of these works was to assist the architect/builder in the practical art of design and construction; these proved popular with educated non-specialists as well, elevating the status of architecture as an art form. Vitruvius's work proved the impetus for this movement in the fifteenth century with the discovery and at times the re-appropriation of *De Architectura*. The trend began with print editions of Vitruvius translated into Italian and manuscripts by Antonio Filarete, Francesco di Giorgio, and continued with other published works. The trend accelerated from the second quarter of the sixteenth century, with treatises by Leo Battista Alberti, Fra Giovanni Giocondo, Serlio, Danile Barbaro, and Andrea Palladio in Italy; Philibert de l'Orme, Jacques Androuet du Cerceau, and Jean Bullant in France; and

---

16. Carpo, *Architecture in the Age of Printing*.

17. Campbell, *Renaissance Art*, 206.

18. Ibid., 9.

Wendel Dietterlin in Germany[19]. Some publications moved into somewhat autonomous conclusions in relation to Vitruvius, Alberti, and Serlio, although these latter works conveyed much influence and served as an impetus for the former. At the time of the transmission of classical and Italian aesthetic ideas into mid sixteenth-century France, for instance, Wendell Dietterlin (Nuremburg, 1598), Rutger Kasemann (Cologne, 1616), and other Germans, while continuing in the treatment of the classical Orders, focused more on exuberant Mannerist decorative elements including herms, grotesques, and other ornamental fantasies. To what do we attribute this explosion of the printed word and image? In the development of Renaissance ideas and the appropriation of ancient knowledge, the printed book occupied a strategic place. It stood between the desire on one hand to remember an oral tradition on which society depended, and the desire on the other for freedom and the diffusion of diverse aspects of knowledge.

These works disseminated Vitruvian ideas on a wider scale, making the column Orders available not only to architects but also to the liberally-educated public. In addition, they worked out proportions and a vocabulary of ornamentation. These works engendered and responded to public interest in architectural representation though perspective, and gave organizational grounding to various forms of built spaces based on varying social content and classes. Serlio's *Architettura* (1559–1562) was, along with Vignola's *Regola delli cinque ordini d' architettura* and Palladio's *I quattro libri dell'architettura*, the most influential Renaissance treatment of the architectural Orders, or columns incorporating base, shaft, capital crowned by its entablature.

19. See also Leo Battista Alberti, I dieci libri dell'architettura . . . novamente de la latina ne la volgar lingua con molta diligenza tradotti da Pietro Lauro (Venise: Vincenzo Valgrisi, 1546); Fra Giovanni Giocondo, M. Vitruvii de architectura libri decem, summa diligentia recogniti, atqu; excusi. . . Additis Iulii frontini de aqueductibus libris . . ., (Lyon, héritiers de B. de Gabiano, 1523) ; Daniele Barbaro, I dieci libri dell'architettura di M. Vitruvio tradutti et commentati da Monsignor Barbaro . . ., (Venise, Francesco Marcolini, 1556.) ; Andrea Palladio, I quattro libri dell'architettura . . ., (Venise, Domenico de'Franceschi, 1570); Philibert de l'Orme, Le premier tome de l'architecture . . ., (Paris, Frédéric Morel, 1567); Jacques Androuet du Cerceau, Duodecim fragmenta structuræ veteris commendata monumentis a Leonardo Theodorico . . ., (Orléans, [Jacques Androuet du Cerceau], 1550.); Jean Bullant, Reigle generalle d'architecture des cinq manieres de colonnes . . ., (Paris, Jérôme Marnef & Guillaume Cavellat, 1564.); Wendel Dietterlin, Architectura (first version) (Architectura und Austheilung der V. Seulen. Das erste Buch, Stuttgart, s. n., 1593).

The earliest major treatise on architecture aside from translations of Vitruvius was not to appear until around 1450 with architect and polymath Leon Battista Alberti's reformulation of the *Ten Books* as *De re Aedificatoria* ("On the Art of Building"), which by 1485 had become an indispensible manual for architects. Intended by Alberti not just for architects and builders, but for "anyone interested in the noble arts," demonstrating to a broader audience his deep understanding of the work of Vitruvius. His work was at the same time lifted up the importance of Vitruvius and also countered his dictates, in which he endeavored to bring together an understanding of the ancient designer while incorporating his own investigation of surviving works of antiquity, thus synthesizing Vitruvius's ideas with the needs of his own time. In so doing, he enlarged the categories of the classical Orders from their original applications and set them to more general usage. For him, Vitruvius's discussion of the Orders served as an impetus for generating an idealized architecture.[20] Alberti explained beauty as "a harmony of all the parts in whatsoever subject it appears, fitted together with such proportion and connection that nothing could be added, diminished or altered, but for the worse."[21]

Indeed, the idea of harmony was reflected in architecture as in the human body as well in perspective, which represented, as painter Piero della Francesca stated, objects seen at a distance "in proportion according to their respective distance."[22] David R. Coffin relates that the Renaissance architect Bruno Brunelleschi first articulated the principles of perspective, which was also construed in terms of balance: "The concern of these architects for proportion caused that clear, measured expression and definition of architectural space and mass that differentiates the Renaissance style from the Gothic and encourages in the spectator an immediate and full comprehension of the building."[23]

From the time of Alberti, then, architectural writing would center on the Orders as the locus for sixteenth-century theoretical templates. These ideas were transmitted via manuscript copies until 1485, thirteen years following Alberti's death, when his treatise first appeared in print form. It

20. I am indebted to Mario Carpo for his sorting out of the many sources on the development of Renaissance architecture and its contemporary treatises. See *Architecture in the Age of Printing.*

21. Alberti, *Ten Books*, VI.II.

22. Coffin, "Renaissance," 938.

23. Ibid.

would not be translated into Italian, and would thus not be available for a wider readership, until 1550, a century after it was first penned, by which time it was surpassed by other works in style and method. Nevertheless, Fil Hearn writes,

> It is a prodigious work, admirable for the quality of the author's research and thought. From the outset, it enjoyed wide repute among the intelligentsia and commanded enormous respect, largely due to its very existence as the first treatise on the theory of architecture since antiquity . . . its almost inestimable importance, then, lay in the precedent it set for future theorists.[24]

Two prominent examples of sixteenth-century architectural treatises were provided by Fra Giovanni Giocondo (1511) and Danile Barbaro (1556), although their reach was limited by a growing taste for illustrated works. Increasingly, treatises were dominated by images for didactic purposes, text explicating the illustrations, as in the work of Serlio (1537) and Andrea Palladio's (1570) *I quattro libri dell'architettura* ("The four Books of Architecture.") These were published in Venice, along with translations of Vitruvius and Alberti, as the city became perhaps the most important producer of architectural thought in the sixteenth century. The publication and dissemination of these works helped establish Renaissance ideas and architectural theory as obligatory for the art of building.[25]

Serlio was a known Protestant who had close contacts with Protestant sympathizers in both Italy and France, and who dedicated his Book V of his *Extraordinario libro (On Churches)* to Margarite de Navarre. In this dedication, he paraphrases the Pauline passage from 2 Corinthians 6:16b, a key Protestant text, "True temples are in the hearts of pious Christians."[26] Mario Carpo sees further indications of Protestant values in Serlio's antipapal attitude following his expulsion from Bologna in 1510 when the city was taken over by Pope Julius II, in the publication of his treatise in Lyons in 1551 by the Protestant Jean I de Tournes, and in his restrained use of the classical Orders, following Calvin's repudiation of ostentation and excessive display. Reflecting on the Protestants' subsequent receptiveness to Serlio, Carpo sees an analogous relationship to that with the written Word of Scripture. He writes,

---

24. Hearn, *Ideas That Shaped Buildings*, 4.
25. Carpo, *Architecture in the Age of Printing*, 48.
26. Serlio, *Domestic Architecture*, 4.

> The relationship between Vitruvianism and Protestantism deserves a more profound investigation. Already in the age of the first humanists, Vitruvius's De architectura had been the object of an almost theological canonization. It thus makes perfect sense that Protestant culture, grounded in the interpretation of a foundational text that was vernacularized and widely disseminated in print, should have adopted almost without question this architectural text of archetypal status. After Trent, the "bible of the architects," translated, annotated, and illustrated, seems to have influenced the architectural culture of the Protestant north more deeply and over a longer time than it did the Counter-Reformation south. . . . A method of architectural composition based on the repetition of visually identical elements required that its components be simple and its rules of assembly rational."[27]

The forms of Greco-Roman classicism intrigued men and women of the Renaissance and particularly those trained in classical humanism and rhetoric. This included both Catholics and Protestants, and was intensified by the rediscovery of the Vitruvian Orders. Yet in time, as the various sectarian divisions hardened and as Catholic taste grew increasingly ornate through the Renaissance and Baroque periods. Carpo draws a tentative conclusion that Protestants, steeped in a culture of Scripture as "the text," were more influenced by Vitruvius's foundational architectural text than were Catholics. More importantly, the unencumbered compositions of classicism appeared more appropriate than ever for differentiating Protestant churches and expressing their values. This was especially the case as architects such as Serlio and de l'Orme took liberties with the Vitruvian dictates.

Serlio's volume, known as *I sette libri dell'architettura* ("Seven Books of Architecture,") began with the fourth book of what he likely intended to be a ten-volume treatise, publishing a total of five. The history of its publication is complicated, but the works were eventually collected into what became known as *Tutte l'opere d'architettura*. These works pressed forward the classical ideal of the "Orders," a foundational unit of architectural design, although they were pressed into service for Serlio's particular program in what Carpo calls "ersatz" antiquity.[28] The five Orders identified by Renaissance architects and theorists were the Tuscan, Doric, Ionic, Corinthian, and Composite. Various Orders from the ornate decoration of the Corin-

27. Carpo, *Architecture in the Age of Printing*, 100.
28. Ibid., 9.

thian to the simplicity and masculine strength of the Doric were preferred at difference times and places. Renaissance stylistic preferences often led to the superimposing of Orders, with a different order of columns employed on each of several stories of a building, beginning on the lower level with the stronger Doric or Ionic capital and progressing to more feminine forms above with Ionic, Corinthian, or Composite. The unifying principle in all its variegated applications was the idea of proportion advanced by Vitruvius and Alberti.

With the invention of the Gutenberg press, the printing of images via woodcut or intaglio prints began to spread at the end of the fifteenth century. The press made possible, as Mario Carpo explains, a revolutionary and explosive expansion of not only the printed word, but also of the printed image. "The theoretically unlimited availability of identical images was an almost absolute novelty in Europe, but it does not seem to have been embraced with immediate enthusiasm by the humanists."[29] The humanists were distracted with another agenda: "fashioning a new rhetoric, inspired by direct imitation of the classical authors." This helps explain why Alberti, following the medieval tradition, resisted the inclusion of images and produced only a text. It also gives perspective on the novelty of Serlio's integral use of illustrations in his treatise. Training in rhetoric entailed extensive memorization. However, with the advent of Gutenberg's press, what previously required mental recollection could now be more easily "carr[ied] in their pockets." Humanist rhetoric developed chronologically before the invention of printing, but it took on a dialectical relationship between "the new media and new ideas." This dialectic is important to Serlio, where image expounds upon the meaning of the text, and the words explicate the meaning of the illustration, a "graphic standardization of the system of the Orders," as Carpo calls it. This is what the Protestant architects sought: a new "visual rhetoric" adequate to expression their faith.

The importance of Serlio, then, lies in his canonizing and reinterpreting the classical Orders of architecture, in popularizing them through his work in France (on the Château de Fontainebleau and the Château d'Ancy-le-Franc in Burgundy,) and especially in his architectural treatise. The latter, unlike that of Alberti, achieved particular influence through the inclusion of illustrations. Serlio's work was the first to deal with the five classical Orders in a systematic fashion, setting the stage for subsequent treatises to follow. Frustrated with the loss of illustrations to which Vitruvius refers in

29. Ibid., 43.

the *Ten Books*, Serlio filled the lack with his own elevations, sections, and plans of his own. In so doing, he was the first to publish his own architectural treatise in Italian with integral illustrations. While Alberti's text was theoretical, Serlio took a practical tack, offering his treatise as a set of rules for design for practicing architects, organizing his work around distinct sections, and establishing his theory of the classical Orders as the foundation for architectural design. In his fourth (but first published) volume, *Regole generali di architettura sopra le cinquemaniere degli ordini* (1537), he put together for the first time the columns of the five Orders.

Serlio was an innovator in his treatment of Vitruvius, not adhering slavishly to his ideas but interpreting them to suit "comfort" and French architectural tastes. He introduced a fifth style, the Composite, to the classical Orders. One of his forms for new church construction was imitated in the building of the Temple du Paradis in Lyons; his housing models, providing practical forms to be employed not just by royalty but by each level of society (which he categorized according to the four types of "artisan," "citizen and merchant," "nobility and officers of the state," and "royalty."[30] In so doing, he developed a typology for a changing social structure, and showed concern for the needs of even the humblest members of society. In a particular irony, even as he expanded the knowledge and appreciation of design beyond professional architectural circles, he also made available building solutions for those who would eschew the services of those professionals.

Serlio's achievements underscore his novel ways of conceiving both space and social realities. In him we see the Protestant mind directed toward reality outside itself. Instead of contenting himself with the ethos of late medieval Catholicism, Serlio perceived a new way of expression that was at the same time ancient, reflecting eternal values. In refusing to look upon idols or put forth his own image of God, he was freed to open the way for the Renaissance in France. The case study of Salomon de Brosse corresponds to the experience of an array of other Protestant architects in France during the sixteenth and seventeenth century. These built upon the foundation of Serlio, accomplishing a distinctively Reformed style as well as a particularly French one as well.

We now turn to several of these architects in France to discern how they turned to classicism to develop a conspicuously Reformed and French visual vocabulary.

---

30. Ibid., 12.

CHAPTER 6

Protestant Architects' Use of
Vitruvian Ideas

FROM HERE, WE WILL outline how classical Vitruvian ideas were disseminated in France through the buildings, and occasionally through the
writings, of Protestant architects. We will examine the lives and work of
Philibert de l'Orme, Jacques-Androuet du Cerceau, Salomon de Brosse,
and Jacques Perret and how they carried on Serlio's ideas (and indirectly,
those of Vitruvius himself). In so doing, we will establish a continuity
of classical ideas, discover ways in which these were altered to achieve a
uniquely French style, and discern a basis for a Neoclassical vernacular in
that country. And, at the same time, their ideas would form the conceptual
basis for a specifically Reformed manner of building churches. Their work
became the basis of Neoclassical architecture, and at the same time served
as the basis for specifically Reformed churches.

It is in this chapter that we see most clearly the Reformed way of seeing
and how it led to a flourishing of architecture and the plastic arts. Aware of
the power of images, sometimes insidious, Protestants insisted on a Word-
based and not an image-based path to the transcendent. Indeed, the image
was dangerous, promising much but in the end serving only to reflect back
the self. Yet in this repudiation, there was a larger affirmation, one that God
meets those who truly seek him and who worship in spirit and in truth. In
learning to really see, Calvinist architects in France invented a uniquely

expressive style and made it available, to their minds, for the purpose of communicating theologically.

Art historian Anthony Blunt described the period of intense artistic creativity in mid fifteenth-century France in his work *Art and Architecture in France 1500–1700*. As in Renaissance Italy, a period of religious and political vicissitudes and tensions marked a blossoming of writing, architecture and the visual arts, including remarkable contributions by Huguenots architects, including de l'Orme, Jean Goujon (1510–1572), Jean Bullant (1515–1578), Jacques Perret (ca. 1540–1610), Salomon de Brosse (1571–1626) and several of the prominent du Cerceau family, including Jacques I Androuet (1510–1584), Jean Baptiste Androuet (1544/47–1590), Jacques Androuet II, (ca 1556–1614), Jean Androuet du Cerceau (ca 1585–1650). Indeed, the majority of architects in the sixteenth to mid-seventeenth centuries in France were Protestants. "It has been known for some time that some of the most important architects in seventeenth-century France were French Calvinists, or Huguenots," notes William Dyrness, "but the religious aspect of their work has been almost entirely ignored."[1] This is an important point to stress, in order to establish that the Protestants were adapting texts in ways Catholics were not, thus ushering the Neoclassical style. It also suggests that the styles of these Calvinist architects was influenced by their faith, and did not arise in spite of their personal beliefs. Huguenots also filled the ranks of other artistic professions as well, including painting, engraving, garden design, ceramicists, and goldsmiths. Fully a quarter of the original members of the Royal Academy were Protestants.[2]

The reign of Francis I and Henry II consolidated more power in the hands of the monarchy. With increasing absolutism came investment in the arts at the same time as attempts to quash deviances from the Catholic Church, and therefore increasing persecution of Protestants. Catharine Randall makes a connection between the immense creativity generated by French Renaissance architects, arguing that Calvinists did conceive of architectural space in terms of their faith. She deals at length with de l'Orme, Bernard Palissy, and Sebastiano Serlio, an evangelical, maintaining that all the royal architects in the era of the 1550s were Protestants:

> It is significant that Philibert's Calvinism has been overlooked, and that all the other architects of the king were Calvinists. The confessional stance cannot fail to have a theoretical and actual impact. A

1. Dyrness, *Reformed Theology*, 109.
2. Ibid.

fuller and more balanced picture of the complexities within which Philibert labored is produced through the mutual consideration of both contextual issues [that of the Protestant faith as well as those seeking validation as artists and architects.][3]

Even when circumstances precluded "the building of a structure conforming to one's belief system, then the text becomes the safe place in which such structures may be dreamed about, hypothesized, and described."[4] All French Calvinist architecture was built upon an "intertext," a conceptual interplay between the words of Scripture and Calvin's *Institutes*, itself a monumental theological commentary on Scripture.

PHILIBERT DE L'ORME

The stream of Vitruvian ideas was appropriated by Serlio, along with virtually all working architects of the Quattrocento, and diffused through publication and through his work in France. He displayed little theoretical apparatus, preferring practical commentary to his illustrations for palaces, churches, or private houses. It was likely Serlio's publications that brought him to the attention of Henry I of France, who invited him to the kingdom to oversee construction of the Château de Fontainebleau. Serlio had begun publication of his treatise in 1537, and it was known in France from that time.

Philibert de l'Orme embraced many of Serlio's ideas, but transformed them through his expansive *Onze Livres,* and pushed what was at the same time a uniquely personal and expressly French vision. Huguenots found in these published works forms consistent with their Calvinist faith; architects such as Salomon de Brosse moved further toward classical forms as a fitting language for expressing their theology and convictions about the nature of the church. This architectural lineage expresses a theological lineage out of which a distinctly Reformed architectural form emerged.

Much of what is known about Philibert de l'Orme stems from his own architectural writings. He is important as an example of an early modern humanist who developed theories and images of a fruitful exchange between ideas and materials through the technology of architecture, moving far beyond the undogmatic and practical pattern books of Serlio. He sorted through a bafflingly wide array of ancient works in order to create

---

3. Randall, "Philibert De l'Orme," 6n13.
4. Randall, *Building Codes*, 102.

a legitimate French style, seen for instance in his extensive rustication and in his "French column" (*Premier tome*), with its double capital and banded column treatment. Virtuosity, indeed, entailed understanding the copiousness of ancient works and judiciously applying them and reinterpreting them for the contemporary situation. This de l'Orme did, mastering the ancient Orders while transforming them into the French context in a way not previously seen in Italy. Anthony Blunt credits de l'Orme as the "most striking single example" of sixteenth-century attempts to achieve a synthesis of the new style from Italy with existing architectural traditions.[5] The medieval pictorial and building traditions were still vital in the century, even as knowledge of classical ruins and Renaissance buildings provided strong impetus for invention. Into this fluctuating situation de l'Orme emerged as an able designer and craftsman, and an advocate of proper classical usage when many were simply applying a decorative overlay of Italian ornament to medieval conventions. His work displayed deep understanding of humanistic learning Renaissance developments in architecture. It replicated the more severe and classical aspects of northern Italian Renaissance building, moving eventually to innovative approaches to vaulting and columns. Further, as the publication of treatises swelled across northern Europe, de l'Orme went beyond the usual presentation of the Orders and developed a conceptual and theoretical foundation of his own.[6]

De l'Orme, the son of a master mason, was born in Lyons around 1510, the same year as Bernard Palissy and Jean Goujon. In addition to the opportunity for learning the building craft in his family context, he would have benefited from the expansive prosperity and growth of Lyons, which was enjoying a period of prosperity as a center of banking and printing that rivaled Paris in the first half of the century. He demonstrated a fascination with classical works of art, collecting pieces for himself and associates in France. Among these associates was his friend François Rabelais, who he seems to have met before his sojourn in Italy and who accompanied Cardinal du Bellay on missions to Rome in 1534 and 1535. Rabelais describes his friend as "le grand architecte du Roi Mégiste," referring to Henry II.

De l'Orme's writing suggests a person well schooled in the arts and sciences of a classical education. In 1533, he travelled to Italy to study, and found employment with Pope John III, and remained for at least three years. Upon his return to France he secured the patronage of du Bellay, and

5. Blunt, *Philibert de l'Orme*, 1.
6. Guillaume, "On Philibert de l'Orme," 219.

settled in Paris to work on the Château de St. Maur-des-Fossés. He built a tomb for Francis I at St. Denis, royal chapels at Villers-Cotteret and St. Germain, and châteaux in Fontainebleau, St. Germain-en-Laye, Meudon, and Anet. He was commissioned to design the Tuileries, although the design was only partially executed. Surviving work includes the Château d'Anet and the royal tomb of Francis I at St. Denis.

De l'Orme displayed an Protestant disposition, which in the early 1500s entailed a desire to reform the Catholic Church from within, à la Erasmus. Well acquainted with the work and writings of Martin Luther, Protestants were "convinced of man's depravity and God's grace, reliant on Scripture and distrustful of 'works of righteousness.'"[7] After the *Affaire des Placards* in 1534, in which Protestants left polemic posters within the royal palace, French Protestants were forced to adopt a strategy of secrecy with their faith in order to survive. Among the evidence of de l'Orme's Protestant sympathies is his association with Serlio, who practiced in Paris at the same time as de l'Orme. De l'Orme clearly followed Serlio's format in his own volumes. More importantly, he reflected Serlio's utilitarian focus and his particular emphasis on the "difference between a simple, plain style and the more ornate . . . idiom of the other major influence on architecture of the period, Vitruvius."[8] Randall concludes that both architects show a certain tentativeness toward their own craft, raising existential questions about its purpose and maintaining "material temples are not really needed for the worship of God."[9] Randall rightly notes the parallel of this attitude with Calvin's distinction between the visible and the invisible church. In particular, de l'Orme's preference for ornamentation that is comparatively sober, simple, and rational echoes the preferences of Serlio. This is the manner in which his "evangelical sympathies are encoded," argues Randall, in his designs.[10] He also followed the Protestant habit of quoting Scripture, was cited by subsequent Protestant architects as their primary inspiration, and was known for his tense relationships with his "more militant Catholic clients." These facts reinforce the idea of de l'Orme's Protestant commitments. He died in Paris in 1570.

About his major work, *Onze Livres d'Architecture*, or *L'Architecture, Œuvres Entières*, de l'Orme explains that he composed this work after a

7. Randall, *Building Codes*, 79.
8. Ibid.
9. Ibid.
10. Ibid., 80.

long period of observing builders who enter into construction carelessly: "Je vous advertiray, que depuis trente-cinq ans en ça & plus, l'ay observé en divers lieux, que la meilleure partie de ceux qui ont fait, ou voulu faire bastiments, les ont aussi soudainement commencez, que légèrement en avaient délibéré."[11] He writes with a sense of mission, struggling against widespread ignorance, in which masons must oversee construction and building is done without adequate plans and elevations. Writing personally (using "I" and "you, the reader"), he betrays his exasperation at insincere toadies who offer false praise: ("C'est bien dict, Monsieur, c'est une belle invention, cela est fort bien trouvé . . . jamais ne sera vue une telle œuvre au monde")[12], and complains of having to deal with an unappreciative audience: ("Dictes-moy, je vous prie, quand celuy qui fait bâtir voit qu'il est repris, que l'on trouve tant de fautes aux œuvres qu'l fait faire, n'a-t-il pas occasion d'avoir grande fâcherie & ennui en son esprit, maudissant quelquefois et les ouvriers & ouvrages?")[13]

De l'Orme shows a keen comprehension of Vitruvius in his work, yet he employs the ancient engineer in a dynamic way. For example, while engaging Vitruvian notions of proportion, de l'Orme exhibits a sense of freedom to modify the rules."[14] De l'Orme considers the history of the development and transmission of Vitruvius, not swallowing his work uncritically but considering the effect of possible multiple sources. For him and his contemporaries, the skilled architect is a master of classical tradition, yet erudite in his interpretation of it. Elsewhere, de l'Orme affirms the dimensions conceived by Vitruvius: "Il faut donc apprendre tels proportions et mesures de notre dit Vitruve, qui sont fort bonnes et très digne d'observer."[15] In embracing the value of Vitruvian regulations, he states his prerogative to use them selectively: "Quant au chapiteau, j'ay ensuvuy les antiquitez, et aussi quelques règles de Vitruve."[16] De l'Orme demonstrates his debt to Vitruvius without

---

11. De l'Orme, *Architecture*, 5. "I tell you that for over thirty-five years, I have observed in many places, that most of those who have built, or have wished to build buildings, have done so lightly and without deliberation."

12. Ibid., 6. "Well said, Sir, that is a fine invention, that is very well conceived . . . never was there seen such a work in the world!"

13. Ibid., 6. "Tell me, I ask you, when he who would build sees that he is criticized, that others find much fault with the works he has made, does it not anger and trouble his spirit, causing him at times to curse the workers and their work?"

14. Ibid., 134b.

15. Ibid., 138a.

16. Ibid., 168a.

using him slavishly in his design for the Tuileries Palace (not executed.)
In that plan, he chooses the Ionic order to lend luster to the queen's palace
since that column was understood to be a feminine form "devised according
to the proportions and beauties of women and goddesses . . . accordingly I
have made use, at the palace of her Majesty the Queen, of the Ionic order,
on the view that it is delicate and of greater beauty than the Doric, and more
ornamented and enriched with distinctive features." In commenting on this
work, l'Orme takes the opportunity to chide his fellow architects who have
not followed the Vitruvian principles as he understands them.[17] At the same
time, de l'Orme insists on the right of the architect to improvise and adapt the
classical vocabulary of architecture—as long as he demonstrates virtuosic use
of ancient sources—to new contexts. His invention of the so-called French
order of columns attests to this, as does his adaptive use of pediment forms in
his building, employing both curved and triangular shapes on the courtyard
entrance of the Tuileries.

De l'Orme finishes his weighty tome with reflection that reveals both
his Protestant sensibility, and the spiritual purpose behind the writing of
this treatise. Writing with an imaginary architect in mind, he insists that in
spite of the challenges of his art, his mind is at peace:

> Mais je ne m'en suis pas beaucoup de soucié, m'asseurant qu'il ne
> m'en pourroit venir aucun dommage, pour n'avoir jamai manié
> aucuns derniers, sinon ceux qu'il a pleu á Dieu me donner: & aussi
> cognoissant que tel travail m'advenoit par la permission de Dieu
> & pour les offenses que je fais journellement contre sa saincte di-
> vinité, qui me suscite des ministres pour me travailler, & me faict
> confesser souvent que je n'ay point de plus grand enemy que moy-
> mesme, & de qui je me doive plus plaindre & douloir, dont j'ay
> plus d'occasion de prendre & faire vengeance de moy, que de tous
> autres, pour estre enemy de moy-mesme.[18]

This last statement is particularly important to understand de l'Orme's
mindset. It displays a Reformed trust in Providence: whatever ills come his
way in the course of his calling are permitted according to the sovereign will of
God. In fact, here de l'Orme echoes the affirmations of the French Confession
(God's purpose and care, and his sovereign direction of all circumstances),

17. Ibid.

18. Ibid., 320. "But I have not many worries, assuring myself that no ills can come
my way apart from those which God allows, and knowing that whatever travails come to
me by his permission; and that even the offenses which daily I commit against his holy
person serve to move me to confess that I am often my own worst enemy."

written by Calvin and adopted by the Synod of Paris in 1559, some eight years before the publication of the *Premier Tome de l'Architecture*:

> Ainsi, en confessant que rien ne se fait sans la providence de Dieu, nous adorons avec humilité les secrets qui nous sont cachés, sans nous poser de questions qui nous dépassent. Au contraire, nous appliquons à notre usage personnel ce que l'Ecriture sainte nous enseigne pour être en repos et en sécurité; car Dieu, à qui toutes choses sont soumises, veille sur nous d'un soin si paternel qu'il ne tombera pas un cheveu de notre tête sans sa volonté. Ce faisant, il tient en bride les démons et tous nos ennemis, de sorte qu'ils ne peuvent nous faire le moindre mal sans sa permission.[19]

> And thus, confessing that nothing takes place apart from God's providence, we humbly bow before the secrets that are hidden to us, without questioning what is beyond our understanding. On the contrary, we personally make use of what Holy Scripture teaches for our peace and security, for God, to whom all things are subject, watches over us with a Father's care, so that not a hair of our heads shall fall without his will. And yet he restrains the powers and all our enemies, so that they cannot harm us without his leave.

De l'Orme was in Paris at that time—this was the year he was replaced as Royal Architect—and it is likely he would have been familiar with this confession of faith, which was under vivid discussion in the Reformed community at the time. His own words reflect this assurance of faith and trust in perseverance of the saints (along with wariness of human tendency to sin.) This conviction moves him to offer this counsel to architects:

> Qui me faict conseiller à nos Architectes de s'efforcer d'estre gens de bien tant que faire se pourra . . . Mais laissons tels propos, & remettons le tout à la volonté de Dieu, qui fait cognoistre la vérité de toutes choses en temps & lieu. Doncques nous reprendrons nostre Architect, lequel je désire estre si advisé, qu'il apprenne à se cognoistre & scavoir quell il est, avec ses capacitez & suffisances: & s'il cognoist qu'aucune chose luy défaille, ie luy conseille d'estre diligent de la demander à Dieu: ainsi que sainct Iacques le nous monstre quand il dict: Si quis vestrum indigent sapientia, postulet à Deo.[20]

19. *La Confession de foi*, Article 8.

20. De l'Orme, *Architecture*, 329. "This moves me to counsel our architects to make every effort, as much as possible, to be persons of quality . . . but let us leave such matters, and leave everything to God's will, who makes known the truth of all things in [his] time and way. Therefore we take up again our Architect, whom I wish to be well advised,

Thus divine wisdom is needed to fulfill the vocation of architect, who after ordering the affairs of his craft, does well to take a contemplative pose, putting before his eyes the vision of "a wise man in a garden before the *Temple d'Oraison*"—an oblique reference to the priority of preaching the gospel.

Figure 8: A depiction of the noble architect, Philibert de l'Orme,
Le Premier tome de l'achitecture, **1567.**

For our purposes, it is important to consider how de l'Orme's faith is expressed, if only in indirect manner, in his designs. Crucial to mastery of architecture was an understanding of classical buildings so that one could bridge the gap between them and newly invented works. Renaissance architects embraced the idea of copiousness, or plenitude, allowing the joining together of ancient and contemporary inventions and expressions. Imitation of nature served as a starting point, leading to associations and analogies. De l'Orme reveals his mastery of this process through designs for architectural embellishment, employing playful associations through features such as caryatids, combinations of Orders, depictions of ruins overtaken by nature, rusticated door frames, and banded columns, in addition

---

that he might learn to know himself, with his capacities and gifts; and might know that nothing need defeat him. I advise him to be diligent in asking of God, just as Saint James shows us when he says, "If any of you lacks wisdom, let him ask of God."

to designs for leaves, vines, trees, and mythical beasts incorporated into buildings. He even seems to make visual puns with columns that morph into men and trees and back again (in more than one engraving of "the architect," he places a tree beside the person—the French word *orme*, "elm," sounds similar to *homme*, or "man," and is his own name.) De l'Orme is making a commentary on himself and his ability to create his own identity, perhaps suggesting his understanding of himself as a Protestant and not a Catholic.

A Calvinistic aesthetic resonates through the excessive embellishment de l'Orme's designs, contrasting with the balance and sense of proportion in Catholic design, embodying a church confident in its historical understanding of itself. Later Reformed buildings would show a preference for more simple designs. The twisting, Mannerist, disproportionate use of forms reminded one of the distortions present in a world of sin, where the true faith of the gospel was endangered. In the hands of de l'Orme, these forms suggested subterfuge, undermining, decay, temporality, and the grotesque; when seen in designs commissioned by Catholic royal power, these hinted at the judgment of God, as Catharine Randall has argued. And yet the meaning is elusive. Just as there is not one single interpretation available, and meaning is more suggestive than mathematical, de l'Orme's Mannerism would not be the only visual language available for Protestant self-expression, as we shall see in the work of Salomon de Brosse. For several years after the death of his patron Henry II, de l'Orme's commissions diminished significantly. This provided him opportunity to write, and he published *Nouvelles Inventions pour bien bastir et à petits Fraiz* in 1561, followed six years later by the more substantial work, *Le premier tome de l'Architecture*, comprised of eleven "books." This was republished the following year and again in 1626 and 1648. In these works he followed the tradition of Vitruvius and Alberti, but as Blunt points out, "both in its general approach and in its plan the book is essentially original and is a characteristic production of French sixteenth-century Humanism."[21]

De l'Orme's original treatise of 1567 comprised nine books addressing construction. Books I and II address initial questions such as qualifications of the architect, choice of site, orientation, materials, and the making of foundations. Books III and IV discuss technical considerations of cellars, foundations, and qualities necessary for sound structures, including vaults, the *trompe*, and the importance of knowledge of geometry. Book V treats

---

21. Blunt, *Philibert de L'Orme*, 109.

the nature of Tuscan, Doric, and Ionic Orders; Book VI description and design of the Corinthian order, and Book VII the design and placement of composite columns. Books VIII and IX discuss gates, entrances, windows and doors, as well as façade composition and fireplaces. The conclusion ruminates on the architectural profession overall. The treatise is noteworthy in its comprehensiveness, treatment of constructions from antiquity, and its inclusion of technical developments, especially on the fabrication of vaults. Yet the treatise stands uncompleted, with the author never finishing the planned second volume containing his own works and his doctrine of the "divine proportions." In consequence, perhaps, he includes diverse material on the subject in the *premier tome*, causing a somewhat haphazard organizational structure. Nonetheless, the treatise is inventive and makes a formidable contribution to the development of a unique French Renaissance style. Rather than simply copying Serlian forms, de l'Orme reflects deeply on models from antiquity, which he sees paradigmatically, and offers his own designs, defending them against "ignorants & fascheux pleins d'envie pourra estre trouvée fort estrange, & peult estre, de mauvaise grace, pour autant qu'ils n'ont accoustumé de voir la semblable & ne peuvent louer ce qu'ils ne sçavent faire & oultrepasse leurs gros esprits."[22] The architect knows his innovations will prove beyond the comprehension of the philistine.

De l'Orme is remarkably personal in his treatise, recounting his journey to Rome and the vicissitudes of his life and career. He provides an insider's look into the architect's profession, and helps open up, as did other writers of treatises, what had been in the medieval era had been carefully guarded trade secrets. The architect employs the term "excogitation" to describe the process of invention, yet not "daring to use the term 'creation' reserved for God alone."[23] He also mines the past for inventive insertions into the Vitruvian templates and medieval models, "cultural parameters" that bring together his working drawings. Potié maintains that later architects would learn from de l'Orme, making "the art of line drawing a rhetoric, allowing the development of a scholarly art of diversity, or even of caprice, which the Mannerist and Baroque eras in particular would exalt."[24] In addition,

22. De l'Orme, *Architecture*, 208. "Ignorant and disagreeable persons full of envy may be found to be very strange, and often, as they are not accustomed to seeing the big picture, they can only see value in what they know. Anything beyond this is too much for their crude spirit."

23. Ibid., 208.

24. Ibid.

his allegory of the good architect not only establishes the position of the architect over that of the critic, but also symbolically elevates the Calvinist faith.[25] If Randall is correct, then much is implied and coded in the writing and physical works of de l'Orme, but he does reveal his aesthetic tendencies in the following passage of *l'Architecture*. In spite of the relative complexity of his ornamentation, he still insists on the importance of fittingness, of soundness of design, lest the Vitruvian value of commodity and solidity be sacrificed to caprice. De l'Orme explains his aesthetic approach in the following extended passage:

> I have always been of the opinion . . . that it is better for the ar-
> chitect, rather than to know how to make ornaments and decora-
> tions for walls or other parts [of a building], to know well what
> is needed for the health and preservation of persons and their
> property . . . I sometimes see that when our nobles build, they wish
> for nothing more than magnificent ornamentation with pilasters,
> columns, cornices, mouldings, bas-reliefs, marble inlays and such,
> rather than understanding the situation and nature of of the site
> of their buildings.
>
> I do not say that it is improper to make beautiful ornaments
> and ornamental façades for kings, princes, and lords when that is
> what they desire. For these give great satisfaction and pleasure to
> the eye, especially when such façades are done with symmetry and
> a sense of proportion, and ornamentation is applied with restraint
> and reason . . . such ornamentation should be done with great
> architectural care, and not of decorative foliage nor of bas-relief,
> which only gathers dirt and filth, birds' nests, flies, and other ver-
> min. In addition, such ornaments are fragile and tend to disinte-
> grate, so that rather than delight the eye, they take on a displeasing
> and dreary appearance.
>
> Therefore, I recommend that architects and all those of the
> building profession study the nature of the sites rather than pro-
> duce grand embellishments, which only serve to dazzle the viewer
> and seek to make money. Truly, it is more honest and useful to
> know how to plan a habitation well and solidly than how to embel-
> lish it without reason, proportion, or measure, most often from
> caprice, without understanding . . . the ornaments and decorations
> of façades should be appropriate, and correspond with the interior
> of the building. The divisions of halls and rooms and the openings
> of windows and casements should not produce a displeasing ef-
> fect on the exterior of the building. Nor would I wish the exterior

25. Randall, *Building Codes*, 136.

ornamentation to prevent proper proportionality of the interior halls, rooms, doors, windows, and fireplaces.[26]

In this passage de l'Orme upholds, in spite of what appears to the modern eye to be a wealth of decoration, the priority of the Vitruvian cardinal virtues of solidity and utility or fittingness. Decorative elements are appropriate, especially when incorporated onto symmetrical and proportionate building fronts. He even cautions that intricacy in architecture embellishment too easily gathers "dust and filth" and is subject to decomposition. More appropriate, he intones, is for the architect to consider carefully the possible solutions to siting. Based on this lucid statement, de l'Orme undoubtedly employed considerable visual irony when he used twisting, seemingly broken columns to adorn a Catholic Church.

Figure 9: Perspective drawing of the chapel of the Château d'Anet, Philibert de l'Orme, *Le Premier tome de l'achitecture*, 1567.

If outer decoration must illustrate the inner purpose and function of a building, de l'Orme was making a commentary on the corruption of the

26. De l'Orme, *Architecture*, 19–20

Catholic faith. His chapel design for the Château d'Anet, for instance (1547–1552; see figure 9), especially as seen from the east elevation, seems absurdly overwrought from the exterior, a pastiche of rectangles and curvilinear forms. A dome over the nave is surmounted by a cupola, whose classical aspect is overcome by high-pitched, pyramidal Gothic stone spires, too close to one another for proportionality, bizarrely conveying an impression of wolves' ears. Visually, it is no stretch to say de l'Orme was giving expression to his view of the rapacious nature of the Catholic Church. Another engraving included with the perspective drawings following chapter 8 in *Architecture* is also enlightening (see figure 10). Closely following the design for the chapel, it depicts a large dome pierced by oval windows and flanked by two pointed towers. This time, however, the building is in ruins, distorted by cracking and overgrown by vegetation, threatened by surging waters. It seems to picture the eventual disintegration of the Roman church.

Figure 10: Drawing for an imaginary building; Philibert de l'Orme,
Le Premier tome de l'achitecture.

De l'Orme claims to have produced designs and ornaments for homes not previously seen and "une belle invention pour bien bastir, et à petit frais." One of his novelties is the "French column," a pillar banded with horizontal strips. This reflected the practical concerns of available local materials—stone was not available in the strength needed for the length of columns. With his design, columns could be fabricated with several joined sections, the joints hidden by the horizontal bands. In so doing, de l'Orme was maintaining an ancient iconography while translating it into the material necessities of another era. As he explains in chapter 8 of Book VIII of *Architecture*, the classical Orders of architecture morphed into different applications in different contexts, producing the Tuscan and Composite designs and assorted local variations. As well, in response to local building materials or concerns of economy, columns were sometimes made from wood. In such cases iron bands were fixed around the column to guard against cracking. In time, the ancients noticed that plants would grow in the cracks behind the bands, and began to imitate this in stone columns. The design followed the copiousness of nature itself in its process of disintegration and growth. This is what de l'Orme recommends: "Vous y colloquerez des plattes bandes accompagnées de feuilles, ou d'autres fortes d'ornements. . ."[27] Aesthetically, it is debatable whether de l'Orme's French column constitutes an invention, but practically segmented columns provided a solution to building based on appropriate use of local materials (see figure 11). More importantly, his columns serve as a reflection on both antiquity and on the processes of nature as they interact with art.

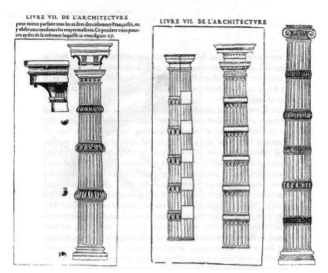

Figure 11: Design for a new "French style" column; Philibert de l'Orme, *Le Premier tome de l'achitecture.*

27. Ibid., 218b.

Viollet-le-Duc maintains that the first half of the sixteenth century in France was a time of architectural capriciousness, and that the effect of de l'Orme's work was to counter this tendency as he introduced increasing sobriety into design.[28] He attributes this in part to the higher nobility, who were "in great part Protestant," who were too occupied, presumably with trying to secure religious rights, to concern themselves with ornate or overwrought building projects. But this seems too facile an explanation; depending on the point of comparison, as we have seen, de l'Orme's work may be read as ornate or as classical in style. The breadth of his stylistic language in his *Onze Livres* ranged from a highly rusticated row of columns to illustrate his discussion of foundations,[29] to a series of wells at the conclusion to Book Eight which appear to be semi-ruins, to an Italianate church. Indeed, his work displays a wide stylistic range with the most classical sensibility seen in his designs for fireplaces and in the Château d'Anet. No doubt the increasing severity of style results in part from his Reformed perspective, which favored the understated, implied, and symbolic rather than the exaggerated, explicit, and Mannerist.

BERNARD PALISSY

Next, we turn to Bernard Palissy (1510–89), ceramicist, architectural planner, designer of grottoes and "rustiques," and hydraulic engineer, who shows us that Huguenot interests were broader than conventional architecture. He demonstrates that, unlike in Catholic use of symbols that sacralized material objects, Protestants saw all of nature as reflective of God's presence and benign purpose. Palissy was born into a family of artisans, it seems, near Agen.[30] After completing an apprenticeship with a glassmaker, he embarked on a tour of France, in which he studied architectural structures, soils and vegetation, and shifted his attention to ceramics. Settling in Saintes, he married and began to raise a family. Anatole France, in his introduction to *Les Oeuvres,* explains that the Palissy home was outside the city walls and enjoyed a garden, as well as proximity to a stream flowing from the Grand-Font à la Charente, where Palissy spent happy hours observing

28. Ibid., 363.

29. De l'Orme, *Onze Livres,* 47.

30. Palissy, *Les Oeuvres,* v.

nature.[31] Rather than "hide his talent in the ground," he sought to "bring to light the things it has pleased God to make me understand."[32]

Figure 12: Engraving of a ceramic platter by Palissy shows typical of his style, including leaves, fish, and amphibians.

His work *Receptes Véritable,* comprising the major part of *Les Oeuvres,* is filled with explorations, in dialogical form, of places of refuge, of fortresses, of waterworks, of the echoes of architectural principles in the natural world, and of rocks, minerals, and the properties of plants and herbs. In these elements, Palissy sought to read the "book of nature" directly, discerning the hand of God in the intricacy and order of the physical world, and saw the principle that "God had given the most industry to the weakest things and not the strongest." Even more than a sense of God's providence and creativity, he perceived in the humblest living things of the created order a tenacious ability to adapt and survive. He saw this characteristic as analogous to his own experience as a member of an oppressed religious minority. The capacity of natural things to endure paralleled his own experience as a Huguenot and highlighted the power of weakness in overcoming strength.

31. Ibid., vii.

32. Palissy, *Discours Admirables*, 1–6.

Palissy appears to have used animals in a symbolic way. On one hand, his rustic basins and platters were straightforward nature studies (see figure 12). On another, they could be read as dramatic tableau of the struggle of faith: snakes, long associated with the Fall in Eden, with original sin and with the devil, swim threateningly toward fish, symbols for the church. This appears to be a commentary on the Reformed, true religion, and the sinister Catholic authority that endangered it.

Palissy describes his work in architectonic ways, using anthropomorphic terms; several times he also describes creation, as well as his own art, as "estrange et monstrueux." This is striking, for Palissy always labors to reproduce painstakingly nature's forms. The strangeness of his works lies in their hybrid quality, realistic and yet artfully composed, artificial yet crafty in their precision and realism, blurring the lines between art and nature as fish, crustaceans, and insects seem to arrange themselves on ceramic platters, even as they maintain their natural coloration and characteristics. In addition, even as architecture imitates and even returns to nature, the grotto is defined by the artifacts of enamel portraying fauna and flora. Palissy suggests trimming trees so as to resemble an entablature, a counterpoint to columns imitating the shape of trees. The "strange and monstrous" quality calls to mind the distortions in de l'Orme's work and the admixture of shapes introduced by Serlio in his *Livre Extraordinaire.*

Most importantly for our investigation, Palissy was a Huguenot. As he labored to unravel various glazing techniques in Saintes in 1546, he heard the message of reform brought by Genevans, and turned to the Reformed community of Saintonge. By the late 1550s, to hold to the Reformed confession meant risking the charge of heresy and a death sentence. As holy war raged in the region of Saintes from 1560, Palissy found a protector in the Duke of Montmorency. His treatise *Receptes Véritables* was published in La Rochelle in 1563, immediately after the Edict of Pacification of Amboise (a peace accord between Protestant and Catholic factions) by the Huguenot printer Barthélemy Berton. Palissy's religious convictions become clear as he recounts the activities of the Reformed church at Saintes; possessing little trust in the peace accord, he turns to designing fortresses and dedicates to his coreligionists a blueprint for a fortress based on the form of a murex shell. In so doing, he suggests through a visual language the wish to protect the Reformed, to withdraw into a shell, and also to trust in the God who works in weakness to accomplish his will and preserve his saints. Palissy appears to have read little, but learned much through deductive reasoning and the observation of nature. He did read Vitruvius, employing him as a design template and human counterpoint to the works of nature. He also steeped himself in the Psalms, to which he regularly refers in *Les Oeuvres*, urging his readers to remember these passages. Palissy sees everything through a scriptural lens: even when speaking of storage for manure as an object lesson for having a right perspective and calling, and pursuing it with diligence; when reflecting on the stones that build the heavenly temple described in the Book of Revelation, he portrays the nature of each stone and its mineral properties. In so doing, he sanctifies base earthly elements and avers that all things have an eschatological purpose. In speaking of buildings made to resemble trees, he applies architectural insights gained from Vitruvius and Serlio, with art imitating nature and vice versa. Often, speaking of plants and animals, he speaks of their proper treatment, a stewardship that fulfills the creation mandate given to man and woman, and explains that God's sovereign care extends even to them.

> Il me semblait que j'apperceu plusieurs choses qui sont déduite et narrées au Pseaume susdit: car je voyais les connils jouant, sautant et pénadans le long de la montagne, près de certaines fosses, trous et habitations que le Souverain Architecte leur avait érigé, et soudain que les animaux apercevaient quelqu'un de leurs ennemis, ils sçavoyent fort bien se retirer au lieu qu'il leur avait esté ordonné pour leur demeurance.[33]

Palissy sympathizes with the natural order because he identifies with it and with the animals who must find shelter in the wild against dangerous beasts, echoing the passage from Hebrews chapter 11, where the faithful are always

> . . . looking forward to the city with foundations, whose architect and builder is God. . . . They went about in sheepskins and goatskins, destitute, persecuted and mistreated— the world was not worthy of them. They wandered in deserts and mountains, living in caves and in holes in the ground.
>
> These were all commended for their faith, yet none of them received what had been promised, since God had planned

---

33 Palissy, *Oeuvres*, 111. ". . . it seemed to me that several things could be deduced from this particular psalm: because I saw rabbits playing and jumping along the mountain near some pits, holes and houses as the Supreme Architect made them, and suddenly noticed that animals caught sight of an enemy, they know well to hide instead of staying where they are."

something better for us so that only together with us would they be made perfect (vv. 10, 37b-40 NIV).

For Palissy, the world is both blessed and cursed, mirroring God's providential design and yet subject to distortion, death, and decay. The creative work of architects and designers was a way of participating with God in the creation mandate, reconstituting Eden in a divine-human partnership. In this Palisssy was in effect aligning himself with agronomist Olivier de Serres and garden theorist Jacques Boyceau. (Huguenots and writers of treatises, both were motivated by aesthic and theological concerns in addition to practical ones. These designers sought to share in a grand project of restoration through a design strategy reflecting the abundance and symmetry of nature.) Through his eccentric vision, Palissy expresses the highest standards of aesthetic value and simultaneously reveals a deeply Protestant vision, one which would sustain both faith and creativity. Built space is not indispensable for worship; the world, albeit blessed, is not the Christian's final home, but rather a prefigurement of his or her heavenly destination.

The marriage of Reformed theology and design tells us that the answer to idolatry is learning a new imagination, one that perceives reality as defined by the Word of God. This understanding enables one to recognize the difference between religious experience and the actuality beyond it, one in which a genuine encounter with God might take place. The buildings and plans of de l'Orme, Palissy and other Protestant architects remind us that valid worship refuses to propose any human image for God. In their designs for Catholic clients we often discern from Calvinist architects an unbalance and impression of disquiet. In contrast, in their designs for Protestant communities we see expressions of the values of order, appropriateness, sobriety, clarity, light, and indeed, beauty. Their artistic imaginations arouse not in a vacuum, but in the theological commitment to unadulterated faith in the biblical God who acts in sovereign freedom.

JACQUES-ANDROUET DU CERCEAU

Jacques-Androuet du Cerceau, born in 1510, was not an architectural theorist but a publisher of practical architectural manuals that focused on illustrations. From 1549 he published a number of books on the construction of houses. His 1559 *Premier Livre d'Architecture*, a manual on country houses from manors to grand châteaux, borrows extensively from Serlio's unpublished manuscript *Sesto libro delle habitationi di tutti li gradi degli homini* (*On the Habitations of People of All Estates;* see figure 13).[34] Du Cerceau's work was an anthology of the best architecture of the French Renaissance, preserving a record of numerous constructions which no longer exist or have been radically altered. The fifty model designs for chateaux do not appear to follow any particular chronological or conceptual order, and there is no particular coherence in the manner of their depiction, done through perspective drawings, plane elevations, and bird's-eye views.

Figure 13: Androuet du Cerceau: Entrance to the Château, Écouen.

Catherine Randall has noted, as have architectural historians, that du Cerceau's presentations of existing buildings often differ extensively from

34. Freigang and Kremeier, "Jacques Androuet," 220.

the actual structures he studied. His drawing of de l'Orme's chapel of the château d'Anet, for example, is scarcely recognizable as the same edifice. Randall argues that this demonstrates du Cerceau's Protestant perspective, constantly reconfiguring reality and seeking a spiritual, not physical, ideal. Fragmentation, alternative perspective, and juxtaposition were the tools he used to conceptually undermine Catholic hegemony and to establish a Protestant "representational space."[35] Randall's argument is cogent, and seems to be the best explanation of the data we possess. Seemingly, differences between du Cerceau's drawings and the buildings they portray are intentional; his books are more than mere documentations of masterpieces from a historical point in time. In addition, the commentary is spare, and the architects seldom named. The books serve as an homage to architecture, but more, they forge a cryptic theological statement, reconfiguring space from the point of view of a Calvinistic and Huguenot world view.

In his introduction to the reader, du Cerceau speaks of divine providence, "selon le don de grâce qu'elle lui avait distribué," echoing the words of the Apostle Paul ("There are different kinds of gifts. . . . Now to each one the manifestation of the Spirit is given for the common good.") He speaks of "vocation," a particular calling which in the Calvinistic perspective each member of the body of Christ possessed. Part of the purpose of that calling was to preserve and refresh what was good and true of the past, a work parallel to the recovery of the gospel which had vanished or lain dormant. The architect praises not the "hauts-faits" of the monarchy, but *buildings* of the realm, "haut bâtiments" reinterpreted as reflections of a Calvinistic metaphysical realm. His work is more art than science, a visual rhetoric ostensibly to the glory of Charles IX, Henry II or Catherine de Médici, but in reality to the glory of God. In contemplating elevations, plans, and iconographic drawings, the viewer may be led, he maintains, to "contemplate profundities." The ostentation and exaggeration of the work is not real but ideal, driven by du Cerceau's unique vision.

In *Livre d'architecture,* du Cerceau furthers the distinctively French habit of separating buildings into wings and pavilions, and architectural embellishment is used sparingly. Existing compilations of buildings concerned works of antiquity, yet this work examines and memorializes contemporary French works. In *Plus excellent bastiments* (1576), apparently encouraged by Catherine de Médici (he dedicates his first volume to her), he writes,

35. Randall, *Building Codes*, 195.

Madame, après qu'il a plu à Dieu nous envoyer par votre moyen
une paix tant nécessaire et désirée de tous, j'ai pensé ne pouvoir
mieux à propos mettre en lumière ce premier livre des bâtiments
exquis de ce royaume, espérant que nos pauvres Français (ès yeux
et entendements desquels ne se présente maintenant autre chose
que désolations, ruines et saccagements que nous ont apportés
les guerres passées) prendront, peut-être, en respirant, quelque
plaisir et contentement à contempler ici une partie des plus beaux
et excellents édifices dont la France est encore pour le jourd'hui
enrichie.[36]

The words of the dedication reference the recent wars of religion, and underscore both the physical devastation and emotional exhaustion of the French people following years of religious wars. Also, as du Cerceau would have been quite aware of the need for royal favor in order to find the space to exercise his own career, gives credit to the queen for at last bringing peace to the realm, while promising a second volume to come, God willing. If she, in her endorsement for the project, hoped to document important houses within the kingdom, it made sense to underscore the pleasure afforded by rendering these drawings (fifteen in the first volume of *Plus excellents bastiments.*) He wishes her peace (which certainly was greatly in the interest of the Huguenots as a persecuted minority population), and the fulfillment of her "holy desires," which may be read two ways: from the queen's standpoint, perhaps her desires ipso facto reflected God's will; from the perspective of a persecuted "righteous" people of God, only those plans and desires which conformed to the sovereign will of God were to be answered.

Catherine de Médici no doubt initiated the project. Du Cerceau affirms this not only in the dedication of the first volume, and also in that of the *Leçons de perspective positive* of 1576,

Madame, si l'injure du temps et troubles qui ont cours, n'eussent
empêché mon accès et vue des châteaux et maisons, que votre
Majesté désire être compris aux livres qu'il vous a plu me com-
mander de dresser et dessiner des plus excellents Palais, maisons

36. Du Cerceau, *Plus excellent bastiments*, A ii. "Madam, since it has pleased God to send us through you a peace which was needed and wished for by all, I thought I could do worse than to bring to light of day this first book of some of the exquisite buildings of the kingdom, hoping that our poor co-citizens, who have seen nothing but desolation, ruin, and siege brought about by the recent wars, would receive some pleasure and contentment in contemplating here some of the most beautiful and excellent edifices which still enrich our France."

Royales et édifices de ce Royaume, dès à présent j'aurais satisfait à votre volonté, qui m'est si précieuse.[37]

Again, the chaotic nature of recent times heretofore prevented the architect from travelling and made viewing of many buildings impossible. Now, however, he has been able to fulfill the wishes of the queen, which are so important to him. Du Cerceau again underscores his desire to garner Catherine's support, and announces that he has been able to complete the task given to him in spite of the difficulties of war (and persecution, or *les troubles*).

The second volume *Les Plus excellents bastiments* is again dedicated to her. In this he repeats his complaint of the difficulty completing his task, and then cites his advanced age (by now nearly seventy years old) that made travel more difficult than previously. From the dedications to his works it is clear they were commissioned by the crown (repeated in the dedication for the second *Livre d'architecture* (1561)), and giving thanks for his audience: "je reçus ce bien de votre accoutumée bénignité et clémence, de me prêter l'oreille à vous discourir de plusieurs bâtiments excellents de votre Royaume . . ." His travel to various places to observe and record the buildings was to "satisfaire à vos commandements."

In the volume, du Cerceau adheres scrupulously to de l'Orme's adaptation of Greek classicism and his interpretation of the Orders. His façades are "devoid of ornamentation" and are discriminatingly proportioned.[38] Hillary Ballon attests to knowledge of Serlio's writings in France, and speculates on the possibility that his ideas passed directly through his writing to the architect du Cerceau and subsequently to his nephew Salomon de Brosse.[39]

[A manuscript version of Serlio's sixth book] seems to have remained in France throughout the seventeenth century . . . in 1673, Francois Blondel referred to Serlio's manuscript: "Il y a un livre de luy qui traite des bastimens des particuliers, à commencer depuis

---

37. Du Cerceau, *Leçons de perspective*, A ii. "Madam, if the calamity of the recent times and 'the troubles' prevented access to châteaux and houses which your Majesty wished to include in the books you commissioned to compile of drawings of the most excellent palaces, royal houses, and edifices of the kingdom, as of now I am able to fulfill your wishes, which are so precious to me."

38. De l'Orme, *L'Architecture*, 47.

39. Ballon, *Paris of Henri IV*, 315–16n.

la cabane de berger jusqu'aux palais du Roy, lequel n'a jamais été imprimé, quoyqu'il pu être de quelque utilité."[40]

Mignot hypothesized that Serlio's manuscript passed from du Cerceau to his nephew Salomon de Brosse.[41]

This draft manuscript for Book Six, acquired by the Avery Library of Columbia University, is known as the Avery Manuscript. It is a draft completed on paper between 1541 and 1549; along with a copy on parchment now in the Bayerische Staatsbibliothek in Munich and a set of printer's proofs of the woodcut illustrations, and the three surviving copies of his works.[42] Although not published until after his death, likely a casualty of Serlio's vacillating career (and his contentious personality,) his Book Six would prove to be widely and lastingly influential. Its presence among the great French family of architects is attested. Myra Nan Rosenfeld writes, "The Avery manuscript passed down through the du Cerceau family to a grandson of Jacques Androuet du Cerceau, the architect Salomon de Brosse, in whose atelier it was probably consulted by Pierre Le Muet."[43] She emphasizes the diffusion of Serlio's ideas and his influence on subsequent urban house-types.

In that way, de l'Orme's principles continued to persuade his architectural progeny of the next generation.[44]

SALOMON DE BROSSE

Salomon de Brosse was born in Verneuil-en-Halatte, probably in 1571, one year after the death of de l'Orme, and died in Paris in 1626. Rosalys Coope asserts that de l'Orme was the greatest French architect of the sixteenth century, and that de Brosse, while not his equal in intellect or inventiveness, was an apt heir to his legacy, "the first outstanding classical architect of the seventeenth century and the vital link between de l'Orme and Francois Mansart."[45] Though nothing of his writings survives, he helped restore French architecture in a time of overwrought Mannerist expressiveness to

---

40. Savot, *bastiments particuliers*, 345.

41. Ballon, *Paris of Henri IV*.

42. Serlio, *Domestic Architecture*.

43. Ibid., 5.

44. Hustin, *Le Palais du Luxembourg*, 31.

45. Coope, *Salomon de Brosse*, 1.

a coherent set of visual and spatial ideas. He was a seminal figure, then, in the development of French classicism, and his plans and extant structures his ideas still communicate. Indeed, without his own explication of his intentions, we are left to exegete the buildings themselves, eloquent in their visual language.

Figure 14: Elevation of Luxembourg Palace, begun in 1615, by Salomon de Brosse.

Coope underscores, in the absence of more extensive source material, the importance of Pasteur Pannier's *un Architecte Français au commencement du XVIIe siècle, Salomon de Brosse* for information of the life of de Brosse. Pannier relies especially on the work of Charles Read, who spent twenty-five years gathering material on the architect. In spite of misleading handling of source material, Pannier demonstrates the importance of de Brosse's upbringing in a family of architects. He was the son of Jean de Brosse, architect, and Julienne, whose father was the famous architect and engraver Jacques I Androuet du Cerceau, author of the folio volumes *Les Plus Excellents Bastiments de France.* Julienne's brothers Baptiste and Jacques II du Cerceau, both architects, seem to have tutored the young de Brosse in the building trade after his father died sometime before 1585. Construction of the château at Verneuil provided employment for the du Cerceau family and their young protégé for twenty years. In addition, the town of Verneuil was an artist colony and an important center of Protestant activity, which strengthened de Brosse's Protestant identity.

De Brosse continued to work for his uncle Jacques II until de Brosse assumed responsibility as architect of the queen Marie de Médici in 1614, at which time he garnered a number of significant contracts. He may be responsible for the Collège de France, and the Hôtel de Soissons, in addition to its *porte-cochère* on the Rue des Deux-Ecus. In 1612 and 1613 he was named as architect for two grand châteaux outside Paris (see figure 14); in 1614 he received the greatest commission of his career, the Luxembourg

Palace, from Marie de Médici, and in 1616 he was invited to design the façade to the late-Gothic church of St. Gervais in Paris. His last project came in 1623 with the second incarnation of the Protestant temple at Charenton. His style can be conceived as linking between the Renaissance and the seventeenth century, and he is as conversant in the Mannerist language of the Château de Coulommiers as in a sober classicism, as in Luxembourg.

Pannier recounts how the personal property of de Brosse's uncles sustained damage at the hands of Catholic rioters because they "aimant mieux quitter [leur] biens que de retourner à la messe"[46] ("Because they preferred to give up their possessions rather than return to the [Catholic] Mass.") Jacques II du Cerceau fled the city in 1588, but church records reveal that de Brosse remained in Verneuil during the internecine conflicts. He raised his seven children in the Protestant faith and remained in this milieu, though he continued to work for Catholic patrons. Through his wife's relations, the architectural dynasty of the extended family was to continue among his descendents in England and Germany. Coope writes that he was personally amiable, a man of modest tastes, and that "all his life de Brosse was neglectful of detail because he was not interested in the minutia of his undertakings. What appears to have seized his imagination was the initial design, the general conception of the building, its effect as a mass or a composition of various masses juxtaposed."[47] Among his few personal effects at his death were a New Testament and a complete Bible in French, as well as three books of architecture. We know of no writings of his that explicate his professional work; he was a practitioner rather than theoretician, underlining his practical and historical significance, and forcing us to guess at his intentions by allowing the work to speak for itself.

De Brosse's career revealed the influence of his predecessors de l'Orme, Vignola, Serlio, and the du Cerceaus. In the course of time, he evidences a progression wherein he strengthened his appropriation of some while distancing himself from others. Coope points out that de Brosse developed in his mastery of the building as a mass, a compositional entity, and a "growing awareness of the three-dimensional approach to architecture," and an "increasing grasp of the fact that classicism should be a quality intrinsic to a building and not merely a decorative adjunct to it."[48] In consequence, he draws less from du Cerceau and Vignola, more toward interpreting de

46. Pannier, *Salomon de Brosse*, 20.

47. Ibid., 13.

48. Ibid., 189.

l'Orme, and more directly, Pierre Lescot, whose influence is more clearly discernible. Direct borrowings are seen from the latter's work from the Louvre for Blérancourt and Coulommiers. A causal relationship can be seen from the façade of de l'Orme's Anet chapel and de Brosse's St. Gervais. Finally, "at the end of his career we find him, at the Temple of Charenton, making a deliberate attempt to reconstruct the Antique according to Vitruvius."[49]

Renaissance classicism made its way into France from Italy via the ideas of Serlio and Primaticcio, amplified by the work of de l'Orme and Lescot, accelerating the formation of a French style. But the du Cerceau satellite appropriated de l'Orme's ideas in more random fashion, taking decorative elements in what was at times a superficial manner. De Brosse learned from de l'Orme's conception of the classical, especially in his adaptation of the Orders and his utilization of massing, yet moved beyond the Mannerist stylistic elements of the late sixteenth century, streamlining and simplifying in his own work.

JACQUES PERRET

Yet another architectural treatise that merits mention is Jacques Perret's *Des fortifications et artifices d'architecture et perspective,* published in 1601 shortly after the Edict of Nantes. Perret (1540/45 to 1610/19) was a Savoyard Huguenot mathematician and designer of military fortifications. His brief treatise, combining both military and ecclesial designs, can be read as an attempt to legitimize the Protestant community. Like Serlio, he organizes his designs according to social status. His treatise comprises twenty-two plates accompanied by textual commentary, dedicated to the king and concluding with the phrase "to God alone the glory."

The frontispiece of Perret's major work, *Des fortifications et artifices: architecture et perspective,* published three or four years after the Edict of Nantes, often describes him as a "gentilhomme savoysien" from Chambéry is described as "lecteur ès arts d'arithmétique et géométrie." Described in biographical notes as a military engineer, he appears to be acquainted with the classic writers Vegetius and Frontinus. He moved to Paris at the end of the sixteenth century after his conversion to Protestantism, and benefited from the protection of Catherine de Parthenay and her son the Duke de Rohan, whose coat of arms appears on several plates of his treatise. In typically

49. Ibid.

Protestant manner, verses from the Old Testament or paraphrases of the Psalms frame the plates, plans and perspective drawings of various models of buildings and fortifications which take inspiration from contemporary military treatises and from the urban building programs of Henry IV.

The work consists of three sections, including Huguenot town plans with row houses and arcades, fortifications and the placement of the Protestant temples, essentially monumental auditoriums, within them, accompanied by brief annotations. These assembly halls, inspired by a Calvinist theology of an elect community (walls separate the town from a potentially hostile world; housing is egalitarian and communitarian) along with hostility toward representational art, were nonetheless monumental and could serve both religious and secular functions and could seat thousands. The churches were unadorned, and yet the city walls were often lined with scriptural quotes (see figure 15). As in Palissy's garden lined with psalms, he thus demonstrates the evangelical proclivity for the Psalter (which Protestants had learned to sing in the famous "Genevan Psalter") even to the extent of wrapping the text or paraphrases of psalms by Clément Marot into the actual wall plan. In doing so, he symbolically places the Reformed community under the protection of the Word of God. Inscriptions underscore the biblical mandate that earthly sovereigns wield the sword in order to punish evil and reward the good; the inscription "In God alone there is repose and true happiness" occurs several times. Catherine Randall points out that the meaning of the biblical texts cuts both ways and opens multiple layers of meaning: rather than simply protect the Protestant faithful, the militant psalms underscore the ability of the Word of God to obliterate godless earthly powers, and its ability to undo Catholic redoubts.[50] The second part of his treatise, addressing ecclesiastical structures, concentrates on Huguenot temples. Providing examples of small, medium, and large edifices, each engraving is supplemented with brief annotations. The coupling of military and religious architecture suggests the situation of Reformed Christians forced to practice their faith in a hostile larger culture.

50. Randall, *Building Codes*, 71.

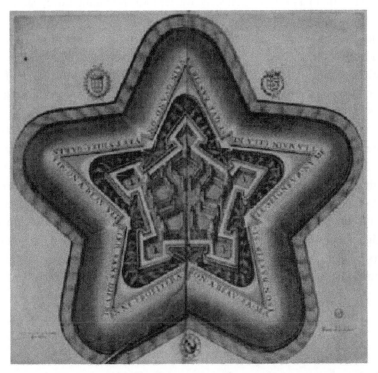

Figure 15: Jacques Perret, *Des fortifications et artifices. Architecture et perspective de Iaques Perret,* **1601.**

Perret's perspective drawings are in fact aerial drawings, shaded and detailed beyond what one would expect in mere plans, suggesting his desire to establish and symbolically reinforce the Protestant religion, as if line drawings alone are too fragile. The perspective intimates that Perret mirrors the sovereign perspective of God. In addition, the treatise displays plans for private architecture, houses, and the royal pavilion, whose style of fenestration reveals a Dutch or English influence. Perret's work reveals indebtedness to Serlio's concerns in his organization according to social roles. Some of the drawings depict a kind of communal Protestant housing with adjacent apartments with access by a single shared front door, calling to mind perspectival designs of Jacques Androuet du Cerceau in his *Premier livre d'architecture.*

Perret's concerns clearly went beyond those of a mere military engineer in the mode of other French designers of fortifications in the seventeenth century, such as Jean Errad de Bar-le-Duc, Sébastien LePrestre Vauban, and

Blaise Pagan, in a period when siege warfare was remaking European cities into the form of gigantic geometric formations. In light of the plans of other designers, the mixed content of Perret's commentaries seemed perhaps an odd hybrid, the product of what Émilie d'Orgeix calls a "utopian Huguenot mathematician."[51] Yet, as has been suggested, his vision, as well as that of de l'Orme, du Cerceau, and de Brosse, would prove integral to the building of a distinctive Huguenot worship space.

The rediscovery of classical ideas, particularly those of Vitruvius, animated the thought and work of sixteenth- and seventeenth-century Calvinist architects working in France. These ideas were introduced through the work of Serlio, and subsequently digested and disseminated by de l'Orme and others, insuring the enduring relevance of classicism for Renaissance architectural experimentation. In the structural forms produced Reformed designers, new possibilities for church buildings appropriate for Protestant worship were conceived. In addition, a subtle critique was engaged against Catholic faith, and the foundations for French Neoclassicism were laid.

51. D'Orgeix, "Perret, Jacques."

CHAPTER 7

The Shaping of Reformed
Worship Space

WE WILL NOW REFLECT on how these ideas worked themselves out in a specific francophone Reformed settings. Our first case study concerns Geneva,
where Protestants adapted spaces they appropriated from the Catholics following the 1535 adoption of the Reform. Secondly, we consider a church
of a Protestant architect which was commissioned by Catholics. Our third
study takes up the situation of Parisian Protestants, comprising a minority
of the population, gathered in a purpose-built structure by that same architect (once they were legally permitted to build a church after the Edict of
Nantes in 1598.) The Genevan church was chosen because it was an ancient
Catholic edifice originally chosen to house the Mass, and later converted
into a house of Protestant worship. As such, it demonstrates the unique
challenges of changing a church's spiritual orientation to conform to the
principles of the gospel as understood by pastors and elders. The second
church reveals the challenges facing a Protestant architect commissioned
to express Catholic theology in stone. The third case study is relevant as
an example of a purpose-built church, showing how Protestant ideas were
expressed in concrete form.

ST. PIERRE

The former Cathedral of St. Pierre in Geneva was founded in the third century, its first structure built in the fourth century on the site of a pagan temple. Building on pagan sites in the Constantinian era and beyond perhaps indicated a desire to declare victory over paganism, although other possible explanations include convenient proximity to the inhabitants of the city or to civic buildings or even an attempt to appropriate and incorporate indigenous beliefs into the newly-introduced Christian faith. Another church was built over the first in the Merovingian era, another in the Carolingian, and, finally, a Gothic building with Romanesque features was started in 1160, taking seventy-two years to complete. The side-chapel, the Chapelle des Macchabées, was added in 1397 (see figure 16).

Figure 16: Engraving of the front of St. Pierre church, Geneva, prior to the addition of a classical porch, shows the irregular façade of the old Gothic church.

The west front of the cathedral was radically transformed from 1752–1756, when a Neoclassical portico was added by Italian architect Benedetto Alfiéri to the front because of structural problems that threatened the integrity of the church. The façade, though stylistically incongruous, projects an austere classical formalism consistent with the Calvinist ethos. Certainly a Renaissance or classical style was favored over the Gothic or Romanesque by Huguenot architects such as de l'Orme from at least the time of the mid-sixteenth century.

The reformer Berchtold Haller in Bern called Guillaume Farel, a student of Lefèvre d'Étaples, to bring Reformed preaching to French-speaking areas in the Pays de Vaud, Neuchâtel, and Geneva. After the Disputation of Bern in 1528, all territories under the control of the Bernese magistrates were free to preach without restriction; Farel partnered with Pierre Viret of Orbe in 1531, and the two would share responsibility for introducing the Reformation to Geneva. Protestant ideas had been disseminated there from the late 1520s via François Lambert and German merchants.[1] With the support of Bernese authorities, Viret and others openly preached by the end of 1533. Public disputations were held the following year; military conflicts with the duchy of Savoy were overcome the following year with the support of Bernese and French troops. In fact, the Savoyard threat enflamed popular support for the Reformation and also helped remove political barriers to reform.

An account from the records of the city magistrates in 1535 reports that even reform-minded ministers hesitated to declare the Mass abolished without the "counsel and support of the magistrates." The decisive moment for reform came on August 8 during a Sunday night vespers service with Farel preaching, when the opening words from Psalm 114 were read: ("When Israel came out of Egypt, Jacob from a people of foreign tongue, Judah became God's sanctuary, Israel his dominion." The account tells us, incredibly, that some twenty children rose up with a collective cry against the idols, and now began to throw them down, "little children throwing themselves upon these little gods."[2] The city magistrates had been unwilling to "abolish the idols" of Catholic worship; now, idols would be swept away in what would be seen as an act of God's grace, inspired by preaching and carried out not by the city powers, but by innocents. The children rushed outside the church, arms full of statues and holy objects, throwing them before a shocked crowd and crying, "We have the gods of the priests! Do you want some?"[3] Whatever the accuracy of the details of the account, it shows the manner in which the citizens of Geneva would come to see their Reformed identity, recalling the words of Psalm 8: "Through the praise of children and infants you have established a stronghold against your enemies, to silence the foe and the avenger." The services that evening would prove to be the last vespers held in St. Pierre; the following day the

1. Fromment et al., *Les actes*, 22.

2. Ibid., 142.

3. Ibid., 145 (translation mine.)

iconoclasm would spread to all the churches of the city, and the day after that the city council would vote to suspend indefinitely the Mass in the city.

For our interests, it is necessary to consider the changes brought about on account of the Reformation of 1535. Protestant adaptability and creativity in response to changing needs can be seen in the re-figuring of medieval basilican space for Reformed worship.

From the outside of the current church, one first notices the portico, added in 1752–1756, with its marble Corinthian columns. It surprises with its incongruous classical façade: surrounding streets follow the ancient medieval pattern, and, the adjacent Place du Bourg-de-Four follows the contours of the former Roman market. The rest of the cathedral is of a Gothic design. However, the immediate neighborhood itself is eclectic, and the church stands adjacent to many eighteenth- and nineteenth-century Neoclassical façades in the Old City of Geneva. Moreover, sandstone cladding and the patina of age lend visual unity to the broad chronological span of buildings in the area. From the front of the Gothic cathedral, one only sees the pitched roof of the porch. Only from a distance can one discern the two Gothic towers above the east end of the structure and the steeple that rises between them. As the modifications to the front of the church follow the Reformation era, however, possible ramifications on the worshiping community there will not be discussed here.

Construction of most of the existing building began in the middle of the twelfth century. Inside the church, the overwhelming impression is of the majestic, conveyed by pleasing proportions and a sense of unity and grandeur in the arches, columns, and vaulting. The church follows a Latin cross design, with two square towers. The church measures approximately sixty-five feet wide at the crossing; the width of the nave is nearly thirty-two feet wide and the length of the transept some one hundred twelve feet. The length of the nave from entryway to apse measured two hundred six feet, though that has been reduced to by the addition of the peristyle. Ten bays (today eight) were divided by five clustered pillars each. The apse comprised a demi-decagonal form, inclining toward the transept. This was an artifice employed by several church architects, recalling the words of the Gospel of John 19:30: *Inclinato capite traditit spiritum* ("He bowed his head and gave up his spirit.")[4]

The apse includes three tiers of windows; four chapels were oriented toward the crossing previous to the Reformation. In the north end of the

4. Blavignac, *Description Monumentale*, 10.

transept, illuminated by small rounded windows framed with columns. The ribs of the vaulting rest on columns in typical Gothic fashion, topped by capitals with figures and grotesques. The bays, composed of large pointed arches, are surmounted by a gallery of six rounded arches (triforium) resting on columns, and a row of openwork including five arches and three clerestory windows above. These all date from repairs done prior to the Reformation. To accommodate the narrower space between the ribs in the transepts, the triforium doubled pairs of arches, with a rose window piercing the extremity of each transept. The ribs separating the bays terminate a massive pillar formed by twelve separate columns, with the central applied column rising to the level of the clerestory windows, where it spreads into the ceiling vaulting, with the key of the vaulting resting sixty-three feet above the floor of the nave.

Prior to the destruction of the façade, a pointed pediment and three or four rows of molding with biblical figures,[5] resting on columns, framed the single arched door. On either side were buttresses at the point where interior nave walls met the west elevation, rising to corbelled pinnacles at the roofline. A trio of windows above the level of the aisles provided light, continuing the pattern of clerestory windows seen in the nave, and a large oculus illuminated each aisle. This was the appearance of the church's front elevation, whose alterations after fire damage in 1430 had already simplified the façade by the time of the Reformation.

Throughout the church, careful masonry work such as ogee moldings and astragals decorate bases and capitals. The capitals themselves depict serpents, mermaids, centaurs, and monsters, some perhaps depicting local legends and others elements of the Apocalypse of John, and others inspired by the Gospels. Stone foliage rings others; the diversity of surviving designs makes clear that Calvin and the Reformed believers of Geneva saw no contradiction between these artistic representations and their biblical faith. All the elements of the church prior to the sixteenth century were eventually painted, including capitals, bases, columns, walls, and vaulting. These were covered with a tempera whitewash beginning in the 1530s and continuing into the next century. The church Bible, hand-written on vellum and dating from the ninth century, survived the iconoclasm of the sixteenth century in spite of its illustrations and illuminated borders.

As we investigate the theological meaning in the utilization of space in St. Pierre, we look to the interstice between the architect's intention and

5. Dating from the eleventh century, according to architect J.-D. Blavignac.

the building's vernacular use, similar to what T. J. Gorringe points out in his discussion of "the great tradition" in architecture, the "written and celebrated, the work of the philosophers, historians, theologians, the learned, and the little tradition, which for the most part comes to us only in scraps, in folk memories, songs, tales and ballads, in pamphlets crudely written."[6] The modifications to the cathedral's interior spaces from 1535 to the first quarter of the seventeenth century rested on the conceptual framework in the accumulated teaching of the reformers, not only in Geneva, but in Strasbourg and elsewhere, but those modifications also took shape as directed by a popular movement. These alterations and the ideas that spawned them formed a theoretical space wherein theology takes shape, as Gorringe states, in "a triangle of text, tradition, and experience."[7] For the reformers, the text was the biblical Scriptures; the tradition, the corpus of Catholic doctrines they worked to undo, but also the visual tradition they modified; and the experience of popular piety. Common Catholic devotional longing to find God as distinct from the rhythms of everyday life was seen in creating an architecture of "otherness" through the idea of sacred space. In contrast, the reformers would emphasize the opposite, seeing God in the everyday and the profane, undoing a division of realms. If God's Spirit was present in the holy community gathered for worship, then God was also present in the home as a "little church."

Sixteenth-century worshipers in Geneva, steeped in the visual traditions of late medieval Catholicism, would have understood the symbolic meanings of carvings, tympanum, statues, paintings, and relics (including a gilded reliquary containing a tooth of St. Peter.)[8] The removal of these objects repudiated powerfully the authority and meanings they had conveyed. Through this process, the import of the building's twelfth- and thirteenth-century architects was modified, and yet as examination of the architectural space itself suggested, there was intentionality about the architecture itself, and not simply its applied decorative elements. The double-five scheme of proportion of the bays suggested the order and rationality of God. The carved figures of the capitals intimated continuity with the themes of classicism and the Old and New Testaments. Pointed arches and vaults served not only a structural purpose, but also evoked the enfolding and providential care of God. The vast span of the nave and the swirling

6. Gorringe, *Theology of the Built Environment*, 8.

7. Ibid., 9.

8. Archinard, *Les Édifices Religieux*.

heights brought to mind the grandeur and sovereignty of God. The stretch of unencumbered walls and ceilings echoed the simplicity and accessibility of the gospel. Abbot Suger had translated a mystical theology of light into glass, inscribing on the bronze doors of the St. Denis abbey,

> Bright is the noble work, but, being nobly bright, the work
> should brighten the minds, so that they may travel, through
> the true lights, to the True Light where Christ is the true door.
> In what manner it be inherent in this world the golden door defines.
> The dull mind rises to truth through that which is material,
> and, in seeing the light, is resurrected from its former submission. . . .[9]

For Catholics, stained glass colored the light and transformed it into a mystical entity that reflected spiritual illumination. However, in St. Pierre as in other Reformed temples, windows needed to simply permit the unobstructed light of the sun; this witnessed to the clarity of God who makes himself present, echoing Calvin's preference for light as a symbol for God. Above all, the effect of light in the cavernous space, now perceived without distraction, would have underscored the light of revelation and the holy essence of God.

The church is unencumbered by paintings, icons, Stations of the Cross, frescoes, mosaics, or other art.[10] When the citizens of Geneva voted to adopt the Reformation, they kept only the practices and embellishments for which they found a positive warrant in Scripture. In consequence, they stripped the church in a fit of iconoclastic fervor that destroyed twenty-four side altars, four chapels, organ, and interior decoration, although grotesques remain on the capitals of the clustered pillars in the nave. André Biéler tells us that when Calvin returned to Geneva in 1541, the interior layout of the cathedral was changed, including eliminating the rood screen and choir, and moving the pulpit from the second pillar on the right to the first pillar across the nave to better allow worshipers to gather around the preaching (as well as putting the Lord's table in place for the periodic celebration of communion.)[11]

9. Suger, "De Administratione," 47.

10. In addition to my indebtedness to Blavignac, the description is based on my own observations and notes from many visits to the church, as well as visits to the Museum of the Reformation in Geneva.

11. Biéler, *Architecture in Worship,* 57.

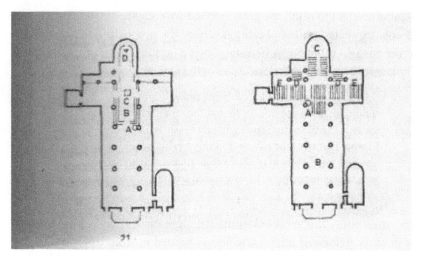

Figure 17: Seating arrangements in the church of St. Pierre prior to and after the Reformation.

Figure 17 represents the interior arrangement of St. Pierre, the left drawing prior to 1535, and the right following the Reformation. (A) marks the pulpit, which following Calvin's adaptations has been moved to the center of the congregation gathered in the apse, transept, and front of the nave. (B) marks the seating of the priests prior to 1535; the Reformation rejected a separate clerical class, and taught that all shared in a priesthood of believers. In the left hand figure, (C) indicates the high altar, and (D) the bishop's throne. In the right hand figure, (C) and (D) indicate pews, now extended into elevated galleries (E).[12] These drawings make clear that significant changes to layout in the years following 1536 reflected changing ideology, and that it is possible to recreate them and understand them through architecture.

In Catholic usage, worshipers would enter the cathedral as several Masses were taking place in side chapels or during the great Mass, but after 1535 worshipers gathered together for the Protestant cult. All objects serving the purpose of the Mass and symbolizing the Catholic view of transubstantiation were removed, including the altar, the tabernacle, and the canopy, with a simple table occupying the space, and reliquaries were removed as well. Nothing conveying a sense that this space was a special sanctuary was allowed to remain. Most stained glass windows were removed, and walls were whitewashed.[13] Devotional practices condemned included lighting of

12. Ibid., 59.

13. Coster and Spicer, *Sacred Space*, 73.

candles, masses and prayers for the dead, and the veneration of saints, and therefore physical objects associated with these practices were removed.[14]

The orientation of worship was turned from the altar toward the pulpit,[15] located on a cluster of columns in the nave, and reached by a series of steps. Geneva's citizens were required to attend weekday and Sunday services. This worship took place in a simplified conceptual space now centered on the spoken Word, and also in a simplified physical space in terms of surface ornamentation. However, the structural contours of the architecture remained, of course, the same. The space itself was still grand. The eye was drawn even more inexorably to the sweep of the vaulted ceiling one hundred twenty feet above. Light from the clerestory windows could be experienced as other-worldly, with no pictorial depictions to distract from the light itself. The space did not specifically instruct the mind or invoke biblical stories as the visual themes before the Reformation did. Nonetheless, the dignity and sense of loftiness in the built space pointed to the sovereign grandeur and transcendent nature of God.

The space was also reconfigured with regard to the placement of the worshipers themselves. Now the faithful converged in the center of the church, fanning around the place where the sermons were preached, from the nave into the transepts, choir, and apse. Whereas the choir had been separated by a rood screen and reserved for clergy prior to the Reformation, now this distinction was dissolved. No longer was seating reserved, as prior to 1535, for clergy. Finally, in a striking innovation, benches were introduced for all worshipers, arranged in perpendicular blocks almost as an amphitheater, eventually accompanied with risers as well.

In his commentary on Exodus 25, in which the Israelites are given instructions for construction of the tabernacle, Calvin reflects on physical symbols of the divine glory. He writes,

> But we must beware of imagining anything inconsistent with the nature of God, for He who sits above the heavens, and whose footstool is the earth, could not be enclosed in the tabernacle; but, because in His indulgence for the infirmities of an ignorant people, He desired to testify the presence of His grace and help by a visible symbol, the earthly sanctuary is called His dwelling amongst men, inasmuch as there He was not worshipped in vain. And we must bear in memory what we have lately seen, that it was

14. Pettegree, *Reformation World*, 513.
15. Coster and Spicer, *Sacred Space*, 72.

not the infinite essence of God, but His name, or the record of His name that dwelt there.[16]

This indicates the grace of God's condescending to meet his people: though heaven and earth cannot contain God (echoing Solomon's prayer at the dedication of the temple, "But will God really dwell on earth? The heavens, even the highest heaven, cannot contain you. How much less this temple I have built!" (1 Kings 8:27) God cannot be contained, and yet demonstrates his grace in making himself accessible. To make allowance for human weakness, he testifies to his presence in the physical symbol of the sanctuary—and yet not in his essence but his name, even "a record of his name," that is his Word. Calvin continues, "God would have His Law deposited in a handsome vessel, in order that its majesty should be recognized. He commanded that the ark itself should be carried with staves, that the hands of the Levites might not touch it, and thus that its sanctity might be the greater."[17] On the surface, Calvin is commending excellence in artistic form, but only as a support for perceiving his true glory, which is his Word. Plastic form as well as artistic action in carrying the Ark of the Covenant, are to reinforce the perception of the sanctity of God in his self-revelation. While there seems to be some margin for artistic expression here, the operative principle is that God is not contained in or limited to such objects.

Changes in Reformed worship push us to ask how the space was used in post-Reformation St. Pierre. Essentially, it was used as a preaching hall, secondarily providing full access to the two biblical sacraments. Calvin's *Ecclesiastical Ordinances* of 1541 of the centrality of preaching, and thus of the pulpit, and called for the sacraments of Lord's Supper and baptism to be celebrated in proximity to the pulpit. "The tables should be set up close to the pulpit so that the mystery can be more suitably set forth nearby." The purpose for this is didactic and practical, because Calvin repudiated any attempt to localize the divine presence or to make one part of the church more sacred than another. He writes, in his commentary on Exodus,

> Now, under the gospel, we have no temple that sanctifies the gold, no altar that sanctifies the gift, but Christ only; and, as to the places of worship, the prophets foretold that *in every place* the spiritual *incense should be offered* (Mal 1:11). And our Savior has declared that those are accepted as true worshippers who

16. Calvin, *Calvin's Commentaries*, 2:173.

17. Ibid.

worship God in sincerity and truth, without regard either to this mountain or Jerusalem (John 4:23).[18]

No particular place was sacred, but the role of preaching was. In consequence, the new orientation of interior space took place in relation to the pulpit. The choir, previously reserved for clerics, no longer had a purpose in the arrangement of space within Reformed worship. Therefore the rood screen no longer served any purpose, having no need to separate the space reserved for clerics from space for the laity, and was dismantled.

In addition to the Protestant service of worship both on Sundays and weekdays, the space was used for council meetings, for teaching, and for other meetings. Overall configuration of space followed practical concerns for hearing and sightlines, and also made an unavoidable visual impression, particularly with what had been before. The pulpit occupied a place of particular prominence, affixed to the columns on the first bay at the transept, mounted by a winding staircase of twelve steps that coiled up to the an ornate Gothic pulpit, elevated some six feet above the floor of the nave. If the prominent—indeed, commanding—position of the pulpit suggested authority, it was an authority of the Word, based on an explanation of Scripture, now intelligible in the French tongue. A great abat-voix attached to the columns above the pulpit helped project the sound of the preacher and insure audibility across the great interior space. The shape of the church space, especially with the innovation of seating on benches, related to the dynamics of worship by allowing persons to focus attentively for longer periods. The central focus of attention was now on the pulpit and a moveable Lord's Table (in fact, two) rather than on altar, retable, choir, or rood screen. The preaching that took place in that setting was intended to elicit a respect for, and indeed an awe, of the sovereign grace of God, rather than a focus on the preacher himself. In that sense, the person was intended to be transparent, causing the audience to look through the preacher to the gospel proclaimed. When communion was celebrated, communicants would proceed to the table, one of which was probably located below the pulpit. The hoped-for outcome in the worshiper would be obedient faith, issuing in a godly life marked by good works. The overall effect on the person entering the newly "cleansed" church might well have been a new appreciation of the clarity of the gospel as embodied and symbolized in the worship space, and perhaps a sense of awe at the judgment of God that had stripped the church of vestiges of idolatry which had previously been so prized by

18. Ibid., 92.

the religious community. One imagines some must have felt a sense of humility or even of being ill-at-ease. If the aesthetic impact of entering the church prior to the Reformation impressed was to impress with a sense of leaving ordinary temporal and spatial reality and entering the sphere of the sacred, the aesthetic impact would now be that of entering a place where one attended to the words of a God who makes a claim on listeners, and a place where one consciously shares in communion with other believers. Intentionally, worship in St. Pierre was not an individualistic experience.

Perhaps this is why Calvin worried that private devotion might degenerate into spiritual fallacy. In his "Ordinances for the Supervsion of Churches in the Country," he insisted,

> Buildings are to remain shut for the rest of the time [apart from times of common worship], in order that no one outside the hours may enter for superstitious reasons. If anyone be found making any particular devotion inside or nearby, he is to be admonished; if it appear to be a superstition which he will not amend, he is to be chastised.[19]

Locked doors to the sanctuary, it was hoped, would prevent individuals from inappropriately venerating the space that was designed for the community of faith and for the purpose of edification by the teaching of God's Word. But Calvin had a further reason for barring access to the church during the week, as William Dyrness points out. Calvin was concerned that the Christian live out the faith in the setting of everyday life.

> He believed that all that goes on in the name of worship need not be confined to church buildings—for example, the believer can pray at home, at work, or while lying in bed. Indeed, for Calvin the focus of Christian worship and discipleship was not on the space of the church but on life in the world, what he frequently called a theatre for the glory of God.[20]

To focus on sacred space at the expense of discipleship in the world was to neglect God's calling to engage with and do justice in the world.

The symbolic resonance within the churches themselves would shift from objects distinguished by their "otherness"—due to their associations with hallowed persons, their artistic conventions that conveyed holiness, or their traditional connection with a venerable site of worship—to objects

19. Calvin, "Ordinances," 79.
20. Dyrness, *Poetic Theology*, 193.

that impress with their everyday character—a common domestic table, a speaker's podium, even the secular garb that replaced the priestly robes. Rather than the focus on artistic or religious richness, a sense of God's presence even through his physical absence brought, ironically, greater spiritual resonance. This was a new sort of sublimity, one in which God occupies the structures of everyday life and materiality.

THE CHURCH OF ST. GERVAIS-ST. PROTAIS, PARIS (1620)

We now turn to our second case study, the classical sacramental church of St. Gervais (the full name is St. Gervais-St. Protais, named in honor of twins martyred perhaps under the reign of Nero.) It is the fourth church in its location, where a church existed from at least the fifth century.[21] It is situated on a slight rise on the Right Bank in Paris, about one hundred yards from the Seine, just northeast of Notre Dame. The church was rebuilt after its destruction by the Normans in 886, and remodeled again in the thirteenth century to accommodate a larger parish, and consecrated in 1420. Of this edifice, only the lower portion of the tower remains, the church having been rebuilt once more in 1494 to allow for a larger congregation. Work continued on the church for over 150 years and was not finished until 1647, although a coherent design was maintained since the original plans were adhered to.

The church's architect is unknown, but Andrew Ayers points out that some have suggested the name of Martin Chambiges, builder of the transepts of the Beauvais cathedral and a parish member at St. Gervais. The interior of the building shows the sure hand of an accomplished designer, with a purity of design unified by Flamboyant Gothic sensibilities "such as vault responds and pier shafts and omission of disruptive components such as capitals."[22] Lancet windows exhibit bar tracery supported and articulated by slender mullions, and flying buttresses support the building with flayed stone tendrils.

Salomon de Brosse, who also designed the temple at Charenton, is generally accepted to be the designer of the façade, although he perhaps collaborated with Clément Métezeau, a royal architect with whom he worked on Marie de Médici's Palais de Luxembourg. Since de Brosse left no writings, we are left to analyze his work visually and compositionally by

---

21. I was helped on the historical data on this church by Ayers, *Architecture of Paris*.

22. Ibid., 90.

an examination of the façade itself. The closest stylistic antecedent for de Brosse's façade is de l'Orme's frontispiece of the Château of Anet, and also reflects a plate in Jacques Androuet du Cerceau's *Grands Temples*. In the St. Gervais church design, as he did with the châteaux he built at Blérancourt (c. 1612–19) and Coulommiers (began 1613), de Brosse eschewed superfluous decoration and emphasized the classical qualities of balance, mass, and clarity. In doing this, he developed a distinctly French form of the Roman Baroque style, moving it toward the clean and unadulterated forms of Neoclassicism. Although the Roman church front had already been built in France his was by far the most innovative in its use of classical vocabulary. Previous examples of the Roman style of the same kind were generally two stories, but de Brosse put three, as in the Anet front. On these three de Brosse affixed three superimposed orders, from Doric, to Ionic, and capped by Corinthian. Wood statues of Saints Gervais and Protais, carved in 1625, adorned interior chapels. Stone statues of the saints fill niches on the façade, although these were placed in the nineteenth century.

The problem confronting de Brosse was the design and construction of a classical façade on an existing Gothic building, and one of distinctly different proportion. In particular, for the architect to cover the projecting aisles and their buttresses would have forced the composition to be significantly wider, and thus taller in order to preserve classical dimensions. To solve this problem de Brosse left the aisles out of his design, allowing them to project beyond the façade but finishing them by rounding off; these remain visible on either side of the façade.

Figure 18: Illustration of the west front of St. Gervais.

It is interesting to compare the style of St. Gervais's façade (figure 18) with that of the church of St. Paul-St. Louis, a church of roughly the same period (1627) sponsored by Louis XIII and designed by architect François Derand, and modeled after the Gesù in Rome. The two churches are located less than seven hundred yards from each other between the Rue St. Antoine and the Rue de la Mortellerie, as seen on Turgot's Plan of 1734. St. Paul-St. Louis was built for the adjacent Jesuit Maison Professe and was first named "Église Saint-Louis de la Maison Professe des Jésuites," wherein the priests were bound by vows of poverty, chastity, obedience, and a fourth vow of special obedience to the Pope.

St. Paul—St. Louis shows the influence of Italian elements and Jesuit dictates combined with French local traditions. Its verticality approaches that of the Gothic style. The very ornate façade consists of three levels, like that of St. Gervais, but with Corinthian columns on the two lower levels, and composite Corinthian on the upper. An elliptical window on the second level pierces the façade above the main doors, the same height as niches to either side. The inspiration for the composition of the façade may indeed be the church of St. Gervais, begun nine years earlier. Both are organized upon three layers with double columns. Derand reverses de Brosse's treatment above the door and at the roofline, putting the rounded form above the entryway and the peaked pediment at the roofline. This creates stolid impression rather than one of lift as the eye moves from the main doors to scan the rest of the design. St. Paul-St. Louis's arrangement makes the columns nearly applied, adhering to the surface of the façade. Contrastingly, St. Gervais's plan makes the columns freestanding, producing deep shadows across the surface of the façade. In Durand's plan the columns, while doubled, are bordered by another column framing the niche, creating a cluster of three. De Brosse's model is more uniform, and thus classical: four pairs of columns on the first two levels create a rhythm that moves the eye laterally, giving pause as one is drawn inexorably upward. This is accomplished because the double columns reduce the horizontal space of the first two floors, creating a sense of upward thrust. A balustrade on the St. Paul-St. Louis façade seems to tamp down the whole.

The effect is more curvilinear than St. Gervais, a fusion of classical and Baroque, and wider than de Brosse's design. The columns are all Corinthian, clustered in threes to each side of the main door and the rose window. Derand has placed a straight pediment over the door and the second story.

Greatly ornamented, the effect is heavy rather than classical, with a bas-relief of garlands festooned between the Corinthian capitals.

In contrast, St. Gervais reads as a dignified and well-proportioned movement from Baroque to classical structure. Fourteen steps rise from the base to the doors. In spite of variations in dimensions to compensate for the psychology of visual perception, the eye reads the first and second stories as the same height, and the space between the exterior and interior double columns as analogous as well. The fluting on the first range of columns begins only a third of the way up from the base, lending a sense of anchoring without resorting to a heavier treatment of the base, preserving the slenderness of the composition and the sense of movement. Still, de Brosse, as had de l'Orme before him, went beyond conventional rules of design, engaging in visual play with displacement and architectural irregularities to intimate that the world is a depraved and disordered place.

If we apply Kieckhefer's method of looking at a church, we begin with two foundational questions. First, how is the space to be used? Second, what emotive reactions is the church meant to generate? In speaking of St. Gervais, the second question is especially applicable when focusing on the west front, as its façade was added to a building in existence for over a century and a half at the time of its construction. The church faces onto a substantial funnel-shaped square, providing perspective of the church front. Its setting establishes the church as an important parish in the urban center of Paris.

While façades often suggest themes carried out in the interior space of a church—frescoes, paintings, altarpieces, and statues, not to mention the repetition of architectural elements—the case of St. Gervais shows a façade style that is strikingly different from the rest of the church. Thus, the meaning of the church is paradoxical in that the architect's intentions and the experience of the building's users were, unlike at Charenton, not necessarily in alignment. The Catholics who commissioned the church front sought a visual statement that confirmed the rightness of the Catholic faith, a confirmation of their spirituality and tradition. De Brosse, according to the visual language he employed, at least desired to make a neutral statement, and perhaps on the contrary, endeavored to undermine the authorities who employed him. He artfully reorganized space, using horizontal planes to repudiate Catholic claims. In understanding the subtleties de Brosse's design, traditional and easy assumptions about patronage and conformity are resisted. Certainly his façade can be read in multiple ways. This is to be expected; if his intentions had been unambiguously clear, his subterfuge would have been ineffective.

The church front makes a particular aesthetic statement: in itself, it serves little purpose other than to close the unfinished edifice. As long as adequate doors pierced the front, any design would have served its basic function of allowing the passage of worshipers into the church. However, de Brosse's work is also sculptural, one that does not accommodate the visual language of the existing church but rather refutes it, alive as it writes contemporary meaning onto a dynamic tradition that is in contradiction with his own purposes. The front windows grow progressively larger as the eye moves from the ground floor entryway, to the second and then the third stories. The two side doors and double central doors seem vaguely inadequate, and the whole structure appears to renounce Catholic understanding of the transcendent, an opposite movement of that of instilling matter with spirit. De Brosse's art does more than emerge from the nature of the materials he uses or from the tradition he ostensibly glorified. It grows from his vision and intentionality, a creative exploit within the constraints of Catholic expectations.

Just as meaning derives from the dialogue (or argument) between the intention of the architect and the experience of the building's users, so also meaning comes from the interplay and intertextuality of vision and materials employed. The great arched doorways of the Gothic style would have logically finished the Gothic interior of St. Gervais, but instead the architect chose both a stylistic language and a specific compositional register that denounced the Catholic faith expressed in the rest of the building. This is in keeping with Kieckhefer's perspective that "the meanings of a church are seldom obvious." Traditional Gothic entrances tend to illustrate, with carved figures lining the tympanum, redemption and judgment.

Hints and echoes of a Reformed theology of creation, covenant, Fall, and redemption can be discerned in the façade, which moves substantially toward a classical style. First, humanity and everything that is not God owes its existence to God. One can only come to an awareness of this through revelation, from God's own self-witness in Scripture. The Apostles' Creed, important to the reformers for pedagogical purposes, affirms that "God the Father Almighty" is "maker of heaven and earth." This affirmation is made by faith, as the creed begins by stating, "I believe." Therefore, creation as well as redemption, which the second article of the creed addresses, is a matter to be received by faith. In the created pattern can be seen order, diversity, unity, intricacy, and beauty. These are characteristics of God himself, reflections of his perfections or attributes. In the church front, these are echoed in the balance, the repetition of form creating pattern—a visual organizational principle analogous for meaning—and the upward thrust, reminding the sensitive viewer that the material order has not been created for its own sake but to enjoy a relationship with its Creator. Creation suggests a hand behind it. De Brosse's church front highlights order, rhythm, and rationality, hallmarks of the creation story and of Christian identity.

The St. Gervais façade ultimately (and intentionally) fails to satisfy; it is meant not as an end in itself but, as with all churches, as a portal into the church interior and into an encounter with the divine. But further, it symbolically witnesses to the futility of self-referential humanity as well as of self-satisfied religion. In addition, creation was an act of grace, the work of God apart from any human merit. Just as humans can only perceive the divine basis and origin of the creation of the cosmos by faith, so creation *ex nihilo* itself is an act for which there is no innate human capacity.

A second important Reformed perspective is that of covenant. In the opening of his *Institutes*, Calvin writes of God's glory shining from creation, which serves to a degree as a mirror in which the invisible God can be considered. Creation portrays God's glory (his radiance, fame, or beauty), calling as such for a response of wonder and worship. Creation testifies that the Triune God is not alone, but wills to draw creation into relationship with his Son and the Holy Spirit. God does not, then, exist to the exclusion of all other forms and life; rather, God created man in the *imago dei* as the summit of creation. The frontispiece of St. Gervais, with its regularity and apparent comprehensibility invites one to approach; the large rounded central door, not set deep in shadow as with a Gothic or even Renaissance elevation, seems to call one to worship, the creature into communion with its Creator. Humanity, as is nature, is the theater for God's covenant of grace, and, as male and female expresses the relational quality of the deity. The classicism of the front draws one closer even as it lifts the spirit upward.

A third Reformed point of emphasis is the fall from grace. In the Augustinian and Reformed way of thinking, the effects of Adam's and Eve's sin are passed on corporately to humanity. As stated in Calvin's *French Confession*, humanity is "par sa propre faute déchu de la grâce qu'il avait reçue» ("by its own fault is torn from the grace it had received." Article IX). Human nature is no longer pristine, but is in rebellion against God by trying to take the place of God. Human persons tend to be enticed by earthly things, but if our attention stops there, then "the world, which has been created as the mirror of God, must be its own creator." (1.5.5) However, in a particularly visual description of fallen humanity in creation, Calvin asserts that "the luster of the world, while it appears great to our eyes, dazzles them so much that "the glory of God" is, as it were, hidden in darkness." (On Titus 2:13; CO 52.424). The effect of this original sin is repeated in each person, who now possesses enough knowledge of God to make him or her guilty and accountable to God, but not enough to affect salvation. We can see, but cannot apprehend, God apart from grace. Appearances are now ambiguous and deceiving. Visually, this is suggested by a kind of push-pull effect: the edifice of St. Gervais invites, but it also seems to push the viewer away; it lifts the eye to heaven, but appears to tamp down human aspiration with its horizontal movement.

A fourth Reformed perspective is redemption. This takes place, paradoxically, when human hopes are demolished, when sinners become aware of their utter incapacity. Any sense of redemption suggested by the exterior of St. Gervais is subtle, not proclaimed with resounding portrayals of Christ in glory or at the Day of Judgment, though perhaps suggested by the presence of angels. But to de Brosse and his Reformed brethren, salvation is not to be found in the Catholic Church, in human endeavor, or in the slightest cooperation with grace. The absence of a clear proclamation of salvation serves as a judgment on Catholic dogma, symbolized by the emphatic down stroke of ten pairs of double columns, calling to mind the Decalogue, a Reformed theme and one judging the false teaching of Catholicism. The renewed classical style, then, is placed in service of Reformed theology.

In the case of St. Gervais the question of how the church is used is at best a secondary issue when considering its façade. In comparison, the question of what sort of reaction the façade intends to stimulate is a complex one. There are at least two possible intended imports, with one meaning aimed for the Catholics and another intrinsic one for Protestants and or perhaps simply for the architect. For the former, surface meaning accentuates Catholic faith. But both communicate a different aspect of creation, one distorted by the Fall, causing disorder and disorientation, a world positioned under God's wrath. The central focus of attention is the upper story with its rounded window, but from there the eye has nowhere to go; the upward thrust is arrested by the round pediment.

The overall configuration exhibits a certain elegance, but a troubled one. The columns convey a restrictive sense, allowing little relief, as if bars to hold a person inside and to contain Catholic power. The horizontal bands, on second look, obstruct the vertical movement and seem to constrict the composition. The windows, of leaded rather than stained glass, are an act of Protestant iconoclasm, removing the means for drawing tinted light into the structure. Due to a series of steps, the church enjoys a position on a slight rise, affording perspective and a sense of grandeur. However, the frontispiece itself has no base. Its only visual foundation is made up of the column bases, a design tactic suggesting that the church itself has no foundation. The Calvinist architect is undermining the validity and authenticity of the Catholic Church.

The inclination of de Brosse and other Reformed architects toward variations of the classical style raises the question of why these were felt to be a fit vessel for expressing their Protestant faith. Reasons for their embracing classicism as an appropriate means of expression seem to include its visual repudiation of the Catholic style, its implementation of the ancient Vitruvian Orders, and its unostentatious dignity a fitting expression of reformed theology.

THE SECOND TEMPLE OF CHARENTON (1623)

> Ne voulez vous pas maintenant vous évertuer, vous élever avec le petit enfant David, prenant votre bâton pastoral, le glaive tranchant, qui est la parole évangélique laquelle Dieu vous a donné par son enfant sortant de sa bouche pour aller sans aucun empêchement a luy, manger du fruit de l'arbre de vie pour résister hardiment à l'encontre de votre ennemie, le grand dragon roux, serpent ancien, qui est la bête épouvantable appelé le grand diable satrape de l'Antéchrist de Rome. [23]
>
> Pour détruire et abolir l'idolâtrie et toutes superstitions qui règne pour aujourd'hui dans l'église de Satan, dont l'Antéchrist en est le chef, a été composé cette présente oraison . . . par laquelle il

---

23. *La Prophétie des petits enfants : Tout est à Dieu: Pseaume 8.* "Will you not now grow in virtue, and lift yourself with the little child David, taking your pastoral rod, the sharp blade that is the evangelical Word by which God gave you in his words of the mouth of his child to protect you from every distraction, to eat the fruit of the tree of life, in order to hardily resist your enemy the great red dragon, that ancient serpent, the terrible beast which is called the devil, the satrap of the Antichrist of Rome."

est défendu de ne faire ni images ni idoles . . . par laquelle nous
est démontré sa grande bonté en l'humanité de son Fils nôtre Seigneur Jésus Christ pour l'édification de son église . . .[24]

The above quote illustrates Protestant theological concerns underlying design issues. In this little scriptural exposition of Psalm 8, written by
an unknown author in 1562 (the same year as the massacre of Vassy), we
see a clear affirmation of Reformed values. It begins with a pastoral appeal,
entreating the reader to humble him or herself and learn from Scripture
("this psalm of David,") wherein God ordains praise for himself from the
lips of infants. Indeed the entire purpose of the people of God is to render
him honor, to give him glory. In turning to Word of God in Scripture one
turns to Christ the Living Word, which will strengthen the true believer to
resist the wiles of the devil, who is the servant of the Antichrist, the Roman pope. The author's purpose in writing is to confront the idolatry and
superstition now reigning in the Catholic Church ("the church of Satan.")
The only way of knowing God is through faith in his son Jesus Christ.

The Physical Structure of the Church at Charenton

These values came to visual expression in the construction of the Protestant Temple of Charenton, our third case study. For the French Protestants,
strict adherence to the words of Scripture was a matter of spiritual life and
death, a commitment to which might put physical life in danger. The alternative was to repeat the idolatries of the Catholic Church, anathema to the
Huguenots. In this following section, we shall investigate the material shape
of the Temple of Charenton and seek to uncover its theological meanings.

In France, Protestants sometimes preferred to (or were forced to)
build new churches rather than use existing churches, monasteries, and
abbeys, even in the territories where they were ascendant.[25] Protestants
regarded Catholic worship spaces as tainted with idolatry. More than in
Geneva, where to be a citizen meant to be a member of the church, the
church was considered the gathered community of believers, the body of

---

24. *La Prophétie des petits enfants.* "To destroy and bring down idolatry and all super-
stitions that reign today in the church of Satan, of which the Antichrist is the head, this
present oration has been composed . . . which forbids the making of images and idols . . .
God the Father shows his great goodness in the humanity of his Son, our Savior Jesus
Christ, for the up-building of his church."

25. Spicer, "Qui est de Dieu," 185.

Christ. The temple constituted the physical place where the community gathered and inevitably served as an embodiment and architectural expression of their convictions. It was here they heard the Word rightly exposited and celebrated the sacraments. It was here, among the various other arenas of their lives, they met together for prayer. Here, too, the consistory met to govern the church, admonish the wayward, and administer the church's discipline.

Many of the same characteristics sought by the Reformed congregation of St. Pierre church in Geneva—spaciousness, light, and orientation to the pulpit—would apply to Charenton as well. In contrast to the ancient St. Pierre, the Temple of Charenton was built in the seventeenth century for the Parisian Protestant community within the period of relative calm under the Edict of Nantes. The edict mandated civil rights for Protestants but also enshrined their status as second-class citizens.[26] Similarly, it made concession for the construction of Protestant temples, but only within restricted areas, and not inside episcopal cities such as Paris. In consequence, the Reformed community erected their building outside the city in Charenton-sur-Pont, to the southeast of the Bois de Vincennes, replacing the first Parisian temple at Ablon near Fontainebleau. The architect of the first Charenton temple in 1607, which subsequently burned, was Jacques-Androuet II du Cerceau, who designed Ablon; his nephew Salomon de Brosse designed the second temple in 1621. Randall maintains that this edifice, a Vitruvian-inspired basilican form, would serve in many ways as the model Protestant temple for other lands,[27] although perhaps not as often as she implies; an octagonal or oval plan proved more popular in many places though more difficult to construct, since those had better acoustics; indeed, the layout of the common space reminds one of a theater, albeit one dedicated to preaching. In addition, a characteristic of Huguenot construction, perhaps for reasons of stewardship as well as for economic ones, is the use of local building materials. The model of the Temple of Charenton was suited for use in that context, using both recycled and local materials, but other contexts demanded their own solutions.

In an era when French Renaissance architects looked to Italy, it is possible that architects of Huguenot churches such as the Temple de Paradis in Lyons or the Temple de Quevilly may have found their inspiration in the Pantheon-influenced drawings of du Cerceau. De Brosse's Charenton stands

26. Randall, *Building Codes*, 12.
27. Guicharnaud, "Architecture," 136.

in contrast to the many octagonal (or as many as twelve-sided) churches in Quevilly, Lyons, La Rochelle, Caen, and other places. Rectangular temples such as Charenton symbolically related the Protestants to the ancients.

Reformed temples in general needed to be differentiated from Catholic churches, and did so overall by giving priority to the preaching of the Word. The structures tended to two basic patterns, the basilican or longitudinal and the centralized plan,[28] harkening back to Roman and ancient Christian meeting places. Both were barn-like buildings without the transepts or apses of Gothic churches, intended to facilitate the act of preaching.

De Brosse's Temple of Charenton fit the former category, a rectilinear shape with a two-story hipped roof punctuated by twenty two-story interior Doric columns, with a tiled floor and a platform and pulpit one third of the way into the space.[29] The building was three stories high, and, in one of the most characteristic touches associated with Reformed temples, ringed with two interior galleries behind balustrades that put more worshipers in proximity to the preacher than would otherwise be possible. These galleries, supported by two-story columns, increased seating capacity and provided sound and a clear view of the pulpit. The building measured nearly one hundred ten feet long and nearly sixty-five feet wide,[30] contained nine bays, and was constructed of sandstone and limestone. Large doors (over six feet wide) pierced the structure at either end and on its sides, allowing large crowds to gather at one time. Twenty-six large windows were placed on each side, alternating between rounded and rectangular, including nine per side that cut into the roofline, allowing the interior maximum light. The walls were plain and whitewashed, and the windows leaded but without stained glass. Many of the materials, including windows and oak beams, had been recycled from the temple at Ablon when it was dismantled. The only exterior embellishment was a square bell tower on the roof, making a landmark visible from some distance. The two Charenton temples, du Cerceau's and de Brosse's, exhibited some continuity with the design of Ablon. Every element was planned so that the worshipers could

28. Ibid.

29. Douen, *La Révocation*, 111–56. I rely on Douen for a detailed history and description of the church. He quotes the description provided in the Mercure Galant, February 1686, as does the Bulletin de la Société de l'histoire du protestantisme français: documents historiques et inédits, XVIe, XVIIe et XVIIIe ciècles, vol. 5, (Paris: 1852), and Jacques-Antoine Dulaure, Histoire physique, civile et morale des environs de Paris, depuis les premiers temps historiques jusqu'à nos jours, vol. 6, (Paris: Guillaume, 1827).

30. Finney, *Seeing Beyond the Word*, 138.

see and hear what took place within its four walls, and the focus was corporate more than individual. As with Reformed churches in general, there was space for assembly in which worshipers had clear sight lines of the preacher/worship leader and of other worshipers. There was an absence of chapels for private contemplation. The effect of these characteristics was that the temple was oriented not toward private mystical experience, but to the experience of common worship. Guicharnaud praises the second temple's "exceptional architectural quality."[31] De Brosse's architectural elevations reveal it to be a structure of proportion and forcefulness.

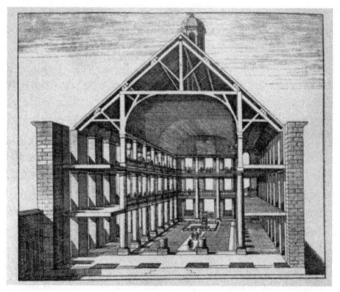

Figure 19: Cutaway view of the front of the Charenton temple.

Aside from the temple interior's simplicity and freedom from statues, stained glass, and paintings, it included pews, a Protestant preference (figure 19). This signaled to the worshipers the importance of sitting still and paying attention to the preaching of the sermon, whereas before the Reformation, the focus had been on the Mass, and the seating had typically been only for the clergy. The seating was arranged in a grid, which can be seen from period engravings of the temple interior. Other objects in the church were for the instruction of the faithful, including a very large plaque inscribed with the Ten Commandments situated above the pulpit.

31. Guicharnaud, "Architecture," 139.

What the Builder Was Attempting to Say

The Temple of Charenton was an expression of the new Calvinist spirit of worship: spare, simple, arresting, and designed to focus on the Word of God, exemplified by the priority given to pulpit, and secondarily, to the sacraments of baptism and the Lord's Supper. If it was clear of many of the traditions and visual expressions of Catholic tradition, it did retain some, including an approximation of an altar in the communion table, and a baptismal font. The purpose in plainness was not to squelch beauty or creative spirit, but that all might participate, hearing and understanding the teaching of Scripture, rather than simply watch as uncomprehending spectators.

James F. White has opined, "Protestants expect to be edified in worship, Catholics to be sanctified."[32] If White is correct, then the purpose of Reformed worship space is not plainness for its own sake, but that the assembled faithful actively participate in worship without distraction, rather than be reduced to distant observers to the Mass they could neither hear nor understand. If the architecture seems spare, it is far from artless; Charenton's design communicated the spiritual aspirations of the congregation.

Charenton calls to mind the severe aesthetic of early Christian meeting places and the dimensions of the Old Testament Temple at Jerusalem. The church's lack of non-essential decoration, such as stained glass, statues, paintings, and reliquaries, is a deliberate attempt to make the message of the gospel clear for all. Its form was adapted to its intended function, which, in turn, reinforced the value of intelligibility, decency, and order. If the Catholic faith displayed more symbols with imaginative meaning, perhaps those of the Protestant temple assumed all the more symbolic power as intensified focal points in the gathered community, regulated by the Word of God as the essential element of Reformed worship. All other aesthetic and architectural concerns are sublimated to that overriding purpose. Catholics might have criticized Protestant temples as looking like secular buildings with a bell tower added to the roof. In poorer communities, simplicity of decoration could simply be the result of financial concerns. But the theological rationale for Huguenot churches meant they *should* resemble secular buildings, with little in the structure to draw attention to itself. Rather it should serve as a call to give proper attention to God.

Like other important Protestant temples, Charenton displayed an elegant system of proportion, even if it was marked by sobriety and severity

---

32. White, "From Protestant to Catholic," 462.

when compared with Catholic churches (see figure 20). Four doors pierced the structure, one on each side of its rectilinear plan, with keystones of shaped stone. Pilasters framed the lines of windows, an entablature tracing the four sides of the building, and a pinnacle crowning the roof. Aside from the practical benefit of the multiple entryways, they symbolically emphasized the accessibility of the Reformed order of worship. The large scale of the windows allowed abundant light, itself a symbol of the glory and revelation of God to flood the space, reminding those in attendance that God is ineffable light. The medieval belief was that all light radiated from God, and now, without stained glass, that light could be seen as an unobstructed reflection of God's splendor. The overall effect was one of monumentality, solidity, and classicism, a striking contrast with the Catholic preference for Mannerist expressiveness. The copy of the tablets of the Ten Commandments on the east wall signaled a commitment to the Law as the appropriate response to the preaching of the gospel, a particular Reformed emphasis. Beyond the apparent simplicity of design, the structure revealed biblical priorities of this place of Reformed worship: sobriety, stewardship, community, attentiveness to the commands of God.

Figure 20: Side elevation of Charenton, showing columns, balustrades, and lantern.

Interior walls were plastered with lime and sand, lending a soft grey or white effect. As with Calvin's church, the temple expressed a preference for lack of color, displaying tints only subtly with scriptural inscriptions such as the letters on the tablets of the Ten Commandments. The church also possessed an organ, a gift of the La Tour d'Auvergne family to aid in congregational singing.

Unlike the Catholics, who employed many visual elements and an array of statues and symbols, Protestant de Brosse worked within the constraints of the streamlined basilican form of temple (see figure 21). Nevertheless, within these restrictions his church at Charenton provided a visible witness to the presence of religious pluralism and the durability of the Reformed faith. The Calvinistic architectural aesthetic of testing all things by Scripture animated de Brosse's vision for this important church building, an echo of the biblical vision of the heavenly Jerusalem. With the simplicity of materials employed at Charenton, de Brosse suggests that faithful stewardship is more important than convention, and that beauty resides in a grace-filled community of the body of Christ. It was not a soul-numbing utilitarianism that comprised the Reformed aesthetic, but rather a biblical symbolism translated into abstract architectural form for the edification of the church.

Figure 21: Perspective drawing of Charenton.

What were the actual patterns of usage in the Charenton temple, and how did these conform to or conflict with the intentions of de Brosse? This is an area unexamined by Catharine Randall. Information is scarce since the temple and all its records were destroyed in 1685 with the Edict of Fontainebleau, and de Brosse himself failed to leave any written record of his architectural work, but some of the patterns of usage at Charenton may be deduced by considering the usage of other temples such as the Temple du Paradis in Lyons.[33]

The temple would have been used for a range of activities from the meeting of the consistory to catechetical instruction of youth. However, the defining use of the building was the Lord's Day worship of the whole gathered community. The very large size, seating four thousand, ensured sufficient room for all the members of the church, and the multiple entries allowed for efficient movement of human traffic. The proportion and elegance of the edifice, as well as the use of building materials, would not have failed to impress worshipers with its beauty and stability.

From the central focus upon the pulpit, one's gaze moved upward to the tablets of the Ten Commandments on the wall high above. Most impressive, however, was no particular object but rather the upward movement of the columns, the generous and impressive endowment of windows, and the quality of light itself, creating an aura of light behind the pulpit and covering the entire east elevation. Together, these structural and aesthetic qualities exemplified the Vitruvian ideals of firmness, commodity, and delight. They suggested a modern style as opposed to that of Catholic tradition, and yet continuity with ancient classicism. The mark of holiness would have been the community of believers itself, symbolized in the space dedicated to Reformed worship. Its symbolic resonance centered on the Word of God and hence was primarily verbal and literary, and yet its visual symbols were significant in their own bracing fashion.

We may safely assume a significant correspondence between de Brosse's intended use of the space and its actual use by the worshiping community, since the architect himself shared the congregation's faith tradition. Since he knew the community, just as he knew du Cerceau, he naturally understood its history, hopes, and conflicts with the larger Catholic culture. That he produced a structure of cultural validity suggests a vital relationship between designer and the users of the space. John Turner's point about housing applies to the congregation's use of worship space, as well: "When dwellers control the major decisions and are free to make their own contributions in the design, construction, or management of their housing, both this process and the environment produced stimulate individual and social

33. Benedict, *Graphic History*, 55.

well-being."[34] The experience of worship at Charenton must have evoked a sense of Israel going out to the desert to worship the Lord because of the physical distance of the temple from the center of Paris. On Sunday mornings, worshipers would leave from the tip of the Ile de la Cité behind Notre-Dame for the short trip upriver to Charenton, singing psalms once they had passed the limits of the city.

Figure 22: The destruction of the Temple de Charenton following the Edict of Fontainebleau in 1685, sixty-two years after its construction.

Being forced to worship outside the boundaries of the city and away from the places they lived and worked would have engendered a sense of alienation and of the Huguenots' identity as a pilgrim people. As members travelled through the suburbs toward their church, a kinesthetic dynamic shaped spiritual consciousness. This church, so formative for Protestant identity, would stand for eighty-two years until the general destruction of Reformed churches following the Edict of Fontainebleau in 1685 (SEE FIGURE 22).

The physical building, just as a human person, is an embodied reality. This means that the second Temple of Charenton existed not just as a material artifact, but in time and space, reminding the Huguenot community housed there of their journey as a scripturally-defined people. This case study shows that while physical movement and physical structure both emphasized the Huguenots' outsider status in society, they also strengthened their communal and theological identity. And when the church at Charenton was no more, its design still served as inspiration for Reformed

34. Turner, *Freedom to Build*, 241.

building in places of the Huguenot diaspora, as well as a place of memory in the Huguenot imagination. Thinking about how we construct spaces of worship not only tells us much about the cultural inheritance of our values from a historical standpoint, but encourages us to think about how to use physical spaces as conduits for the spiritual.

In sum, the example of Charenton has shown the intentionality of design in French Protestant churches. This suggests the importance of physical space in creating theological space for renewal, but it also raises questions about its limitations: the design qualities of the church underscored the theological tenets of the Reformed faith with their clarity and apparent simplicity. But were they also capable of misinterpretation or misreading? Certainly, the efficacy of these qualities depended on their sanctification by the reading and the clear preaching of the Word of God.

CHAPTER 8

A Distinctively Reformed Voice

There is certainly nothing so obscure or contemptible, even in the smallest corners of the earth, in which some marks of the power and wisdom of God may not be seen; but as a more distinct image of him is engraved on the heavens . . . their splendor might lead us to contemplate all parts of the world. When a man, from beholding and contemplating the heavens, has been brought to acknowledge God, he will learn also to reflect upon and to admire his wisdom and power as displayed on the face of the earth, not only in general, but even in the minutest plants.[1]

THE CREATED WORLD CAN only be apprehended through aesthetic perception, which takes place through feeling. Architecture is a visual rhetoric analogous to Calvin's use of rhetoric, and is similarly meant to teach and persuade—to instruct, and to move the viewer through one's emotions towards a higher ideal. These faculties are not far from a sense of the sacred. Philip Sheldrake has suggested that space should not be seen as "absolute, infinite, empty, and a priori."[2] It is rather always experienced locally and particularly as place. Yet this dynamic exists in tension with the Christian expectation of future fulfillment, and with the rootless condition of those called to go into all the world, a pilgrim people who encounter God not just in particular places but everywhere.

1. Calvin, *Commentary on the Psalms*, 19:1.
2. Sheldrake, *Spaces for the Sacred*, 6.

Reformed faith and Catholic faith are two distinct ways of seeing reality and of perceiving religious truth. Catholics in the Reformation era experienced God through a heightened sensitivity to sacred space. Yet Protestants did as well, though in different modes. To say that only explicit illustration, or pictorial artistic depiction has the capacity to express the sacred, is to overlook the power of negation, the *via negativa,* as with the post-exilic Jerusalem temple from which the ark of the covenant had disappeared since the time of the Babylonian captivity. Sometimes, what is absent evokes more strongly than what is present. The stripped churches of Geneva and Charenton both conveyed the values of a biblical, anti-idolatry, rigorous faith that depended on hearing and doing the Word, of willingly living under the (empty) cross, and not on attaching oneself to sacred objects. The same value would come through with Calvin's instructions that he was to be buried in an unmarked grave when he died, leaving no monument to himself but for the church reforming according to Scripture. Calvin's words on communion provide a fitting conclusion to his understanding of the possibility of sacred space:

> For though he has taken his flesh away from us, and in the body has ascended into heaven, yet he sits at the right hand of the Father—that is, he reigns in the Father's power and majesty and glory. This Kingdom is neither bounded by location in space nor circumscribed by any limits as the symbols invite us to him in his wholeness.[3]

In the Renaissance view of plenitude, the talented artist is the master of erudition and invention. We see those qualities in the Reformed architects discussed above, and a forging of a new Reformed style combining functionality, stylistic restraint, and harmony in which each aspect of decorative design was deliberated afresh. In addition to their contribution to a Reformed and Huguenot style, we see their involvement in creating a Neoclassical architecture, one that came to be seen in France as a distinctive national style, as was seen in nascent form in the churches of St. Gervais and Charenton.

This study has sought to understand two divergent ways of perception, Catholic and Protestant, and to recognize the implications of these ways of seeing in distinct architectural forms. These forms are either seen as significant in themselves as conduits of grace, as in the case of Catholic space, or, with representational Protestant space, intended to lead to an

3. Calvin, *Institutes,* 4.17.18.

objective encounter with the God who is present even in his apparent absence. The Catholic imagination focused on images, which it found to be icons of grace, and indeed this is the crux of the Reformation controversy over idolatry. Images were "idolatrous" because they were subjective, only able to reflect back to viewers representations of themselves. The experience of an icon, relic, or altar was only able to engender an experience of the self, which was then projected upon the divine. The reason idolatry seemed so abhorrent for Huguenots and other Reformed Christians was that it blocked the possibility of a true encounter with God. For them, Catholic rejection of Scripture entailed exchanging the glory of God for self-glory. The result of self-serving worship is heaven's condemnation; only worship according to the regulative principle of Scripture, in the view of French and Swiss Protestants, is capable of pleasing God. Faith centered on material realities is inseparable from one's own projections and imaginings. The clearest image of grace, then, is not the Eucharistic host, nor even the cross, but a covenant community of believers who hear the Word of Scripture and come to the obedience of faith. In this alone may we be addressed by God, and learn to see objectively.

The works of de Brosse and other Protestant architects who shared these convictions helped shape the visual rhetoric that came to express the new Reformed imagination. They did this first by resisting the embellishment characteristic of Mannerist, and later Baroque design, as expressive of idolatrous wanderings and instead uniquely gave rise to a visual, Protestant rhetoric. This was largely accomplished through recovering the classical Orders and their structure—inscribing Protestant faith onto the classical pattern—as coherent with the plan of God who shaped creation and calls his people into covenant community. Architecture was therefore integrated into the Protestant expression of faith in unprecedented ways. Yet its significance in understanding Reformation ideas on buildings and sacred space has been largely overlooked; to continue to do so risks neglecting important insights into how ideas of visuals and sacred space contributed to the formation of a rational and articulate Reformation theology, and in turn to the practice of piety. Reformed iconoclasm was a statement—not merely a peevish payback for Catholic oppression, but a statement of the core belief that the idolatry expressed by images obscured God's true glory.

Protestant architects and designers working in France and Switzerland believed themselves to be participating in a recovery of nature as part of a larger work in which God was restoring creation and making a new Eden, presaging the scientific revolution. This is tied to the concept of civility as an improvement of space—important to the developments of towns, buildings that promoted "true" values and pure faith, and to keeping people in a state of understanding and dignity. Rather than alienation, the vision of the whole realm of nature as the Lord's lent a sense of gratitude and stewardship. In this innovative Reformed visual rhetoric, new symbols reflected the transcendence and immanence of God through light, space, community, and a visual language distinguished by sobriety, simplicity, power, and even elegance. It is not impossible to discern in this development the beginnings of the Neoclassical movement in French architecture.

Since the Huguenots were forced to practice their faith in a hostile larger culture, they developed a unique style of church building in which space was not seen as sacred in itself, but was nonetheless able to communicate powerfully the presence and purpose of God among his people. The repudiation of idols and the embrace of the single authority of the Word also insured a hundred fifty years of irreconcilable conflict between the Church of Rome and the new Reformed faith, each on opposite trajectories springing from divergent ways of seeing.

Therein lies the paradox, that God transcends space, but that if there is no set dwelling place for God, then perhaps he can reside in naturalism, in spiritualism, in every religion, and in the subjectivism of the individual mind. Huguenot architects like de Brosse recognized the difficulty in drawing worshipers towards holiness through space, insisting that God does not need that space and cannot be limited by it. The human imagination and our ways of seeing need constraints. The architects mentioned above worked to provide these boundaries while acknowledging the inherent contradiction between human structures and the boundlessness of God.

The Huguenot preoccupation with the idolatry of "superstition" and its redefinition of iconology reflect a Reformed way of seeing, one that has helped change the way we perceive architectural space even today. Their habits of theology, worship, and design can still raise pertinent questions about straightforwardness, community, and how we understand the ability of Scripture to shape our manner and places of worship.

Appendix

ARCHITECTURAL MANUSCRIPTS OR PRINTS PUBLISHED IN FRANCE, WRITTEN IN FRENCH OR TRANSLATED INTO FRENCH (SIXTEENTH AND SEVENTEENTH CENTURIES)[1]

Albenas, Jean Poldo d' (1508–1580)

Alberti, Leo Battista (1404–1472)

Androuet du Cerceau, Jacques (1511–1585/86)

Aviler, Augustin-Charles d' (1653–1701)

Bachot, Ambroise (15?–16?)

Barbaro, Daniele (1513–1570)

Barbet, Jean (ca. 1605–av. 1654)

Bartoli, Cosimo (1503–1572)

Bassi, Martino (1542–1591)

Bernard, Jean (15?–16?)

Béroalde de Verville, François (1556–1626)

Bertin, Dominique (15?–1578)

Besson, Jacques (ca. 1530–1573)

Binet, Étienne (1569–1639)

Bitainvieu, Silvère de, also Du Breuil, Jean (1618–1686)

---

1. Lemerle and Pauwels, "Architecture, Textes, et Images."

Blondel, François (1618–1686)

Blunt, Hans (ca. 1520–ca. 1560)

Böckler, Georg Andreas (seventeenth century)

Boillot, Joseph (1545/50–1605)

Bosse, Abraham (ca. 1604–1676)

Bouquet, Simon (sixteenth century)

Bourdin, Pierre (1595–1653)

Boyceau de la Barauderie (15?–16?)

Brosse, Salomon de (ca. 1571–1626)

Bullant, Jean (15?–1578)

Bullet, Pierre (1639–1716)

Cataneo, Girolamo (15?–1584)

Cataneo, Pietro (15?–1569)

Catherinot, Nicolas (1628–1688)

Caus, Salomon de (1576–1626)

Cesariano, Cesare (1483–1543)

Chastillon, Claude (ca. 1560–1616)

Coecke van Aelst, Pieter (1502–1550)

Collot, Pierre (seventeenth century)

Colonna, Francesco (1433?–1527)

Common, Charles (seventeenth century)

Cousin, Jean (ca. 1490–ca. 1560)

Crescenzi, Pietro de (1230–1320?)

Dan, Pierre (seventeenth century)

Daret, Pierre (1604–1678)

De l'Orme, Philibert (1514–1570)

Derand, François (1588?–1644)

Desargues, Girard (1591–1661)

Desgodets, Antoine (1653–1728)

Deville, Antoine (1596–1657)

Dietterlin, Wendel (ca. 1550–1599)

Dögen, Matthias (1605:1606–1672)

Du Breuil, Jean (1602–1670)

Dürer, Albrecht (1471–1528)

Errard, Jean (1554–1610)

Estienne, Charles (1504–1564)

Fabre, Jean (15?–16 ?)

Faventinus Marcus Cetius (third century)

Félibien, André (1619–1695)

Félibien des Avaux, Jean-François (1658?–1733)

Flamant, Claude (1570–1626)

Fournier, Georges (1595–1652)

Francart, Jacques (1583–1651)

Francini (Francine) Alessandro (Alexandre) (15?–1648)

Fréart de Chambray, Roland (1606–1676)

Freitag, Adam (1602–1664)

Gardet, Jean (sixteenth century)

Gentillâtre, Jacques (1587–1623?)

Giocondo, Giovanni Monsignori Fra (1433–1515)

Girard, Albert (1595–1632)

Girard, Jean (1639–ca. 1708)

Goldmann, Nicolaus (1611–1665)

Goujon, Jean (ca. 1510–ca. 1566)

Grapaldi, Francesco Maria (1464?–1515)

Grapheus (De Schrijvers) Cornelius (Cornelis) (1482–1558)

Guarini, Guarino (1624–1683)

Hondius, Hendrik (1573–1650)

Jousse, Mathurin (ca. 1575–1645)

Kasemann, Rutger (ca. 1589–1645)

Labacco, Antonio (1495–ca. 1568)

La Hire, Gabriel-Philippe de (1677–1719)

Lauro, Pietro (ca. 1510–ca. 1568)

Le Blond, Jacques (seventeenth century)

Leclerc, Sébastien (1634–1714)

Le Muet, Pierre (1591–1669)

Lepautre, Antoine (1621–1679)

Lepautre, Jean (1618–1682)

Leu, Thomas de (1560–1612)

Liébault, Jean (ca. 1534–1596)

Lochom, Michel van (1601–1647)

Loris, Daniel (seventeenth century)

Loyseleur de Villiers, Pieter (ca. 1530–1590)

Malthus, Francis (16?–1658)

Manesson Mallet, Allain [Alain] (1630–1706)

Marolois, Samuel (ca. 1572–1627)

Marot, Jean (1619–1679)

Martellange, Étienne (1569–1641)

Martin, Jean (ca. 1507–ca. 1553)

Mauclerc, Julien (ca. 1543–ca. 1608)

Menessier, B. (seventeenth century)

Meynier, Honorat (ca. 1570–1638)

Milliet de Chales, Claude-François (1621–1678)

Mollet, André (ca. 1600–1665)

Mollet, Claude I (ca. 1557–1647)

Nicéron, Jean-François (1613–1646)

Ouvrard, René (1624–1694)

Pagan, Blaise-François de (1604–1665)

Palissy, Bernard (ca. 1510–1589)

Palladio, Andrea (1508–1580)

Pasini, Aurelio (15?–16?)

Pélerin, Jean, also Viator (ca. 1445–ca. 1524)

Pérelle, Gabriel (1603–1677)

Perrault, Charles (1628–1708)

Perrault, Claude (1613–1688)

Perret, Jacques (1540/45–1610/19)

Philandrier, Guillaume (1505–1565)

Prado, Jeronimo (1547–1595)

Procope de Césarée (ca. 500–ca. 562)

Ramelli, Agostino (1530–1608 ?)

Renty, Gaston de (1611–1649)

Ryff, Walther Hermann (1500–1548)

Sagredo, Diego de (ca. 1490–1528)

Sambin, Hugues (1520?–1601)

Sardi, Pietro (1560–1642?)

Sauval, Henri (1620–1676)

Savot, Louis (ca. 1579–1640)

Scamozzi, Vincenzo (1552–1616)

Scève, Maurice (ca. 1500–1563)

Serlio, Sebastiano (1475/90–1553/57)

Serres, Olivier de (1539–1619)

Silvestre, Israël (1621–1691)

Stevin, Simon (1548–1620)

Tappe, Eberhard (?–ca. 1541)

Tory, Geoffroy (ca. 1480–1533)

Valladier, André (ca. 1565–1638)

Valle, Giovanni Battista della (?–1535)

Vallet, Pierre (15?–1642)

Végèce, Flavius Vegetius Renatus (fourth to fifth centuries)

Viator, Jean Pélerin (1445?–1524 ?)

Vigenère, Blaise de (1523–1596)

Vignole, Barozzi, Jacopo (1507–1573)

Villalpando, Juan Bautista (1552–1608)

Viola Zanini, Giuseppe (ca. 1575/80–1631)

Vitruvius, Marcus Pollio (first century BC)

Vredeman de Vries, Jan (Hans) (1527–1609)

Vredeman de Vries, Paul (1567–ca. 1630)

Zanchi, Giovanni Battista de (1515–ca. 1586)

Bibliography

Adorno, Theodor. *Aesthetic Theory.* Minneapolis: University of Minnesota Press, 1998.

Alberti, Leon Battista. *Ten Books on Architecture.* 1755 Leoni Edition. Mineola, NY: Dover, 1986.

Anderson, Ray S. *The Shape of Practical Theology: Empowering Ministry with Theological Praxis.* Downers Grove, IL: InterVarsity, 2001

Aquinas. *Contra Gentiles, IV.61.2.* Online: http://genius.com/St-thomas-aquinas-summa-contra-gentiles-book-iv-annotated.

Archinard, André. *Les Édifices Religieux de la Vieille Genève.* Geneva, CH: Joël Cherbuliez, Libraire, 1864.

Arnheim, Rudolf. *Art and Visual Perception: A Psychology of the Creative Eye.* Rev. ed. Berkeley, CA: University of California Press, 1969.

Augustine. *The City of God.* Translated by H. Bettenson. London: Penguin, 2003.

Ayers, Andrew. *The Architecture of Paris.* Stuttgart: Merges, 2004.

Bachelard, Gaston. *The Poetics of Space.* Boston, MA: Beacon, 1994.

Backus, Irena, and Philip Benedict, eds. *Calvin and His Influence, 1509–2009.* New York: Oxford University Press, 2011.

Ballon, Hilary. "Constructions of the Bourbon State: Classical Architecture in Seventeenth-Century France." In *Cultural Differentiation and Cultural Identity in the Visual Arts,* edited by Susan J. Barnes and Walter S. Melion, 136–48. Studies in the History of Art 27. Washington, DC: National Gallery of Art, 1987.

——. *Louis Le Vau: Mazarin's Collège, Colbert's Revenge.* Princeton, NJ: Princeton University Press, 1999.

——. *The Paris of Henry IV: Architecture and Urbanism.* Cambridge: MIT Press, 1994.

Baskins, Cristelle, and Lisa Rosenthal, eds. *Early Modern Visual Allegory: Embodying Meaning.* Aldershot: Ashgate, 2007.

Baumgartner, Frederic J. *France in the Sixteenth Century.* New York: St. Martin's, 1995.

Baxandall, Michael. *Patterns of Intention: On the Historical Explanation of Pictures.* New Haven, CT: Yale University Press, 1985.

Begbie, Jeremy. *Voicing Creation's Praise: Towards a Theology of the Arts.* 1st ed. Edinburgh: T. & T. Clark, 2000.

Beik, William. *Urban Protest in Seventeenth-Century France: The Culture of Retribution.* Cambridge: Cambridge University Press, 1997.

Benedict, Philip, "Calvinism as a Culture?" In *Seeing Beyond the Word: Visual Arts and the Calvinist Tradition,* edited by Paul Corby Finney, 19–49. Grand Rapids: Eerdmans, 1999.

Bibliography

————. *Christ's Churches Purely Reformed: A Social History of Calvinism.* New Haven, CT: Yale University Press, 2002.

————. *Cities and Social Change in Early Modern France.* London: Unwin Hyman, 1989.

————. *The Faith and Fortunes of France's Huguenots, 1600–85.* St. Andrew's Studies in Reformation History. Aldershot: Ashgate, 2001.

————. *Graphic History: The Wars, Massacres and Troubles of Tortorel and Perrissin.* Geneva: Librairie Droz, 2007.

Biéler, André. *Architecture in Worship: The Christian Place of Worship.* Philadelphia: Westminster, 1965.

Benoist, Élie. *Histoire De L'édit De Nantes: Contenant Les Choses Les Plus Remarquables Qui Se Sont Passées En France Avant & Après Sa Publication.* Charleston, SC: Nabu, 2010.

Birmingham, David. *Switzerland: A Village History.* Athens, OH: Ohio University Press, 1999.

Blavignac, J.-D. *Description Monumentale de l'Église de St. Pierre, Ancienne Cathédrale de Genève.* Geneva: Jullien et Fils, 1845.

Blunt, Anthony. *Art and Architecture in France 1500–1700.* Rev. ed. New Haven, CT: Yale University Press, 1999.

————. *Philibert de L'Orme.* London: A. Zwemmer Ltd., 1958.

Boer, Wietse de, and Christine Göttler, eds. *Religion and the Senses in Early Modern Europe.* Leiden: Brill, 2012.

Bonney, Richard, and D. J. B. Trim, eds. *Persecution and Pluralism: Calvinists and Religious Minorities in Early Modern Europe: Studies in the History of Religious and Political Pluralism,* Vol. 2. Oxford: Peter Lang, 2006.

Bowen, David Anderson. *John Calvin's Ecclesiological Adiaphorism: Distinguishing the "Indifferent," the "Essential," and the "Important" in His Thought and Practice 1547–1559.* PhD diss., Vanderbilt University, 1985.

Brand, Stuart. *How Buildings Learn: What Happens After They're Built.* New York: Penguin, 1995.

Briggs, Robin. *Early Modern France, 1560–1715.* Rev. ed. Oxford University Press, 1998.

Browning, Don S. *A Fundamental Practical Theology: Descriptive and Strategic Proposals.* Minneapolis: Augsburg Fortress, 1995.

Bruce, Steve. *A House Divided: Protestantism, Schism, and Secularization.* London: Routledge, 1990.

Bruening, Michael W. *Calvinism's First Battleground: Conflict and Reform in the Pays de Vaud, 1528–1559.* New York: Springer, 2006.

Bryson, Norman. *Word and Image: French Painting of the Ancien Régime.* Cambridge University Press, 1981.

Bullinger, Heinrich. *The Second Helvetic Confession, XXII.4.* Christian Classics Ethereal Library. Online: http://www.ccel.org/creeds/helvetic.htm.

Burke, Peter. *Popular Culture in Early Modern Europe.* Aldershot: Ashgate, 2009.

Calabi, Donatella. *The Market and the City: Square, Street and Architecture in Early Modern Europe.* Aldershot: Ashgate, 2004.

Calvin, John. "Articles Concerning the Organization of the Church and of Worship." In *Calvin: Theological Treatises,* edited by J. K. S. Reid, 48–55. Philadelphia: Westminster, 1954.

————. *Catechism of the Church of Geneva,* from *Treatises on the Sacraments: Tracts by John Calvin.* Grand Rapids: Reformation Heritage, 2002.

Bibliography

———. *Commentaries on the Last Four Books of Moses Arranged in the Form of a Harmony.* Translated by Charles William Bingham. Grand Rapids: Calvin Translation Society, n.d.

———. *Commentary on the Psalms.* Translated by James Anderson. Grand Rapids: Christian Classics Ethereal Library. Online: http://www.ccel.org/ccel/calvin/calcom08.titlepage.html.

———. *Habakkuk, Zephaniah & Haggai.* Edinburgh: Banner of Truth, 1986.

———. *Harmony of the Law, vol. 2, Exodus.* Christian Classics Ethereal Library. Online: http://www.ccel.org/ccel/calvin/calcom03.pdf.

———. *The Institutes of the Christian Religion.* Edited by John T. McNeil. 2 vols. Philadelphia: Westminster, 1960.

———. "Ordinances for the Supervsion of Churches in the Country." In *Theological Treatises,* edited by J. K. S. Reid, 76–82. Louisville, KY: Wesminster John Knox, 1954.

———. *Writings on Pastoral Piety.* Translated by Elsie Anne McKee. New York: Paulist, 2001.

Campbell, Gordon. *Renaissance Art and Architecture.* Oxford University Press, 2004.

Canlis, Julie. *Calvin's Ladder: A Spiritual Theology of Ascent and Ascension.* Grand Rapids: Eerdmans, 2010.

Carpo, Mario. *Architecture in the Age of Printing: Orality, Writing, Typography, and Printed Images in the History of Architectural Theory.* Translated by Sarah Bensen. Cambridge, MA: MIT Press, 2001.

Caruthers, Mary, and Jan M. Ziolkowski, eds. *The Medieval Craft of Memory: An Anthology of Texts and Pictures.* Philadelphia: University of Pennsylvania Press, 2002.

Cavallo, Sandra. *Domestic Institutional Interiors in Early Modern Europe.* Aldershot: Ashgate, 2009.

Cave, William. *Primitive Christianity: Or, the Religion of the Ancient Christians in the First Ages of the Gospel.* London, 1672. WorldCat. Online: http://www.worldcat.org/title/primitive-christianity-or-the-religion-of-the-ancient-christians-in-the-first-ages-of-the-gospel-in-three-parts/oclc/613939234.

Cazeaux, Clive. *The Continental Aesthetics Reader.* New York: Routledge, 2000.

Coffin, David R. "The Renaissance: Early Renaissance in Italy, 1401–95," Encyclopedia Britannica. Online: http://www.britannica.com/EBchecked/topic/32952/Western-architecture/47340/The-Renaissance?anchor=ref488858.

Cole, Michael. *The Idol in the Age of Art: Objects, Devotions, and the Early Modern World.* Aldershot: Ashgate, 2009.

Coope, Rosalys. *Salomon de Brosse and the Development of the Classical Style in French Architecture 1565 to 1630.* London: Zwemmer, 1972.

Conner, Philip. *Huguenot Heartland: Montauban and Southern French Calvinism during the Wars of Religion.* Aldershot: Ashgate, 2002.

Cornelison, Sally J. "Art Imitates Architecture: the Saint Philip Reliquary in Renaissance Florence." *The Art Bulletin* 86.4 (2004) 642–58.

Cornwall, Robert D. and William Gibson. *Religion, Politics and Dissent, 1660–1832.* Aldershot: Ashgate, 2010.

Coster, Will, and Andrew Spicer, eds. *Sacred Space in Early Modern Europe.* Cambridge: Cambridge University Press, 2005.

Cowling, David. *Building the Text: Architecture as Metaphor in Late Medieval and Early Modern France.* Oxford: Oxford University Press, 1998.

Crowther-Heyck, Kathleen. "Wonderful Secrets of Nature." *Isis* 94.2 (2003) 253–73.

Bibliography

D'Orgeix, Émil. "Perret, Jacques." In *Architectura: Architecture, Textes, et Images, XVI—XVIIe siècles*. Online: http://architectura.cesr.univ-tours.fr/traite/Auteur/Perret. asp?param=.

Daneau, Lambert. *A Fruitful Commentary on the Twelve Small Prophets*. Cambridge: University of Cambridge, 1594. The Digital Library of Classic Protestant Texts.

Davis, Natalie Zemon. *Society and Culture in Early Modern France*. Stanford, CA: Stanford University Press, 1975.

Davis, Thomas J. *The Clearest Promises of God: the Development of Calvin's Eucharistic Teaching*. New York: AMS, 1995.

de Boer, Wietse, and Christine Göttler, eds., *Religion and the Senses in Early Modern Europe*. Leiden: Brill, 2012.

Debuyst, Frédéric. *Modern Architecture and Christian Celebration*. Atlanta: John Knox, 1968.

De l'Orme, Philibert. *L'Architecture, Oeuvres Entières*. Liège: P. Mardaga, 1981.

De Tervarent, Guy. *Attributs et Symboles dans l'Art Profane 1450–1600: Dictionnaire d'un Langage Perdu: Travaux d'humanisme et Renaissance*. Geneva: Droz, 1958.

Diefendorf, Barbara B. *Beneath the Cross: Catholics and Huguenots in Sixteenth-Century Paris*. Oxford University Press, 1991.

Douen, O. *La Révocation de l'Édit de Nantes à Paris d'après des Documents Inédits*, Vol. 1. Paris: Librairie Fischbacher 1894.

Du Cerceau, Jacques-Androuet. *Les Plus excellents bastiments de France*. Translated and edited by C. Ludet. 2 vols. Paris: Aventurie, 1955.

Dyrness, William A. *Poetic Theology: God and the Poetics of Everyday Life*. Grand Rapids: Eerdmans, 2011.

———. *Reformed Theology and Visual Culture: The Protestant Imagination from Calvin to Edwards*. Cambridge University Press, 2004.

Eco, Umberto. *Art and Beauty in the Middle Ages*. New Haven, CT: Yale University Press, 2002.

Eire, Carlos M. N. *War Against the Idols: The Reformation of Worship from Erasmus to Calvin*. Cambridge University Press, 1989.

Elliott, J. H. *History in the Making*. New Haven, CT: Yale University Press, 2012.

Elwood, Christopher. *The Body Broken: The Calvinist Doctrine of the Eucharist and the Symbolization of Power in Sixteenth-Century France*. New York: Oxford University Press, 1999.

Erling, Bernhard. *Nature and History: A Study in Theological Methodology With Special Attention to the Method of Motif Research*. Lund: C. W. K. Gleerup, 1960.

Eurich, Amanda. "Sacralising Space: Reclaiming Civic Culture in Early Modern France." In *Sacred Space in Early Modern Europe*, edited by Will Coster and Andrew Spicer, 259–81. Cambridge: Cambridge University Press, 2005.

Evans, E. P. *Animal Symbolism in Ecclesiastical Architecture*. London: W. Heinemann, 1896.

Evers, Bernd. *Architectural Theory from the Renaissance to the Present*. Cologne: Taschen, 2006.

Finney, Paul Corby. *Seeing Beyond the Word: Visual Arts and the Calvinist Tradition*. Grand Rapids: Eerdmans, 1999.

Fischer, Ernst. *The Necessity of Art*. London: Verso, 2010.

Bibliography

Fréart de Chambray, Roland. *Parallèle de l'architecture avec la moderne*. Paris, 1650. Édition critique établie par F. Lemerle, suivie de l'*Idée de la Perfection de la peinture*, édition établie par M. Stanic. Paris: École Nationale Supérieure des Beaux-Arts, 2005.

Freedberg, David. *The Power of Images: Studies in the History and Theory of Response*. Chicago: University of Chicago Press, 1989.

Freigang, Christian, and Jarl Kremeier. "Jacques Androuet du Cerceau." In *Architectural Theory From the Renaissance to the Present*, edited by Bernd Evers, 220–22. Köln: Taschen, 2003.

Frommel, Sabine. *Sebastiano Serlio, Architect*. Translated by Peter Spring. Milan: Electa Architecture, 2003.

Fromment, Anthoine, et al. *Les actes et gestes merveilleux de la cité de Genève: nouvellement convertie à l'évangile fait du temps de leur Réformation, et comment ils l'ont recue rediger par éscript en forme de Chroniques, Annales, ou Hystoyres commençant l'an MDXXXII*. Geneva: Jules Guillaume Fick, 1854.

Gadamer, Hans-Georg. *Truth and Method*. 2nd ed. Translated by Joel Weinsheimer and Donald G. Marshall. New York: Continuum, 2011.

Garrisson-Estèbe, Janine. *Protestants du Midi 1559–1598*. Toulouse: 1980.

Germann, Georg, "Les Temples Protestants dans les traités d'architecture du dix-septième siècle." Bulletin de la Société de l'Histoire du Protestantisme Français, Tome 152. Geneva: Droz.

Giedion, Siegfried. *Space, Time, and Architecture: the Growth of a New Tradition*. Cambridge, MA: Harvard University Press, 2009.

Gietmann, Gerhard, and Herbert Thurston. "Basilica." *The Catholic Encyclopedia*. Vol. 2. New York: Robert Appleton Company, 1907. Online: http://www.newadvent.org/cathen/02325a.htm.

Girouard, Mark. *Cities and People: A Social and Architectural History*. New Haven, CT: Yale University Press, 1987.

Glorieux, Guillaume. *Le Château de Condé: Une Demeure de Plaisance au siècle des Lumières*. Paris: Somogy, 2004.

Gorringe, T. J. *A Theology of the Built Environment*. Cambridge: Cambridge University Press, 2002.

Gorski, Philip S. "Historicizing the Secularization Debate: Church, State, and Society in Late Medieval and Early Modern Europe, ca. 1300 to 1700." *American Sociological Review* 65.1 (2000) 138–67.

Grosse, Christian. "Liturgical Sacrality of the Genevan Reformed churches." In *Sacred Space in Early Modern Europe*, edited by Will Coster and Andrew Spicer, 60–80. Cambridge: Cambridge University Press, 2005.

Guicharnaud, Hélène. "An Introduction to the Architecture of Protestant Temples Constructed in France before the Revocation of the Edict of Nantes." In *Seeing Beyond the Word: Visual Arts and the Calvinist Tradition*, edited by Paul Corby Finney, 133–61. Grand Rapids: Eerdmans, 1999.

Guillaume, Jean. "On Philibert de l'Orme: a Treatise Transcending the Rules." In *Paper Palaces: The Rise of the Renaissance Architectural Treatise*, edited by Vaughan Hart and Peter Hicks, 219–31. New Haven, CT: Yale University Press.

Guillot, Alexandre. *L'Église de St. Pierre à Genève: Notice Historique, in Saint-Pierre, Ancienne Cathédrale de Genève*. Whitefish, MT: Kessinger Legacy Reprints, n. d.

Hamling, Tara. *Everyday Objects: Medieval and Early Modern Material Culture and Its Meanings*. Aldershot: Ashgate, 2010.

Bibliography

Harries, Karsten. *The Ethical Function of Architecture*. Cambridge, MA: MIT Press, 2000.

Hart, Vaughn, and Peter Hicks, eds. *Paper Palaces: The Rise of the Renaissance Architectural Treatise*. New Haven, CT: Yale University Press, 1998.

Hearn, Fil. *Ideas That Shaped Buildings*. Cambridge, MA: MIT Press, 2003.

Heller, Henry. *The Conquest of Poverty: The Calvinist Revolt in Sixteenth-Century France*. Leiden: Brill, 1986.

Hillerbrand, Hans J. *The Oxford Encyclopedia of the Reformation*. New York: Oxford University Press, 1996.

Hesselink, I. John. *Calvin's First Catechism: A Commentary: Featuring Ford Lewis Battle's Translation of the 1538 Catechism*. Louisville, KY: Westminster John Knox, 1997.

Hills, Helen. *Architecture and the Politics of Gender in Early Modern Europe*. Aldershot: Ashgate, 2003.

Hodges, Elisabeth. *Urban Poetics in the French Renaissance*. Aldershot: Ashgate, 2008.

Holder, R. Ward. *John Calvin and the Grounding of Interpretation*. Leiden: Brill, 2006.

Hustin, Arthur. *Le Palais du Luxembourg: Ses Transformations, Son Agrandissement, Ses Architectes, Sa Décoration, Ses Décorateurs*. Paris: P. Mouillot, 1904.

Jacobsen, Eric. *The Space Between: A Christian Engagement with the Built Environment*. Grand Rapids: Baker Academic, 2012.

Jones, Lindsay. *The Hermeneutics of Sacred Architecture: Experience, Interpretation, Comparison, Vol. 1: Monumental Occasions: Reflections on the Eventfulness of Religious Architecture*. Cambridge, MA: Harvard University Press, 2000.

Jones, Serene. *Calvin and the Rhetoric of Piety*. Columbia Series in Reformed Theology. Louisville, KY: Westminster John Knox, 1995.

Kamil, Neil. *Fortress of the Soul: Violence, Metaphysics, and Material Life in the Huguenots' New World, 1517–1751*. Baltimore, MD: Johns Hopkins University Press, 2005.

Kieckhefer, Richard. *Theology in Stone: Church Architecture from Byzantium to Berkeley*. New York: Oxford University Press, 2008.

Kilde, Jeanne Halgren. *Sacred Power, Sacred Space: An Introduction to Christian Architecture and Worship*. Oxford University Press, 2008.

Knecht, Robert. *The Rise and Fall of Renaissance France, 1483–1610*. 2nd ed. Hoboken, NJ: Wiley-Blackwell, 2002.

Krautheimer, Richard, and Slobodan Curçic. *Early Christian and Byzantine Architecture*. New Haven, CT: Yale University Press, 1986.

Kruft, Hanno-Walter. *History of Architectural Theory From Vitruvius to the Present*. Princeton, NJ: Princeton Architectural, 1996.

Kümin, Beat. *Political Space in Pre-industrial Europe*. Aldershot: Ashgate, 2009.

La Confession de foi de 1559, dites de la Rochelle. Aix-en-Provence: Édition Kerygma, 1998.

Lefebvre, Henri. *The Production of Space*. Oxford: Blackwell, 1991.

Lemerle, Frédérique, and Yves Pauwels. "Architecture, Textes, et Images, XVIe—XVIIe siècles." *Architettura*. Online: http://architettura.cesr.univ-tours.fr/Traite/index.asp?param=en.

Léry, Jean de. *Histoire d'un voyage fait en la terre du Brésil, autrement dite Amérique, 1578*, as *History of A Voyage to the Land of Brazil, Otherwise Called America*. Edited by Janet Whatley. Berkeley, CA: University of California Press, 1990.

Lucas, Herbert. "Ecclesiastical Architecture." *The Catholic Encyclopedia*. Vol. 5. New York: Robert Appleton, 1909. Online: http://www.newadvent.org/cathen/05257a.htm.

Luria, Keith. "Separated by Death? Burials, Cemeteries, and Confessional Boundaries in Seventeenth-Century France." *French Historical Studies* 24.2 (2001) 185–222.

Bibliography

Luscombe, Desley. "The Architect and the Representation of Architecture: Sebastiano Serlio's Frontispiece to Il ferzo libro." *Architectural Theory Review* 10.2 (2005) 36–39.

Machiavelli, Nicolo. "A Letter to Francesco Guicciardini." In *The Portable Machiavelli*, edited by Peter Bandanella, 53–76. New York: Penguin, 1979.

Margolf, Diane C. "Religion and Royal Justice in Early Modern France: The Paris Chambre de 'Edit, 1598–1665." Sixteenth Century Essays and Studies 67. Kirksville, MO: Truman State University Press, 2003.

Marguerite de Navarre. "The Heptameron of Margaret, Queen of Navarre." Translated by Walter K. Kelly. Paris: Société des Bibliophiles Français. Online: http://digital.library.upenn.edu/.

McGowen, Margaret M. *The Vision of Rome in Late Renaissance France*. New Haven, CT: Yale University Press, 2000.

McGrath, Alister E. *A Life of John Calvin: A Study in Shaping of Western Culture*. Oxford: Blackwell, 1993.

Meland, Bernard E. *Fallible Forms and Symbols: Discourses of Method in a Theology of Culture*. Philadelphia: Fortress, 1976.

Mentzer, Raymond A. *La Construction de l'identité réformée aux XVIe et XVIIe siècles*. Paris: Honoré Champion, 2006.

———. "The Persistence of 'Superstition' and 'Idolatry' among Rural French Calvinists." *Church History* 65.2 (1996) 220–33.

———. *Sin and the Calvinists: Morals Control and the Consistory in the Reformed Tradition* Kirksville, MO: Truman State University Press, 2002.

Mentzer, Raymond A., and Andrew Spicer, eds. *Society and Culture in the Huguenot World, 1559–1685*. Cambridge: Cambridge University Press, 2002.

Middleton, Robin, and David Watkin. *Neoclassical and 19th Century Architecture: The Diffusion and of Classicism and the Gothic Revival*. Reprint. New York: Electa/Rizzoli, 1993.

Mignot, Claude. "Palladio et l'Architecture Française du XVIIe Siècle, Une Admiration Critique." *Annali di architettura* 12 (2000) 107–15.

Millet, Olivier. *Calvin et la dynamique de la parole. Étude de rhétorique réformée*. Paris: Bibliothèque littéraire de la Renaissance, série 3, tome 28, 1992, 176–181. Online: http://www.worldcat.org/title/calvin-et-la-dynamique-de-la-parole-etude-de-rhetorique-reformee/oclc/768060313.

Milner, Matthew. *The Senses and the English Reformation*. Aldershot: Ashgate, 2011.

Mirzoeff, Nicholas. *The Visual Culture Reader*. 3rd ed. London: Routledge, 2012.

Montaigne, Michel de. "Of Sumptuary Laws." In *Essays of Montaigne*, vol. 2, translated by Charles Cotton. London: Reeves and Turner, 1902.

Morgan, David. *The Sacred Gaze: Religious Visual Culture in Theory and Practice*. 1st ed. Berkeley, CA: University of California Press, 2005.

Moriarty, Michael. *Taste and Ideology in Seventeenth-Century France*. Cambridge: Cambridge University Press, 2009.

Mugerauer, Robert. *Interpreting Environments: Tradition, Deconstruction, Hermeneutics*. Austin, TX: University of Texas Press, 1995.

Muir, Edward. *Ritual in Early Modern Europe*. Cambridge: Cambridge University Press, 2005.

Muller, Richard A. *Post-Reformation Reformed Dogmatics. Vol. 2, Holy Scripture: The Cognitive Foundation of Theology*. Grand Rapids: Baker, 1993.

Bibliography

—. Review of Serene Jones, *Calvin and the Rhetoric of Piety*. *Calvin Theological Journal* 31.2 (1996) 582–83.

Murray, Peter. *The Architecture of the Italian Renaissance*. New York: Schocken, 1986.

Naphy, William G. *Calvin and the Consolidation of the Genevan Reformation*. Louisville, KY: Westminster John Knox, 1994.

Navarre, Marguerite de. "The Heptameron of Margaret, Queen of Navarre by Marguerite de Navarre (d'Angoulême), Duchesse d'Alençon (1492–1549)." In *L'Heptameron des Nouvelles de très haute et très illustre Princesse Marguerite D'Angoulême, Reine de Navarre*, 3 vols., translated by Walter K. Kelly. Paris: Société des Bibliophiles Français, 1853.

Opitz, Peter. Review of Randall Zachman, *Image and Word in the Theology of John Calvin*. *Scottish Journal of Theology Scottish Journal of Theology* 64.1 (2011) 117–20.

Orgeix, Émilie de. "Perret, Jacques." In *Architettura: Architecture, Textes, et Images, XVIe –XVIIe siècles*. No pages. Online: http://architettura.cesr.univ-tours.fr/Traite/Notice/ENSBA_LES1698.asp?param=en.

Palladio, Andrea. *Four Books on Architecture*. Boston: MIT Press, 2002.

Palissy, Bernard. *Les Œuvres de Bernard Palissy*. Paris: Charavay Frères Éditeurs, 1880.

—. *Discours Admirables*. Paris: Martin le Jeune, 1580.

Pannier, Jean. *Salomon de Brosse, un architecte Français au commencement du XVII siècle*. Paris: Librairie centrale d'art et d'architecture, 1911.

Panofsky, Erwin. *Gothic Architecture and Scholasticism*. New York: Arch Abbey, 2005.

—. *Perspective as Symbolic Form*. New York: Zone, 1991.

—. *Studies in Iconology: Humanistic Themes in the Art of the Renaissance*. New York: Harper and Row, 1962.

Pelikan, Jaroslav. *Reformation of Church and Dogma (1300–1700)*. Chicago: University of Chicago Press, 1984.

Pericolo, Lorenzo. *Subject as Aporia in Early Modern Art*. Aldershot: Ashgate, 2010.

Pettegree, Andrew. *The Reformation World*. London: Routledge, 2000.

—. *Reformation and the Culture of Persuasion*. Cambridge University Press, 2005.

Pevsner, Nikolaus. *A History of Building Types*. Princeton, NJ: Princeton University Press, 1979.

Philips, Henry. *Church and Culture in Seventeenth-Century France*. Cambridge: Cambridge University Press, 2002.

Poisson, Michel. *Paris: Buildings and Monuments, An Illustrated Guide*. New York: Abrams, 1999.

Proctor, Robert E. "Beauty as Symmetry: The Education of Vitruvius' Architect and Raphael's Stanza Della Segnatora." *Newington-Cropsey Cultural Studies Center*. Online: http://www.nccsc.net/2010/3/3/beauty-as-symmetry.

Racaut, Luc. *Hatred in Print: Catholic Propaganda and Protestant Identity during the French Wars of Religion*. Aldershot: Ashgate, 2002.

Raguin, Virginia Chieffo. *Art, Piety and Destruction in the Christian West, 1500–1700*. Aldershot: Ashgate, 2009.

Randall, Catharine. *Building Codes: The Aesthetics of Calvinism in Early Modern Europe*. Philadelphia: University of Pennsylvania Press, 1999.

—. *Earthly Treasures: Material Culture and Metaphysics in the Heptameron and Evangelical Narrative*. West Lafayette, IN: Purdue University Press, 2007.

Bibliography

———. "Philibert De l'Orme, Protestantism and Architecture: Peculiarities of Style." In *Studies in Reformed Theology and History*, no. 2. Princeton, NJ: Princeton Theological Seminary, 1999.

———. "Structuring Protestant Scriptural Space in Sixteenth-Century Catholic France." *Sixteenth Century Journal* 25.2 (1994) 341–52.

Reymond, Bernard. *Le Protestantisme et les Images: Pour en finir avec quelques clichés*. Geneva: Labor et Fides, 1999.

———. *Temples de Suisse romande: à la découverte d'un patrimoine*. Morges: Éditions Cabédia, 1997.

Ricoeur, Paul. *Interpretation Theory: Discourse and the Surplus of Meaning*. Fort Worth, TX: Texas Christian University Press, 1976.

Roussel, Bernard. "'Ensevelir honnestement les corps': Funeral Corteges and Huguenot Culture." In *Society and Culture in the Huguenot World, 1559–1685*, edited by Raymond A. Menzter and Andrew Spicer, 193–208. Cambridge: Cambridge University Press, 2002.

Rubin, Patricia Lee. *Images and Identity in Fifteenth-Century Florence*. New Haven, CT: Yale University Press, 2007.

Ruesens, Le Chanoine. "Éléments d'Archéologie Chrétienne." *ATLA Historical Monographs Collection* 1 (1885) 1–627.

Savot, Louis. *L'Architecture Françoise de bastiments particuliers*. In *Architectura: Architecture, Texte, et Images XVIe—XVIIe ciecles*, edited by F. Blondel. Online: http://architectura.cesr.univ-tours.fr/traite/Notice/Savot1642.asp?param=.

Selderhuis, Herman J. *The Calvin Handbook*. Grand Rapids: Eerdmans, 2009.

Schaff, Philip. *The Creeds of Christendom: With a History and Critical Notes, Vol. 3*. New York: Harper and Brothers, 1877.

Schwartz, Regina. *Sacramental Poetics at the Dawn of Secularism: When God Left the World. Cultural Memory in the Present*. Stanford, CA: Stanford University Press, 2008.

Scruton, Roger. *The Aesthetics of Architecture*. Princeton University Press, 1979.

Serlio, Sebastiano. *On Architecture, Vol. 1, Books 1–4. Tutte l'Opere d'Architecttura et Prospetiva*. Translated by Vaughn Hart and Peter Hicks. New Haven, CT: Yale University Press, 2005.

———. *Serlio on Domestic Architecture*. Text by Myra Nan Rosenfeld. Mineola, NY: Dover, 1978.

Sheldrake, Philip. *Spaces for the Sacred: Place, Memory, and Identity*. Baltimore: Johns Hopkins University Press, 2001.

Silverman, Lisa. *Tortured Subjects: Pain, Truth, and The Body in Early Modern France*. Chicago: University of Chicago Press, 2001.

Smith, Thomas Gordon. *Vitruvius on Architecture*. New York: Monacelli, 2003.

Spicer, Andrew. *Calvinist Churches in Early Modern Europe*. Manchester: Manchester University Press, 2007.

———. "Qui est de Dieu oit la parole de Dieu." In *Society and Culture in the Huguenot World, 1559–1685*, edited by Raymond A. Menzter and Andrew Spicer, 175–92. Cambridge: Cambridge University Press, 2002.

Suger, de Saint-Denis. *Abbot Suger on the Abbey Church of St.-Denis and Its Art Treasures*. 2nd ed. Translated by Erwin Panofsky. Princeton, NJ: Princeton University Press, 1979.

Bibliography

———. "De Adminisratione, XXVI—XXVIII." In *Abbot Suger on the Abbey Church of St-Denis and Its Art Treasures*, 2nd ed. Translated by Edwin Panofsky. Princeton, NJ: Princeton University Press, 1979

Sunshine, Glenn S. *Reforming French Protestantism: The Development of Huguenot Ecclesiastical Institutions, 1557–1572*. Sixteenth Century Essays and Studies 66. Kirksville, MO: Truman State University Press, 2003.

Sutherland, N. M. *The Huguenot Struggle for Recognition*. New Haven, CT: Yale University Press, 1980.

Tanner, Kathryn. *Theories of Culture: A New Agenda for Theology*. Minneapolis, MN: Augsburg Fortress, 1997.

Thomson, David. *Renaissance Paris: Architecture and Growth, 1475–1600*. Southampton: Camelot, 1984.

Teilhard de Chardin, Pierre. *Le Milieu Divin*. Glasgow: Collins, 1967.

Thurston, Herbert. "Symbols." *The New Catholic Encyclopedia*, vol. 14. New York: Robert Appleton, 1912. Online: http://www.newadvent.org/cathen/14373b.htm.

Tillich, Paul. *On Art and Architecture*. Chestnut Ridge, NY: Crossroad, 1989.

Torgerson, Mark A. *An Architecture of Immanence: Architecture for Worship and Ministry Today*. Grand Rapids: Eerdmans, 2007.

Tornare, Alain-Jacques. *Commission du 700me*. Marsens: n.p., 1991.

Turner, Harold W. *From Temple to Meeting House: The Phenomenology and Theology of Places of Worship*. Hague: Mouton, 1979.

———. *The Ritual Process: Structure and Anti-Structure*. Lewis Henry Morgan Lectures. Chicago: Aldine, 1969.

Van Eck, Caroline. *Classical Rhetoric and the Visual Arts in Early Modern Europe*. Cambridge: Cambridge University Press, 2007.

Van Eck, Caroline, and Edward Winters. *Dealing With the Visual: Art History, Aesthetics, and Visual Culture*. Aldershot: Ashgate, 2005.

Van Til, Henry R. *The Calvinistic Concept of Culture*. Grand Rapids: Baker, 1972.

Vassaux, Eugène and Francis Messner, *Églises réformées d'Europe francophone: Droit et fonctionnement*. Paris: L'Harmattan, 2008.

Verhoeven, Gerrit. "Calvinist Pilgrimages and Popish Encounters: Religious Identity and Sacred Space on the Dutch Grand Tour (1598—1685), Imagery and Identity." *Journal of Social History* 43.3 (2010) 615–34.

Viret, Pierre. *Instruction Chrétienne en la Doctrine de la Loi et de L'évangile*. Geneva: Jean Rivery, 1564. Digital Library of Classic Protestant Texts.

———. *L'office des mortz, fait par dialogues, en manière de devis*. Geneva: Jean Girard, 1552. Bibliothèque de Genève. Online: http://www.e-rara.ch/doi/10.3931/e-rara-2443.

Vitruvius. *The Ten Books on Architecture*. Translated by Morris Hicky Morgan. New York: Dover, 1960.

Von Kalnein, Wend. *Architecture in France in the Eighteenth Century*. New Haven, CT: Yale University Press, 1995.

Von Simson, Otto. *The Gothic Cathedral*. Princeton, NJ: Princeton University Press, 1988.

Wandel, Lee Palmer. *The Eucharist in the Reformation*. Cambridge: Cambridge University Press, 2001.

———. *The Reformation: Towards a New History*. Cambridge: Cambridge University Press, 2011.

Bibliography

———. *Voracious Idols and Violent Hands: Iconoclasm in Reformation Zurich, Strasbourg, and Basel*. Cambridge, UK: Cambridge University Press, 1999.

Wanegffelen, Thierry. *Ni Rome ni Genève: Des fidèles entre deux chaires en France au XVIe siècle*. Paris: Honoré Champion, 1997.

Watkin, David. *Morality and Architecture*. Chicago: University of Chicago Press, 1984.

Webb, Benjamin. "Sketches of Continental Ecclesiology, or, Church Notes in Belgium, Germany, and Italy." *ATLA Historical Monographs Collection* 1 (1848) 1–612.

Weber, Max. *Essays in Sociology*. Edited and translated by H. H. Gerth. Oxford: Oxford University Press, 1958.

White, James F., and Susan J. White. *Church Architecture: Building and Renovating for Christian Worship*. Nashville: Abingdon, 1988.

———. "From Protestant to Catholic Plain Style." In *Seeing Beyond the Word: Visual Arts and the Calvinist Tradition*. Grand Rapids: Eerdmans, 1999.

Whyte, William. "How Do Buildings Mean? Some Issues of Interpretation in the History of Architecture." *History and Theory* 45.2 (2006) 153–77.

Wolters, Albert M. *Creation Regained: Biblical Basics for a Reformational Worldview*. 2nd ed. Grand Rapids: Eerdmans, 2005.

Wolterstorff, Nicholas. *Art in Action*. Grand Rapids: Eerdmans, 1980.

Yates, Frances A. *The Art of Memory*. Chicago: University of Chicago Press, 1966.

Zachman, Randall C. *Image and Word in the Theology of John Calvin*. South Bend, IN: University of Notre Dame Press, 2007.

Zerner, Henri. *Renaissance Art in France: The Invention of Classicism*. Paris: Éditions Flammarion, 2003.

Zuidervaart, Lambert. *Adorno's Aesthetic Theory: The Redemption of Illusion*. Boston: MIT Press, 1993.

#0010 - 270317 - C0 - 229/152/12 - PB - 9780718894696